C000243861

Land Law

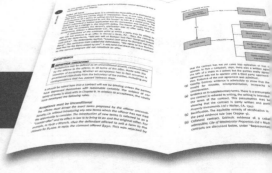

NUT**CASES**

Land Law

SIXTH EDITION

by
CHRIS CHANG
LLB, Barrister (UK)
Advocate and Solicitor (Malaysia)

SWEET & MAXWELL

THOMSON REUTERS

First Edition – 1997
Second Edition – 2001
Third Edition – 2003
Fourth Edition – 2005
Fifth Edition – 2009

Published in 2012 by Sweet & Maxwell, 100 Avenue Road, London NW3 3PF, part of
Thomson Reuters (Professional) UK Limited (Registered in England and Wales,
Company No.1679046. Registered Office and address for service: Aldgate House,
33 Aldgate High Street, London EC3N 1DL).

*For further information on our products and services, visit *www.sweetandmaxwell.co.uk.*

Typeset by YHT, London.
Printed in Great Britain by Ashford Colour Press, Gosport, Hants.

*No natural forests were destroyed to make this product;
only farmed timber was used and re-planted.*

A CIP catalogue record for this book is available from the British Library.

ISBN-978-0-414-02271-3

Contents

v

Using this Book

Welcome to our new look NUTCASE revision series. We have revamped and improved the existing design and layout and added new features, according to student feedback.

NEW DETAILED TABLE OF CONTENTS for easy navigation.

REDESIGNED TABLES OF CASES AND LEGISLATION for easy reference.

NEW CHAPTER INTRODUCTIONS to outline the key concepts covered and condense complex and important information.

Protection of
in Land

INTRODUCTION

The estates and interests cap
Law of Property Act 1925. W'
law depends on its requir
on the Formal and In'
Upon th

NEW BOXED "THINKPOINT"
at the end of each chapter with
further case analysis and questions
to encourage critical thinking.

THINK POINT

Although an owner of land owns t.
to the heavens, there are statutory
the land. Think about what these ai
use of the land.

In addition, other third party ri
owner's use of the land. Consid'
be.

ial tests for whethei
ie two tests set out in *Hollan*
.ords in *Elitestone Ltd v Morris* [1997]
ecided that a bungalow erected on pillar:
These cases were also approved in *Che*
(2000) 22 E.G. 147, where it was held that a hc
ropes and connected to utilities was a chatte
nature of the tenancy of a houseboat was
annexation. In *Cinderella Rockerfellas Ltd v Ru*
decided that a vessel which was moored per
of the land for the purpose of assessing its '
at it was nonetheless a chattel rather th
for rating purposes.
'ssex Reserve Forces & Cad

NEW COLOUR CODING throughout
to help distinguish cases and
legislation from the narrative.
At the first mention, cases are
highlighted in colour and italicised
and legislation is highlighted in
colour and emboldened.

Table of Cases

TABLE OF CASES

Table of Statutes

The Meaning of Land
The definition of land

INTRODUCTION

The legal definition of land is much broader than what the lay person traditionally understands from the term "land". Section 205(l)(ix) of the Law of Property Act 1925 defines land as including land of any tenure, and mines and minerals, whether or not held apart from the surface, buildings or parts of buildings (whether the division is horizontal, vertical or made in any other way) and other corporeal hereditaments; also a manor, an advowson, and a rent and other incorporeal hereditaments, and an easement, right, privilege or benefit in, over, or derived from land. Apart from the soil, ground or earth, the word land includes the buildings on the land, fixtures attached to the land, mines and minerals and incorporeal hereditaments (such as easements and profits à prendre). The presumption in the case of where a stream divides two adjoining properties is that the boundary is divided laterally in the middle of the stream: *Herbert v Pegrum* [2005] EWCA Civ 120.

In addition to the statutory definition, two Latin maxims are often quoted to define land. The first is "cuius est solum eius est usque ad coelum et ad inferos" which means the person that owns the land owns everything from the depths of the earth up to the heavens and "quic quid plantatur solo, solo cedit" which means that things which are attached to the ground becomes part of it. As will become apparent, there are exceptions to these general principles, especially, in the context of airspace and ownership of minerals in the land and how the law has determined what becomes part of the land by nature of its attachment to it.

FIXTURES AND CHATTELS

Key Principle

The ownership of land includes ownership of fixtures on the land. Section 62 of the **Law of Property Act 1925** provides that a conveyance of land is deemed to include, inter alia, fixtures unless specifically excluded.

HOLLAND v HODGSON 1872
The question arose as to whether spinning looms, which were attached to the stone floors of the rooms in a mill formed part of the land.

Held ....
❖ (Ex Chamber) The spinning looms were to be regarded as fixtures and were therefore part of the land. (1871-1872) L.R. 7 C.P. 328.

Commentary ....
Blackburn J. suggested that the degree of annexation and object (or purpose) of annexation were the important criteria for deciding whether an item is a fixture or not. Subsequent cases have applied this. For example, in *HE Dibble Ltd v Moore* [1970] 2 Q.B. 181 CA (Civ Div), the court decided that moveable greenhouses (standing on their own weight on dollies which were not fixed to the ground) did not pass to the new owners of the property under s.62 of the **Law of Property Act 1925**; in *Elwes v Maw* (1802) 3 East 37 Ct of King's Bench, a Dutch barn which rested on its own sockets let into the ground was held not to be a fixture.

Two further cases indicate the importance of ensuring that the contract or conveyance is clear as to what is to be included or excluded by contract. In *Taylor v Hamer* [2002] EWCA Civ 1130, the Court of Appeal held that upon its true construction a conveyance did include flagstones in a landscaped garden. The flagstones had been removed after the purchaser inspected the property. Damages for breach of contract were awarded including the cost of replacing and re-laying flagstones. In *Jones v Forest Fencing Ltd* [2001] EWCA Civ 1700, the Court of Appeal ruled that s.2 of the **Law of Property (Miscellaneous Provisions) Act 1989** did not mean that agreements for the removal of equipment could not be incorporated into the contract. In the case, there was sufficient evidence of an agreement that the electrical infrastructure be removed between contract and completion, which was incorporated into the contract of sale. However, equipment, which was fixed in concrete and was not removed (as intended) before the final transfer of the freehold, could not be subsequently removed as they were fixtures attached to the land which merged with the freehold upon completion.

Key Principle ....
The two tests set out in *Holland v Hodgson*, are still relevant in deciding whether an item is a fixture or a fitting.

TSB Bank Plc v Botham 1996

The court had to decide whether items such as fitted carpets, light fittings, gas fires, curtains and blinds, towel rails, soap dishes, a Victorian bath, tap fittings and shower head, mirrors attached to the walls, kitchen units, sink and electrical items such as the oven, dishwasher, integrated washing machine, extractor fan, gas hob, refrigerator and freezer were fixtures or chattels.

Held

❖ (CA) Applying the two tests set out in *Holland v Hodgson*, the gas hob, the extractor fan, freezer, oven, dishwasher, an integrated washing machine, refrigerator, fitted carpets and curtains, gas fires and a Victorian bath standing on its four short legs were not fixtures. The other items referred to above were, however, regarded as fixtures. (1997) P. & C.R. D1.

Commentary

At first instance, the court decided that all the items were to be regarded as fixtures. This appeared to demonstrate the courts' preference for the purpose of annexation test rather than the degree of annexation test. This preference has been seen in earlier cases, as dicta from Lord Scarman in *Berkley v Poulett* (1977) 241 E.G. 911 CA (Civ Div) has suggested. In *Leigh v Taylor* [1902] A.C. 157 HL, tapestries which were affixed to the walls of a house were held to be chattels and not fixtures as the purpose of annexing them to the wall was for the better enjoyment of the chattel. In contrast, in *D'eyncourt v Gregory* (1866-67) L.R. 3 Eq. 382 Ct of Chancery, it was held that marble statues of lions were held to be fixtures as their presence on the land was for the better enjoyment of the land. The first instance decision in *Botham* surprised many as it was assumed that electrical items such as freezers, and dishwashers would be chattels, which could be removed by the vendor on a conveyance of the land, in the absence of any agreement. The practical effect is that it would have increased the value of the property that the mortgagee could have obtained from the sale. The Court of Appeal has now overturned this decision and reverted back to the original tests for whether an item is a chattel or a fixture.

The two tests set out in *Holland v Hodgson* were applied by the House of Lords in *Elitestone Ltd v Morris* [1997] 1 W.L.R. 687 HL where their Lordships decided that a bungalow erected on pillars was a fixture as this had all the attributes of a house and none of the features of for example a houseboat which could be easily removed.

These cases were also approved in *Chelsea Yacht & Boat Co Ltd v Pope* [2000] 1 W.L.R. 1941 CA (Civ Div), where it was held that a houseboat moored by cables and ropes and connected to utilities was a chattel. It was also decided that the nature of the tenancy of a houseboat was not relevant for determining annexation. In *Cinderella Rockerfellas Ltd v Rudd (Valuation Officer)* [2003] EWCA Civ 529 the court decided that a vessel which was moored permanently was regarded as part of the land for the purpose of assessing its rates. However, Potter L.J. made it clear that it was nonetheless a chattel rather than fixture. It was only regarded as land for rating purposes and hence there is no conflict between this case and *Chelsea Yacht & Boat Co Ltd v Pope*. More recently, in *Mew v Tristmire Ltd* [2011] EWCA Civ 912, the Court of Appeal held that two houseboats which were rested on wooden platforms supported by wooden piles driven into, and in some cases cemented into, the bed of the harbour were not fixtures. They were structures which could have been removed without being dismantled or destroyed in the process. The case of *Wessex Reserve Forces & Cadets Association v White* [2005] EWHC 983 (QB) illustrates that the issue as to whether objects on the land are fixtures or chattels can apply to situations where the renewal of a lease is in question.

AIRSPACE

Key Principle
The owner of land has rights over his airspace. Invasion of the airspace at the lower stratum (the portion of airspace extending to about 200 metres above roof level), prima facie, amounts to a trespass.

> **KELSEN V IMPERIAL TOBACCO CO 1957**
> An advertising sign erected by the defendants encroached into the airspace above the plaintiff's property. The plaintiff applied for a mandatory injunction for the removal of the sign.

Held
❖ (QBD) The invasion of the plaintiff's airspace amounted to a trespass and therefore a mandatory injunction would be granted. [1957] 2 Q.B. 334.

Commentary
The Latin maxim "cuius est solum eius est usque ad coelum et ad inferos" applies here. It is clear that where there is an invasion of the lower stratum of the airspace, this amounts to trespass. It would have caused economic interference and loss of enjoyment to the owner of the land. McNair J. suggested that where there is an invasion of, at a height which might interfere with the owner's use of the land, this would amount to a trespass rather than a nuisance. In *Laiqat v Majid* [2005] EWHC 1305 (QB) it was confirmed that an overhanging extractor fan protruding 75cm and 4.5 metres above ground level did constitute an interference with airspace. A similar conclusion was

reached in *Stadium Capital Holdings (No.2) Ltd v St Marylebone Property Co Plc* [2009] All E.R. (D) 166.

Key Principle

Where an injunction is granted to restrain the invasion of airspace, it is generally inappropriate to suspend the injunction.

> ### JAGGARD V SAWYER 1995
> The plaintiff brought proceedings for an injunction to restrain the defendants' breach of covenant and trespass over her part of a road. The plaintiff had earlier threatened to bring proceedings but had taken no action until sometime later.

Held

❖ (CA (Civ Div)) Since the use of the road would cause minimal damage to the plaintiff and having regard to the defendants' conduct and the plaintiff's delay in applying for an injunction, the grant of an injunction would be oppressive. In the circumstances of the case, it was appropriate to award damages in lieu of granting an injunction. [1995] 1 W.L.R. 269.

Commentary

In *Anchor Brewhouse Developments Ltd v Berkley House (Docklands Developments) Ltd* (1987) 284 E.G. 625, Scott J. granted an injunction to prevent the invasion of the landowner's airspace by the booms of tower cranes belonging to the defendants, but suspended it for 21 days. Further, in *Woolerton and Wilson Ltd v Richard Costain Ltd* [1970] 1 W.L.R. 411 Ch D, an injunction granted on similar facts was suspended for 12 months to allow the building work to be completed. These two decisions were disapproved of in *Jaggard v Sawyer*, which suggested that it was inappropriate to suspend the injunction in this type of case.

Key Principle

Invasion of airspace in the higher stratum does not amount to an actionable trespass.

> ### LORD BERNSTEIN V SKYVIEWS AND GENERAL LTD 1977
> The defendants took an aerial photograph of the country house belonging to the plaintiff. They offered to sell the picture to him. The plaintiff alleged, inter alia, that the defendants were liable for trespass.

Held ....

❖ (QBD) The defendants did not infringe the plaintiff's rights and therefore no trespass was committed. [1978] Q.B. 479.

Commentary ....

Griffiths J. stated that a landowner did not have unlimited rights over his airspace. His rights over the airspace were limited to such height as was necessary for the ordinary use and enjoyment of the land. Above that height, the landowner had no better rights than any other individual. This is one of the limitations to the latin maxim—"cuius est solum eius est usque ad coelum et ad inferos" in that the owner of the land does not strictly own his airspace right to the heavens but merely to such height as is necessary for his enjoyment of the land. In addition, s.76 of the Civil Aviation Act 1982 makes it clear that there is no actionable trespass or nuisance for aircraft flying over a property at a reasonable height.

MINES AND MINERALS

Key Principle ....

The owner of the land owns the land down to the depths of the earth.

> BOCARDO SA v STAR ENERGY UK ONSHORE LTD 2010
> The defendants had obtained a licence under the Petroleum (Production) Act 1934 from the Secretary of State to search for and extract petroleum from land. In extracting the petroleum, the defendants drilled from its own land, but, in doing so had encroached into the strata underneath the claimant's land.

Held ....

❖ (Supreme Court) The owner of the land also had ownership of the strata underneath the land and this included minerals in it, unless the owner had disposed of those rights by contract or as a result of common law or statute. The encroachment by the defendants amounted to trespass and hence damages would be awarded. [2010] UKSC 35.

Commentary ....

The owner of the land owns the strata under the land unless this right had been disposed of. Although under the Petroleum (Production) Act 1934 the property in petroleum existing in the strata lies with the Crown, permission from the landowner is needed in order to extract this. If this is not possible then the Mines (Working Facilities and Support) Act 1923 enable a minerals operator to go to court to acquire compulsorily the right to work minerals and it gave powers to enable persons entitled to work minerals to acquire compulsorily "ancillary rights" to enable the operator to work minerals. The defendants failed to do so in this case and hence had trespassed onto the land of the claimant. Note also the provisions of the Coal Act 1938 in respect of ownership of coal and the *Case of Mines* [1586] 1 Plowd 310 in respect of ownership of gold and silver.

OBJECTS FOUND ON OR IN LAND

Key Principle
An object found buried in the ground belongs to the owner of the land.

> **ELWES V BRIGG GAS CO 1886**
> The question arose as to whether a prehistoric boat which was buried in the soil, six feet below the surface, belonged to the owner of the land.

Held
❖ (Ch D) The prehistoric boat, which was buried in the ground, belonged to the owner of the land, regardless of the fact that the owner of the land was unaware of the existence of the boat. (1886) L.R. 33 Ch. D. 562.

> **WAVERLEY BC V FLETCHER 1995**
> The defendant, who was lawfully present in a park owned by the plaintiff, used a metal detector and found a medieval gold brooch, which was buried in the ground. The plaintiff had a policy of prohibiting the use of metal detectors in the park, which the defendant was unaware of. The brooch was held by a coroner's court not to be treasure trove and returned to the defendant. The plaintiff commenced an action against the defendant to claim the brooch.

Held
❖ (CA (Civ Div)) Where an object was found in or attached to the land, the owner of the land had a better title to the object than the finder. In the circumstances, the plaintiff's appeal against the first instance decision would be allowed. [1996] Q.B. 334.

Commentary
Both these cases make it clear that where an item or object is found buried or attached to the ground the owner of the land has a better claim to it as

against the finder. In such a situation, there is no need for the owner of the land to have manifested any intention to retain control over such items or objects. It was also irrelevant whether the finder was a trespasser or a lawful invitee onto the land.

Key Principle

Where the object or item found buried in the ground amounts to treasure, the rightful owner is the Crown. This principle is now subject to the Treasure Act 1996.

ATTORNEY GENERAL OF THE DUCHY OF LANCASTER V GE OVERTON (FARMS) LTD 1981
A hoard of about 7,811 Roman coins was discovered buried in a field in Lincolnshire. A coroner's court found that they were treasure trove and therefore belonged to the Crown. The defendants claimed that the hoard was not treasure trove as it did not consist of silver coins.

Held

❖ (Ch D) The Crown's right to claim treasure trove did not extend to items not made of gold or silver. It was a question of fact for the court to decide whether a coin was a silver coin and in reaching that decision, the court was not compelled to apply any rigid rule as to the required silver content. On the facts of the case, the coins were not treasure trove. [1981] Ch. 333.

Commentary

The importance of this case is that it clarifies the position as to what amounts to treasure trove. Dillon J. suggested that treasure trove is when the object contains a substantial amount of gold or silver, is concealed in the land, and the owner is unknown. However, this rule is now subject to the **Treasure Act 1996.**

The **Treasure Act 1996** abolishes treasure trove and replaces it with the concept of treasure and new rules relating to it. Section 1 of the Act defines treasure as any object which is at least 300 years old, which if not a coin has a metal content of at least 10 per cent silver or gold. Where the find concerns a coin, it will be regarded as treasure if it is one of at least two coins having a metal content of least 10 per cent silver or gold or where it is one of at least 10 coins, both of which must be at least 300 years old. Section 4 of the **Treasure Act 1996** provides that when treasure is found, subject to prior interests and rights, it would vest in the franchisee (as defined in s.5 of the Act) if there is one, otherwise it vests in the Crown. The Act also makes provision for the holding of inquests in the coroner's court (s.7) and makes it a summary offence of failing to report the find to the coroner (s.8). The other important part of the Act relates to the payment of a reward, where the Secretary of State determines that a reward is payable. Section 10 expressly provides that the reward may be paid to the finder or the occupier of the land on which the item is found or any other person having an interest in the land. The reward is not to exceed the value of the treasure at market value. The Secretary of State is directed by s.11 of the Act to prepare a code of practice relating to treasure which has since been published.

Key Principle

An object or item found on the ground belongs to the finder unless the owner of the land manifested his intention to retain control over such items or the finder is a trespasser.

> PARKER V BRITISH AIRWAYS BOARD 1982
>
> The plaintiff was in the international executive lounge at terminal one of Heathrow Airport when he found a gold bracelet lying on the floor. He gave it to the defendant's employee with his name and address and made it clear that if the owner of the bracelet did not claim it, it should be returned to him. As there was no claimant for the bracelet, the defendant sold it and retained the proceeds. The plaintiff claimed the proceeds of sale from the defendant.

Held

❖ (CA (Civ Div)) The plaintiff acquired rights of possession of the bracelet by having taken it into his care and control. The defendant could have better rights to the bracelet if they manifested an intention to exercise control over the airport lounge and things in it. As the defendant failed to manifest such an intention, it had no rights over the bracelet, and as such, the proceeds of sale had to be given to the plaintiff. [1982] 1 Q.B. 1004.

Commentary

It is clear that where a person is an invitee onto the land, any objects found on the property by that person will belong to him, unless the owner of the land has made it clear that any such objects found on the land belongs to him. This intention must be manifested prior to the objects being found, for example, by a notice stating clearly that items found on the premises would not be returned. The court also suggested that where the finder is a trespasser, his or her rights are frail. In such a case the owner of the land has a better claim to the objects found on the land.

OWNERSHIP OF WILD ANIMALS AND FISH FOUND ON THE PROPERTY

Key Principle

The owner of the land has a qualified property in wild animals and fish which are found within the boundaries of his land.

> WILLIAM BLADES V WILLIAM HIGGS 1865
> The plaintiff chased and killed rabbits on land belonging to the Marquis of Exeter without permission. He sold these rabbits to a third party.

Held

❖ (HL) The servants of the Marquis were entitled to take possession of the dead rabbits as they belonged to the Marquis. (1865) 11 H.L. Cas. 621.

Commentary

This means that the owner of the land has the right to hunt and catch the wild animals or fish (unless they are a protected species) and once they are caught and killed, he acquires ownership of them. See also *Nicholls v Ely Beet Sugar Factory Ltd (No.2)* [1936] Ch. 343.

THINK POINT

Although an owner of land owns the land from the centre of the earth to the heavens, there are statutory restrictions of what he can do with the land. Think about what these are and how they affect the owner's use of the land.

In addition, other third party rights may exist which restrict the owner's use of the land. Consider what these proprietary rights may be.

Protection of Interests in Land

. . . .

2

INTRODUCTION

The estates and interests capable of existing in law are set out in s.1 of the **Law of Property Act 1925**. Whether the estate or interest in fact takes effect in law depends on its required mode of creation and registration. See Ch.3 on the Formal and Informal Methods of Acquisition of Interests in Land.

Upon the sale of land it is necessary to have a system for protecting third party interests in that land. Historically, there have been three stages of development in protecting third party interests. Prior to any system of registration, legal rights bound the world whilst equitable rights bound all except a bona fide purchaser for value of a legal estate without notice.

In the unregistered land system, the above prevailed except that certain interests were registrable as Land Charges and protection of such interests depended on their registration in the Land Charges Register. In addition, certain rights such as interests under a trust were overreachable (s.2 of the **Law of Property Act 1925**).

In the registered land system, estates are substantively registrable, mortgages need to be protected as registered charges, certain interests are specified as being overriding without needing registration, the remainder of interests should be protected by entry on the register either as a notice (agreed or unilateral) or a restriction in order to be protected and be binding on a subsequent owner of the land (s.29 of the Land Registration Act 2002). The system of land registration is governed by the **Land Registration Act 2002**. This makes various changes to the registered title system—one of the more fundamental changes is the change from "registration of title" to "title registration". This means in effect that legal estates in registered land can only be created registration and will not be a legal estate unless it is completed by registration: s.27 of the **Land Registration Act 2002**. It also authorises the use of electronic contracts and transfers therefore providing the basis for the introduction of e-conveyancing. In addition, the Act attempts to encourage total registration of all land in England and Wales by requiring registration of short leases, promotes voluntary registration and introduces two additional situations which trigger first registration. However, the grades of title remain the same as under the **Law of Property Act 1925**.

UNREGISTERED TITLE

Key Principle

Historically, protection of equitable interests has depended on the doctrine of notice.

> ### JONES V SMITH 1841
> The mortgagee enquired of the mortgagor as to interests affecting the security offered. The mortgagee was informed that the marriage settlement included only the wife's property and not the husband's estate being offered as security. The mortgagee advanced money without seeing the settlement, which in fact did include the husband's estate.

Held

❖ (Ch D) The mortgagee was not affected with constructive notice of the settlement's true contents. Constructive notice applies in two cases: first, where the party has notice that the property is encumbered or in some way affected, then he is deemed to have knowledge of facts to which he would have been led by due enquiry from the knowledge he actually had; secondly, where the party had a suspicion that the land was charged and wilfully or fraudulently determined to avoid receiving actual notice thereof. (1841) 1 Hare 43.

Commentary

A purchaser is caught by notice of prior interests. Sufficient knowledge can be actual knowledge, constructive knowledge as described in this case or imputed knowledge, i.e. knowledge attributed to the purchaser by the actual or constructive knowledge of one's legal representative. It should be noted that constructive knowledge includes knowledge that the purchaser would have if he made all the proper enquiries in respect of an inspection of the land and the title. It would also include situations where the purchaser refused to make enquiries and is deemed to have notice of all those matters which such proper enquiries would normally disclose. Compare *Hunt v Luck* [1901] 1 Ch. 45 where it was held that knowledge that rents were paid to an estate agent did not constitute notice of an intermediate interest adverse to the vendor.

Key Principle

A transferee takes free of a prior interest of which he has no knowledge.

PILCHER V RAWLINS 1872

The mortgagor conveyed land to trustees of a settlement in return for trust money. The surviving trustee later conveyed part of the land back in return for part-payment of the loan which he then misappropriated. The mortgagor then conveyed that part of the land to new mortgagees concealing, with the trustee's connivance, the prior mortgage and re-conveyance. The beneficiaries of the trust sought to recover the unpaid debt by asserting that the new mortgagees took subject to the original mortgage.

Held

❖ (CA) The new mortgagees took the estate free of the prior interests. (1871–72) L.R. 7 Ch. App. 259.

Commentary

The original conveyance recorded the terms of the trust. The subsequent conveyance did not, so it appeared to the new mortgagees that the land was unencumbered.

Key Principle

An interest, which fails to bind a purchaser, is also destroyed for the purposes of subsequent owners of the land.

WILKES V SPOONER 1911

The lessee of 137 High Street, East Ham, carried on the business of pork butcher and covenanted not to carry on any other business there other than a pork butcher. He was also lessee of 170 High Street, East Ham, under a different landlord where he carried on the business of general butcher. He assigned No.170 covenanting with the plaintiff that in effect he and his successors would not use No.137 to compete as general butchers. He surrendered the lease of No.137 to the landlord who then leased it to the now former lessee's son. The lease contained a covenant not to carry on any business other than a butcher (not specifying pork butcher as before). At the time of the surrender the landlord was not aware of the covenant made with the plaintiff, though the son was.

Held

❖ (CA) The landlord was not affected with constructive notice when he acquired back the lease. The grant to the son of a new lease was thus free of any such restriction and the son could carry on business as a general butcher. [1911] 2 K.B. 473.

Commentary

Whilst apparently unfair on the facts, this case makes clear the destructive effect of a conveyance (in this case a surrender) upon unprotected interests. This serves the interests of certainty of dealings, in that subsequent owners of the land will not get caught up in old and undiscoverable interest that could affect the use and value of the land.

Key Principle

To be registrable as a land charge, an interest in land must be proprietary and not just personal.

PRITCHARD V BRIGGS 1980
In 1944, L and his wife sold a hotel and surrounding land to R retaining a house, lake and petrol pumps. The sale contained a covenant to the purchaser and successors that so long as the vendors and purchaser were alive, the vendors and successors would not sell the retained land without giving the purchaser an option to buy the retained land. The covenant was registered under the Land Charges Act 1925. In 1947, R sold the hotel with the benefit of the covenant to M, who similarly sold on the land to the first and second defendants in 1954. In 1953, L and his wife had granted a weekly lease of the retained land other than the house to the plaintiff. In 1959, a five-year lease was granted to the plaintiff with a covenant that the plaintiff would have the option to buy all the retained lands upon giving notice within three months after the death of the survivor of L and his wife. In 1964, a further lease of 25 years was granted also containing the option. The option was registered under the Land Charges Act 1925.

The wife died, L's health deteriorated, and funds were urgently needed for looking after him. His nephew, the third defendant, was appointed receiver and agreed to sell the retained lands to the first and second defendants in pursuance of the 1944 pre-emption, conditional upon them indemnifying L and his nephew against any claim by the plaintiff. L died and the land was conveyed to the first and second defendants. The plaintiff served notice purporting to exercise his option.

Held ....

❖ (CA (Civ Div)) A right of pre-emption grants no proprietary right in land. There was no right to call for a sale until the grantor satisfied the conditions of the grant. The pre-emption could only bind once the conditions were satisfied. The registration of the option, which was a proprietary right, took priority over the pre-emption. [1980] Ch. 338.

Commentary ....

The registration of the pre-emption was therefore ineffective. A pre-emption could only be effectively registered once the conditions of the pre-emption were met. This will be impractical if other rights have been granted and registered in the meantime.

Key Principle ....

An option is a registrable interest at the time of its grant and binds subsequent purchasers when registered.

> ARMSTRONG & HOLMES LTD V HOLMES 1993
> In 1986 the first defendant granted the plaintiff an option to buy land. This was subsequently registered under the Land Charges Act 1972. The plaintiff sought to exercise the option but the first defendant would not co-operate in setting a price. The first defendant sold part of the land to a third party subject to the option insofar as it subsisted. The third party then sold that part of the land to the second defendant subject to the option.

Held ....

❖ (Ch D) The second defendant took subject to the option. The option was a registrable interest and had been protected by registration. The exercise of the option was not a separately registrable interest. [1993] 1 W.L.R. 1482.

Commentary ....

The case represents the converse of *Pritchard v Briggs* [1980] Ch. 338 (see above) in two senses. First, an option is registrable upon grant but a pre-emption is registrable only when it becomes exercisable. For an explanation of the distinction between a right of pre-emption and an option, see *Coaten v PBS Corporation* [2006] EWHC 1781 (Ch). Secondly, an unprotected interest is extinguished in respect of subsequent owners of land whereas a protected interest binds such owners. In *Phillips v Mobil Oil Co Ltd* [1989] 1 W.L.R. 888 CA (Civ Div) it was held that an option to renew a lease was a registrable estate contract and failure to protect it by registration made it void as against a purchaser of the land.

Key Principle

An easement arising by estoppel on the grounds of mutual benefit and burden and acquiescence does not have to be registered and binds successors to the land.

ER IVES INVESTMENT V HIGH 1967

The defendant's neighbour, W, built foundations that encroached into the substratum of the defendant's land. It was orally agreed that the defendant would allow this trespass to continue and that W would allow the defendant to have a right of way across W's backyard to get access to a side road. W sold his property to purchasers who knew of the agreement.

The defendant built a garage, which could only be used in conjunction with the right of way. The purchasers made no objection to the garage or use of the right of way. They got the defendant to resurface the yard for which he paid one fifth of the cost. The property was sold to the plaintiffs. Both the auction notice and the conveyance said that the sale was subject to the right of way. The right of way was never registered as a land charge. The plaintiffs sought a declaration that the right of way was void against them for want of registration and asked for damages and injunction for the alleged trespass.

Held

❖ (CA) By the mutual benefit and burden and acquiescence there was an estoppel-based easement which was not required to be registered as a land charge. [1967] 2 Q.B. 379.

Commentary

On the evidence, it was unfair to deny the defendants' right of way. It would not be logical to demand a right be registered where its existence comes about by estoppel.

Key Principle

A spouse's matrimonial home rights under the Family Law Act 1996 is strictly not a proprietary right, but can be registered as a land charge. Its registration stalls dealings in the land until family law issues are resolved.

WROTH V TYLER 1974

The defendant agreed to sell his bungalow with vacant possession to the plaintiff. Before completion his wife entered a notice on the Register of her right of occupation under the Matrimonial Homes Act 1983 (now known as matrimonial home rights under the **Family Law Act 1996**). The plaintiff sought specific performance and/or damages.

Held

❖ (Ch D) To grant specific performance with vacant possession would require the husband to litigate against his wife. To grant specific performance with the wife in occupation would split the family, not protect the defendant or daughter and would leave the wife open to eviction once the purchase was complete. The court granted damages in lieu of specific performance to the value of the difference between the offer price and current value. [1974] Ch. 30.

Commentary

Section 31 of the **Family Law Act 1996** replaces the rights of occupation under the **Matrimonial Homes Act 1983** with matrimonial home rights. Whilst strictly not a property right but a personal one, a spouse's matrimonial home right has the characteristic of a charge on the property when registered as a Class F land charge. This then binds future purchasers of the property (s.198 of the **Law of Property Act 1925**).

Key Principle

Failure to register an estate contract does not matter as between the parties but leaves the agreement void as against purchasers.

HOLLINGTON V RHODES 1951

Seven-year underleases were agreed between the defendant landlord and the plaintiffs. Documents were signed but not formally completed. The agreements were not registered as land charges. The defendant assigned the head lease to D subject to tenancies, on the property. D served notice arguing that the plaintiffs only enjoyed periodic annual tenancies. The plaintiffs had to renegotiate new leases of the full term at a higher rent and with a premium payable. The plaintiffs sought a declaration that they were entitled to the original lease agreed and damages for failure to complete that agreement.

Held

❖ (Ch D) The contract had never been completed. Had there been a contract they would have been entitled to their claim to damages against the defendant. [1951] 2 T.L.R. 691.

Commentary

There is no obligation to register an interest. As between grantor and grantee it is binding in contract law without the need for registration. However, failure to register makes the agreement void as to successors in title to the property.

Key Principle

An unprotected interest falling under class C(iv) or D of the **Land Charges Act 1972** will not survive a sale to a purchaser for money or money's worth. Such a purchaser need not act in good faith nor have to provide a commercial price as long as there is valuable consideration.

> MIDLAND BANK TRUST CO LTD V GREEN (NO.1) 1981
>
> A father granted his son an option to buy a property. The son did not register his estate contract. The father conveyed the land to his wife for £500 when the property was worth £40,000, almost twice the fixed sum which the option was set at. The conveyance was done with some haste and secrecy. On the evidence the sale was made in order to defeat the unprotected option. The son purported to exercise the option but the mother refused to sell. The son sought a declaration that the option was binding. By the time the case reached the House of Lords the property was worth £400,000. The dispute became one between the son's widow and children against his parents' estate. The difference in the widow and children's inheritance would be huge depending on the outcome of the case.

Held

❖ (HL) The House of Lords found that the mother took free of the son's unprotected interest. To take free of an unprotected interest such as this, s.13(2) of the **Land Charges Act 1925**, now s.4(6) of the 1972 Act, requires that there be a purchaser for money or money's worth. Money or money's worth did not have to be a fair commercial price but merely valuable consideration. This could even be nominal consideration. The meaning of purchaser did not, according to the statute, require that the purchase be in good faith. This requirement was one of the problems in the old system of discerning motive and intention, which the Act sought to remove. [1981] A.C. 513.

Commentary
The decision may look unfair given the apparent intention to take advantage of the son. However, in the long run justice is served better by a system that provides for certainty of dealings. The answer to plaintiffs in such a position of the son is to register their interest. Failure to do so will otherwise lead to people taking a legal advantage of one's carelessness. It is not a fraud to take legal advantage of another's failings. A similar conclusion was reached in *Lloyds Bank Plc v Carrick* [1996] 4 All E.R. 630.

Key Principle
In unregistered land a purchaser takes free of beneficial interests which he has no notice, actual, constructive or imputed.

CAUNCE V CAUNCE 1968
A husband and wife agreed to buy a house in their joint names with the help of a loan. Without the wife's knowledge the husband had the house put in his sole name and obtained three different bank loans using the house as security. The husband was declared bankrupt and he left the matrimonial home. The wife who stayed in the home sought declarations that:

[i]   the husband held the home on trust for herself and the banks;
[ii] the banks' mortgages were charged only against the husband's beneficial interest;
[iii] her interest had priority over that of the banks; and
[iv] the bank, who were also her bankers, had constructive notice of her equitable interest.

Held
❖ (Ch D) The bank took free of her interest unless they had constructive notice of it. An enquiry into the wife's account was not an enquiry that the bank should have reasonably made and there were no special facts which should have brought to their notice her interest. Mortgagees were not affected with notice of equitable interests of people residing in the property where that residence was not inconsistent with the title offered as security. They were not fixed with constructive knowledge by failure to enquire. The

mere fact of it being a matrimonial home did not raise a need to enquire. [1969] 1 W.L.R. 286.

Commentary ....

Section 199 of the **Law of Property Act 1925** provides in effect that a purchaser (s.87 puts a mortgagee in the same position) takes free of interests of which he has no actual or constructive notice. The case implies that a bank need not go behind the circumstances of a matrimonial home held in the name of one spouse. Compare this with the recent shift in the courts' attitude towards the degree to which a bank should enquire as to beneficial interests in property. (See Ch.8 on Mortgages).

REGISTERED TITLE

In the registered title system the estate is substantively registered. Third-party interests are either entered on the register against the substantive registration or are overriding. Legal mortgages are entered as Registered Charges. All other interests not being substantively registrable estates, registered charges or interests capable of being overriding, should be protected by entry on the register in the form of a notice or restriction. This area of the law has been reformed by the **Land Registration Act 2002** which was brought into force on October 13, 2003. As a result of the changes, a number of the cases on the Land Registration Act 1925 are no longer applicable.

[a] Interests which are capable of being overridden

Key Principle ....
A beneficial interest can form the basis of an interest which is capable of being overridden.

> WILLIAMS & GLYN'S BANK LTD V BOLAND 1980
> The case merges two actions on materially the same facts. A husband was a registered proprietor of a house. The wife had contributed a large part of the purchase price and the mortgage loan repayments. She therefore had a beneficial interest in the house. He mortgaged the house to the bank, which made no enquiries of the wife. The house was the matrimonial home in which husband and wife resided. The loan was defaulted upon and a possession order was granted.

Held
....

❖ (HL) The wife had an overriding interest of actual occupation under s.70(l)(g) of the **Land Registration Act 1925,** to which the bank's interest was subject. Her actual occupation based upon her beneficial interest was more than just a minor interest. Of itself a beneficial interest is registrable as a minor interest. [1981] A.C. 487.

Commentary
....

The **Land Registration Act 2002** reduces the number and extent of the application of the interests which are capable of being overriding and requires some of these interests to be noted on the register and for such interests to lose its overriding status on being noted on the register. The purpose is so as to enable the register to be as complete as possible. The Act makes a distinction between interests that override first registrations (Sch.1) and those that override registered dispositions (Sch.3). The two schedules contain an overlap but there are also significant differences relating to some others.

Interests which are the same:

There are interests which are the same in both Schs 1 and 3. In paras 4–9 of the schedules, a customary right, a public right, coals and coal mines and associated rights and certain mineral rights in land registered before 1925 retain their overriding status indefinitely.

Paragraphs 10–14 of both Schedules provide for interests which lose their overriding status after 10 years (so as not to breach the Human Rights Act 1998)—hence these will cease to have effect from October 2013. These are a franchise, manorial right and right to rent which was reserved to the Crown on the grant of any freehold estate, a non-statutory right in respect of an embankment or sea or river wall and a right to payment in lieu of tithe.

Interests which differ:

The interests where Schs 1 and 3 differ are as follows:

- Leases granted for less than seven years are interests which are capable of being overriding. Schedule 3 excludes a lease, the grant of which constitutes a registrable disposition from having overriding status. The reason is that a notice protecting such an interest is entered on the title of the superior estate.
- Easements and profits à prendre—A legal easement or profits à prendre is an interest that can override first registration. The **Land Registration Act 2002** states clearly that equitable easements are not overriding interests. However, Sch.3 para.3, read together with s.27 of the **Land Registration Act 2002** reduces the types of legal easements and profits that can override a registered disposition. For the first three years from the date of the coming into force of the Act, the position of such

easements and profits are the same as for first registration, i.e. that they bind the proprietor. After October 13, 2006, an unregistered legal easement or profit will override a registered disposition if it is obvious from a reasonable inspection of the land, known to the person to whom the disposition is made, exercised within the year before the disposition or it is registered under the Commons Registration Act 1965.

The effect of these provisions is that the only easements or profits capable of overriding a registered disposition are the easements arising from implied grant or reservation, by the operation of s.62 of the Law of Property Act 1925 or by prescription. Section 27 of the Land Registration Act 2002 imposes a requirement that an easement arising by express grant or reservation has to be completed by registration and that it does not operate until it is so registered. Therefore, such interests are not capable of overriding a registered disposition. Once completed by registration, it will be protected by entry on the register of a notice and although such interests could be legal, it is not an overriding interest.

- Interests of persons in actual occupation—this is more narrowly defined than in s.70(l)(g) of the Land Registration Act 1925. In order for such persons to claim an interest that is capable of overriding the claimant's interest, he or she must be in actual occupation of the property. The Land Registration Act 2002 removes the category of a person in receipt of rents and profits from claiming an overriding interest. If the claimant occupies only part of the land, his interest is only protected as regards that part and not the whole property (*Ferrishurst Ltd v Wallcite Ltd* [1999] Ch. 355 is no longer good law)—applied in *Thompson v Foy* [2009] EWHC 1076 (Ch). The interest of a person in actual occupation is not overriding if inquiry is made of that person and he does not disclose his interest when he could reasonably be expected to have done so or if the interest is not obvious on a careful inspection of the land—applies to registered dispositions and not to first registration.

Key Principle

An interest of a person in actual occupation must be founded on a proprietary right of some kind.

LLOYDS BANK PLC V ROSSET 1990

A couple wished to purchase a semi-derelict house as their home. As the purchase price was to be paid out of the husband's trust fund, its trustees insisted that the legal title be in the husband's sole name. The vendors allowed the purchasers access to the property before the exchange of contracts. Renovation work was commenced with the wife carrying out some decorating work as well as undertaking the supervision of the builders. The husband took out an overdraft with the plaintiffs to cover the renovation costs. Upon the husband's default of the loan, the plaintiffs sought possession of the property.

Held

❖ (HL) The wife's activities in respect of the renovation work prior to completion did not provide sufficient evidence on which the court could infer a common intention that she should have a beneficial interest in the property. In the absence of any express common intention, the finding that the husband held the property as constructive trustee for himself and his wife could not be supported. [1991] 1 A.C. 107.

> NATIONAL PROVINCIAL BANK LTD V HASTINGS CAR MART LTD 1964
> See Ch.7 on Licences.

Commentary

Contractual licences should not be regarded as proprietary rights. The reasoning is that these are rights enforceable against the person, which should not bind the land. Similarly a question had been raised in *Collings v Lee* [2001] 2 All E.R. 332 CA (Civ Div) whether mere equities could give rise to a proprietary right. However, s.116 of the **Land Registration Act 2002** makes it clear that mere equities can bind purchasers of registered land and as such could be an interest that is capable of being overriding. This also applies to estoppel claims and rights of pre-emptions (ss.115 and 116).

The law recognises for example, in *Hammond v Mitchell* [1991] 1 W.L.R. 1127 (Fam Div) that beneficial interests can be impliedly acquired by cohabitees, where there is an agreement or understanding that property be beneficially shared, upon which the claimant has detrimentally relied giving rise to a constructive trust or proprietary estoppel. This decision was followed in *Lloyds Bank v Rosset*. It should be noted that Lord Bridge stated in *Rosset*, that in the absence of any express common intention, it was doubtful if any conduct short of direct financial contribution will be sufficient to infer a common intention to share the property beneficially. The Court of Appeal in *Drake v Whipp* [1996] 1 F.L.R. 826 CA (Civ Div) emphasised that in the case of a constructive trust, the court can adopt a "broad brush approach" in determining the cohabitee or spouse's share of the beneficial interest in the property. In *Oxley v Hiscock* [2004] EWCA Civ 546, Chadwick L.J. stated that where a couple buys a home to be used as a family home in the sole name of one of the parties and each makes some financial contribution to the purchase and there is no express declaration of trust the approach to be taken was by way of asking two questions:

1. whether there is a common intention that each shall have a beneficial interest in the property. If there was such a common intention then there is no problem. Even where there is no communication of this nature this can be inferred from the financial contribution made by the parties. If the answer to this question is yes then as a constructive trust arises, there should be detrimental reliance but this is satisfied by virtue of the financial contribution.

2. what is the extent of the parties' beneficial interest? Often the evidence of their discussions at the time would provide the necessary solution but if no such discussion took place then the court will have to look at the course of dealings between the parties.

The approach in *Oxley v Hiscock* has been followed in *Stack v Dowden* [2007] UKHL 17 (see Ch.4) where the court stressed that the court will look at all the circumstances of the case in order to decide the parties' intention as to their beneficial interests.

The following are examples of the different types of interest which were held to be sufficient to support a claim of overriding interest:

- *Skipton Building Society v Clayton* (1993) 66 P. & C.R. 223—a couple who had been promised a right to occupy rent free for the rest of their life had a tenancy rather than a licence which thereby gave her a proprietary interest.
- *Redstone Mortgages Plc v Welch* [2009] 36 E.G. 98 CC (Birmingham)— the second and third defendants who had an assured tenancy had an overriding interest which had priority as against the mortgage company.
- *Nurdin & Peacock Plc v DB Ramsden & Co Ltd* [1999] 1 E.G.L.R. 119—a potential claim to rectify a lease was an overriding interest.
- *Malory Enterprises Ltd v Cheshire Homes (UK) Ltd* [2002] EWCA Civ 151—the right to rectify was a proprietary interest in land.
- *Goodger v Willis* (1999) E.G.C.S. 32—the claimant had an overriding interest on the basis of building works carried out on the land. The proprietary interest forming the basis for the occupation was the beneficial interest under a bare trust.

An interest that is capable of being overriding cannot be claimed where the interest upon which it is founded does not itself have priority over the transferee.

> PADDINGTON BUILDING SOCIETY V MENDELSOHN 1985
> A mother and son agreed to buy a flat. The mother contributed roughly half the purchase price. The flat was put in the son's name so that he could raise a loan for the remainder of the purchase price in return for mortgaging the flat to the building society. The society had no knowledge of the mother. The son and girlfriend moved into the house in July. The mother moved into the flat in August and the mortgage was registered in October. The son defaulted and the society obtained a possession order. The mother claimed that she had an overriding interest.

Held ....

❖ (CA (Civ Div)) Without any express trust or agreement at the time of the purchase, the intention must be imputed to the mother and son that her interest could not take priority over the first mortgagee. This is because they both knew that they could not buy the flat without the loan from the building society. The mother could not claim an overriding interest against the mortgagee because although she was in occupation at the relevant time (by the law prevailing then and since changed by *Abbey National v Cann*, below), the beneficial interest upon which she founded her occupation impliedly ceded priority to the bank. (1985) 50 P. & C.R. 244.

Commentary ....

The fact of occupation does not improve any interest upon which it is based. One cannot claim against the lender who enables you to acquire the property. This approach was followed in *Bank of Scotland v Hussain* [2010] EWHC 2812 (Ch) where the Bank claimed possession of the second defendant's house but the latter claimed that the Bank was bound by her overriding interest under s.70 (1) (g) of the **Land Registration Act 1925** (as the mortgage was created prior to the **Land Registration Act 2002**). The court held that on the facts the second defendant was in actual occupation through having her furniture and personal belongings in the property and having lived at the property from time to time with her intention to continue residing at the property. However, as the second defendant was aware that there would be a mortgage and that she would be bound by it she could not claim an overriding interest against the Bank.

Cases on overriding interests usually involve situations where a prior beneficial interest exists.

Key Principle
Actual occupation may be actual or apparent occupation.

> **CHHOKAR V CHHOKAR 1983**
> A husband held the legal title on matrimonial home on trust for himself and his wife. He entered into an arrangement to secretly transfer the title to a friend at an undervalue. They arranged to complete the purchase whilst the wife was in hospital giving birth. The husband took the proceeds himself and left the country. When the wife returned from hospital she found the locks changed and was excluded from the property. The husband's friend put the house up for sale at market value. The wife claimed an overriding interest of actual occupation.

Held
❖ (CA (Civ Div)) The wife was not literally in actual occupation at the time of the husband's friend becoming the proprietor. The continuing presence of her furniture with and her continuing intention to occupy was sufficient to constitute actual occupation for the purposes of s.70(l)(g) of the **Land Registration Act 1925**. [1984] Fam. Law 269.

Commentary
This approach has recently been followed in *Link Lending Ltd v Bustard* [2010] EWCA Civ 424 where the court held that the respondent, who was in psychiatric care and had not been allowed to live in her house for her own personal safety, was in actual occupation for the purposes of establishing an overriding interest under Sch.3 para.2 of the **Land Registration Act 2002**. Although she was not physically at the property at all times, she still considered this as her home and visited the house weekly on supervised visits. It is also crucial that the claimant maintains an intention to be in occupation. In *Thompson v Foy* [2009] EWHC 1076 (Ch), the claimant had moved some (but not all) of her belongings from the property and had expressed an intention not to return. The court held that she failed in her claim for an overriding interest on the basis that she was no longer in actual occupation.

In *Hodgson v Marks* [1971] Ch. 892 CA (Civ Div) the test was said to be more literal. There, the fact of occupation was effective notwithstanding that the vendor-registered proprietor was also in occupation. The onus is on the purchaser to enquire as to possible claimants to overriding interests. Whilst

Williams & Glyn's Bank Ltd v Boland suggests that the test is one of fact not law, the courts have not allowed claims based on short-term, (*Abbey National Building Society v Cann*, below), or transient presence, (*Lloyds Bank v Rossett* [1991] 1 A.C. 107 HL). In *Kling v Keston Properties Ltd* (1985) 49 P. & C.R. 212 Ch D the presence of the plaintiff's car was held to be sufficient actual occupation where the defendant maliciously blocked the plaintiff's car. In *Epps v Esso Petroleum Co* [1973] 1 W.L.R. 1071 Ch D, below, it was held that parking at unknown times in an unidentified place did not amount to actual occupation. It is important to note the dicta in *Abbey National Building Society v Cann* [1991] 1 A.C. 56 HL where Lord Oliver suggested that actual occupation "is a concept which may have different connotations according to the nature and purpose of the property". He went on to state that " ...it does ... involve some degree of permanence and continuity which would rule out mere fleeting presence". It has also been recognised in *Bank of Scotland v Hussain* [2010] EWHC 2812 (Ch) that a person can be in actual occupation of more than one property at the same time.

In *Hypo-Mortgage Services Ltd v Robinson* [1997] 2 F.L.R. 71 it was held that a child could not have an independent right of actual occupation even though half the beneficial interest in the house was held on trust for them. Further in *Bhullar v McArdle* [2001] EWCA Civ 510, the court stressed that the claimant had to be personally in actual occupation—it was not possible to be in actual occupation through a third party except in the case of occupation through a caretaker or employee of the claimant which is a company, see below.

The court in *Link Lending Ltd v Bustard* [2010] EWCA Civ 424, approved a useful summary of the law in respect of actual occupation in *Thompson v Foy* [2009] EWHC 1076 (Ch) which is as follows:

"(i) The words 'actual occupation' are ordinary words of plain English and should be interpreted as such. The word 'actual' emphasises that physical presence is required: Williams & Glyn's Bank v Boland [1981] A.C. 487 per Lord Wilberforce at 504;

(ii) It does not necessarily involve the personal presence of the person claiming to occupy. A caretaker or the representative of a company can occupy on behalf of his employer: Abbey National BS v Cann [1991] 1 A.C. 56 per Lord Oliver at 93;

(iii) However, actual occupation by a licensee (who is not a representative occupier) does not count as actual occupation by the licensor: Strand Securities Ltd v Caswell [1965] Ch. 958 per Lord Denning M.R. at 981;

(iv) The mere presence of some of the claimant's furniture will not usually count as actual occupation: Strand Securities Ltd v Caswell [1965] Ch. 958 per Russell L.J. at 984;

(v) If the person said to be in actual occupation at any particular time is not physically present on the land at that time, it will usually be necessary to show that his occupation was manifested and accompanied by a continuing intention to occupy: compare Hoggett v Hoggett (1980) 39 P. & C.R. 121 , per Sir David Cairns at 127."

Key Principle

Actual occupation must exist at the time of the creation of the transferee's interest in order to override the transferee.

ABBEY NATIONAL BUILDING SOCIETY V CANN 1990

The first defendant applied to the plaintiff for a loan to purchase a house on the basis that she would be sole occupier. He intended to live there with his mother and her future husband, the second and third defendants. The plaintiff inspected the property and the loan was formally offered and accepted. Contracts were exchanged on July 19, 1984, the money was advanced on August 6, the mortgage was executed before August 13, completion took place on August 13. The first and third defendant arrived at 10am that morning and began moving their furniture in at 11.45am. On September 13 the first defendant was registered as sole proprietor. The first defendant defaulted on the loan. The Building Society brought repossession proceedings. The second defendant claimed a beneficial interest by virtue of her contribution to the purchase of a previously shared home and an assurance by the first defendant that she would always have a roof over her head. She also claimed to have an overriding interest.

Held

❖ (HL) The relevant date for determining the existence of overriding interests was the date of registration of the estate not transfer or creation. However, for the purposes of s.70(l)(g) (of the **Land Registration Act 1925**) the person claiming must have been in actual occupation at the time of creation or transfer of the legal estate. The transactions of acquiring the estate and granting the mortgage were indivisible. There was no scintilla of time from the acquisition of the estate to the grant of the mortgage in which the second defendant's actual occupation based on a claimed beneficial interest could fit to bind the mortgagee. Occupation from 11.45am on the day till 12.20pm could not make for an overriding interest. In any case, the acts on the day were preparatory to moving in to reside and did not have a sufficient degree of permanence and continuity to constitute actual occupation. [1991] 1 A.C. 56.

Commentary

In respect of actual occupation, the date of occupation has been moved back from registration of the transferee's (mortgagee's) interest to the creation of the interest. This closes the registration gap between creation and registration where another interest could be fitted. This decision finds statutory recognition in s.29 of the **Land Registration Act 2002**. The date of registration remains the effective date for the transfer of interests to take effect in law for other purposes. The case also closes the gap between acquisition of an estate and grant of a mortgage. Logically one cannot grant something out of a property until it is owned. The court, however, recognised the reality that for practical purposes they are one transaction where the purchase is dependent upon a loan secured by the mortgage.

Curiously, in *Barclays Bank Plc v Zaroovabli* [1997] Ch. 321 Ch D, it was held that a protected tenancy which was created after the creation of a mortgage over the land but before registration of the mortgage would bind the mortgagee and thus prevent re-possession. The case can be distinguished on the grounds that the right claimed was not specifically one of actual occupation and there was a gap of six years between the creation and registration of the mortgage.

Key Principle

The actual occupation must be obvious on a reasonably careful inspection.

THOMAS V CLYDESDALE BANK PLC 2010

B was the sole registered owner of a property which he subsequently mortgaged to the Bank. He defaulted on the repayments to the bank who then sought possession of the property. The issue was whether the Bank was bound the beneficial interest of his partner, T, and in particular whether she was in actual occupation in accordance with para.2 Sch.3 of the **Land Registration Act 2002**. Before T and B moved into the property, they undertook renovations with builders and interior designers in the property. T visited the property almost on a daily basis. T and B subsequently moved into the property. The Bank contended that under para.2(c)(i) of Sch.3, T's interest was not one which was obvious on a reasonably careful inspection of the land at the time of the mortgage.

Held

❖ (QBD) T had reasonable prospects of establishing that her physical presence at the property and the presence of the builders and interior designers were of such a nature and extent that could be expected of T and B having regard to the renovation works being carried out to amount to actual occupation. There was a degree of permanence and continuity in her presence and that her intention was that she would reside permanently at the property. In respect of whether it was obvious on a reasonably careful inspection of the land, it is the visible signs of occupation which have to be obvious on inspection and in the circumstances the Bank would have been aware of T's interest if they had undertaken the inspection. [2010] EWHC 2755 (QB).

Commentary

The court in reaching its decision followed the earlier decision of *Lloyds Bank v Rossett* and *Abbey National Building Society v Cann* in that actual occupation was dependent on the circumstances of the case and in appropriate cases this would be affected by the state of the property. In the present case it was not fit for their occupation and therefore their occupation was through the builders and the interior designers with T's regular visits to the property and her intention to move in the property permanently. If a reasonable careful inspection of the property had been undertaken, T's presence would have been discovered. The court also followed the view of Mummery L.J. in *Link Lending Ltd v Bustard*, above, where he stated that the earlier authorities on actual occupation as found in the previous land registration legislation and now found in the **Land Registration Act 2002** were binding on the court.

[b] Interests that should be protected by entry on the register

The **Land Registration Act 2002** has made changes to the way that such interests are protected. Under this Act only two forms of protection by entry on the register exist—by notice and restriction. However, these two forms of protection have been extended to cover situations where cautions or inhibitions would have been used under the **Land Registration Act 1925**. It should be noted that the 2002 Act makes no reference to the minor interests but it is useful to continue to use this terminology.

Notice: Section 32 of the **Land Registration Act 2002** defines a notice as "an entry in the register in respect of the burden of an interest affecting a registered estate or charge". It goes on to provide in s.33 a list of interests that may not be protected by way of a notice. This includes an interest arising under a trust of land or strict settlement (which should be protected by a restriction), a lease for not more than three years and a restrictive covenant in a lease. The Act makes provision for two different types of notices:

Agreed Notice—the notice is entered with the agreement or on the application of the registered proprietor; and

Unilateral Notice—can be entered without the agreement of the registered proprietor. The Registrar will however inform the registered proprietor of the entry of the unilateral notice and the latter can apply for the entry to be cancelled. This is effectively the replacement for the caution but the difference is that it has the same effect as an agreed notice if no objection is forthcoming from the registered proprietor. In *Valais Ltd v Clydesdale Bank Plc* [2011] EWHC 94 (Ch), the court made it clear that the distinction between a caution and a unilateral notice was that the unilateral notice conferred priority for a valid interest. If the registered proprietor objects to the notice, the Land Registration Rules 2003 make provision for the resolution of this.

Restriction: Section 41 of the **Land Registration Act 2002** defines the restriction as

"an entry in the register regulating the circumstances in which a disposition of a registered estate or charge may be the subject of an entry in the register".

Section 40 provides that a restriction can be entered on the Register either for an indefinite period, for a limited period or until the happening of a specific event—which could include notice being given, or an order by the Registrar or court or consent being obtained. The restriction under the **Land Registration Act 2002** is broad enough to cover the interests that were formerly protected by way of restriction or inhibition under the **Land Registration Act 2002**. Sections 42 and 44 of the Act provides when the Registrar may and when he must enter a restriction. The restriction can be entered with or without the consent of the registered proprietor. In cases where the restriction is entered without the registered proprietor's consent, he or she must be informed of the entry. The Rules make provisions as to how the disputes are to be dealt with. The Act makes it clear that the restriction is not intended to be an alternative to the notice and that it must not be used to protect an interest that should be protected by way of a notice: ss.42(2) and 46(2) of the **Land Registration Act 2002**).

Schedule 12 of the **Land Registration Act 2002** makes it clear that existing entries in the Register by way of restriction, inhibition, notice and caution shall continue to have effect.

Key Principle ....
A cautioner who consents to a grant of a legal charge cannot later prevent dealings in the land by the chargee.

> CHANCERY V KETTERINGHAM 1993
> Property developers agreed to grant a lease to the defendant in con-sideration of £95,000. A caution was entered in the defendant's name. The developers negotiated a loan from the plaintiff for £570,000. The plaintiff asked for and received from the defendant consent for a mortgage of the freehold to be granted. The mortgage was duly entered as a Registered Charge. The defendant went into occupation though a lease had not formally been granted. The plaintiff sought to enforce its charge free of the defendant's lease agreement.

Held ....
❖ (Ch D) The proprietor of a legal charge entered on the register with the consent of a cautioner could deal with the land free of the rights of that cautioner. [1994] Ch. 370.

Commentary ....
Whilst apparently harsh, it is almost certainly true that the plaintiff would not have exposed himself to risk without obtaining the defendant's consent. In theory, the same principle would apply to unilateral notices under the **Land Registration Act 2002**.

Key Principle ....
The doctrine of notice as illustrated in cases such as *Peffer v Rigg* no longer has relevance under the **Land Registration Act 2002**.

> PEFFER V RIGG 1976
> In 1962 the plaintiff and first defendant bought a house as an invest-ment and home for the first defendant's mother-in-law. The house was put into the first defendant's name on trust for the plaintiff and first defendant. The house was divided into two flats. The lower flat was occupied by their mother-in-law and the upper one was rented out. The rental income covered the loan repayments on the house. The first defendant's wife moved into the lower flat. The plaintiff was concerned at this. An express trust was drawn up to reflect the original agreement. Further lettings of the upper flat became problematic, as it would

involve granting a protected tenancy. The first defendant, however, re-let the upper flat without the plaintiff's knowledge. The first defendant and his wife divorced. As part of the settlement he transferred the freehold of the house to her as beneficial owner and for consideration of £1. It was intended that she took over the mortgage repayments from the letting income from the upper flat. The plaintiff claimed that the re-letting of the upper flat and selling of the freehold were in breach of trust and that the house was held on trust 50 per cent for the plaintiff.

Held

❖ (Ch D) The re-letting was not in breach of trust. The first defendant acted reasonably as rental income was needed to cover the shortfall caused by the plaintiff's refusal to contribute maintenance of the house. The second defendant knew that the property had been held on trust. If the consideration was regarded as nominal then under s.20(4) she took the house subject to the plaintiff's unregistered interest. If there was valuable consideration in the context of the overall divorce settlement, it was still a requirement under ss.20(1) and 59(6) of the **Land Registration Act 1925** for the second defendant to be a purchaser in good faith. Even then, as she knew the property was held on trust she took it on general equitable grounds under a constructive trust for herself and the plaintiff. [1977] 1 W.L.R. 285.

Commentary

The question that arises is whether *Peffer v Rigg* will survive the **Land Registration Act 2002**. Although the Act does not specifically reject the principle in *Peffer v Rigg*, the Act does not replicate s.59(6) of the **Land Registration Act 1925**, upon which *Peffer v Rigg* relied on and arguably there is no longer any room for the application of the principle in *Peffer v Rigg*. It was also made clear by the Law Commission that neither actual notice of the unprotected interest nor bad faith would have any effect on the purchaser.

BENEFICIAL INTERESTS

Key Principle

Where a beneficial interest is overreached an interest in the property is converted into an interest in the proceeds and can thereafter not be an interest that is capable of being overriding.

> CITY OF LONDON BUILDING SOCIETY V FLEGG 1987
> A couple bought a house for £34,000 for themselves and the wife's parents to reside in. The parents contributed £18,000. The remainder

was to be raised by the couple from a loan. The couple was registered as proprietors and as joint beneficial tenants under a trust for sale. The parents lived in the house. The couple executed two further mortgages without the knowledge of the wife's parents. All three charges were discharged by an advance made by the plaintiffs of £37,500 in return for another mortgage. No enquiries were made of the wife's parents. The couple defaulted and the plaintiff took repossession proceedings. The parents claimed a prior beneficial interest by virtue of their contribution to the purchase price. They also claimed that their interests plus occupation at the time of execution of the plaintiff's mortgage gave them an overriding interest.

Held

❖ (HL) The parents' interests were overreached by the payment, which was properly made to two trustees. Given that their beneficial interests in the house were overreached, they no longer had a property interest upon which an overriding interest of actual occupation could be based. [1988] A.C. 54.

BIRMINGHAM MIDSHIRES MORTGAGE SERVICES LTD V SABHERWAL 1999
Two sons purchased a house for £185,000 with the assistance of a mortgage loan of £136,000. The house was occupied by the sons, their wives, children and their mother. The mother had made significant contribution over the years to the family homes and businesses. The sons re-mortgaged the house and subsequently defaulted on the loan re-payments. The claimants sought re-possession of the house. They relied on the principle of overreaching as in *Flegg*, above, and the fact that consent forms had been signed declining priority against the lender. The mother asserted that she had an overriding interest in the house. This was based on a beneficial interest derived from years of contributions to family homes and the fact that she was in occupation at the time of the re-mortgages. She asserted that her beneficial interest was not overreached. This was argued on a number of grounds: (1) *Flegg* and the law on overreaching were no longer good law after the Trusts of Land and Appointment of Trustees Act 1996 ("TLATA 1996"); and (2) If (1) was not correct *Flegg* could be distinguished on the grounds that the law on overreaching was invalid under art.8 of the European Convention on Human Rights and her interest arose under a constructive trust by virtue of proprietary estoppel.

Held

❖ (CA) **TLATA 1996** had not removed overreaching from the law. Article 8 had no application not least because the **Human Rights Act 1998** was not in force at the time and the **European Convention on Human Rights** was not part of domestic law at the time. Whether an interest was overreachable did not depend on whether it arose from proprietary estoppel. The mother's interest was overreached because the re-mortgage loan had been paid to the sons being two trustees. 80 P. & C.R. 256.

Commentary
The property legislation sought to balance the need to protect beneficiaries with the need to make land alienable when held under a trust. In *Flegg*, once the wife's parents' interests had been overreached they had no separate interest in the house that would affect the mortgagees. Their claim should lie against the trustees. They should not be in a better situation than a beneficiary who happens not to be in residence.

An interesting issue arose in *National Westminster Bank Plc v Malhan* [2004] EWHC 847 (Ch) where the court was asked to consider whether overreaching was discriminatory under arts 8 and 14 of the **European Convention for Human Rights**. The court stated that it did not have to answer the question as the **Human Rights Act 1998** was not retrospective and therefore was not applicable to the case.

REGISTERED CHARGES AND PRIORITIES

Key Principle
Registration normally determines the survival of an interest.

> MORTGAGE CORP LTD V NATIONWIDE CREDIT CORP LTD 1993
> The registered owners executed a legal charge in favour of the plaintiffs in return for a loan of £367,500. The plaintiffs did not enter this as a registered charge or protect it as a minor interest. The proprietors executed a second mortgage in return for a loan of £60,000 from the defendants. This was entered as a notice under s.49 of the **Land Registration Act 1925**. As the proceeds of sale were insufficient to meet both loans, the issue arose as to which mortgage had priority.

Held
❖ (CA (Civ Div)) A charge protected by notice only takes effect in equity until entered as a registered charge. The first mortgage, also unregistered, takes effect in equity. The second mortgage taking effect in equity (albeit entered as a notice) lost priority to the earlier mortgage. [1994] Ch. 49.

Commentary

The rule as to priority for the first time is now covered in s.28 of the **Land Registration Act 2002**. Under this the priority is dependent on the date of creation and it is not dependent on whether the equities are equal.

ALTERATION AND INDEMNITY

Key Principle

The Register can be altered in appropriate circumstances.

> **EPPS V ESSO PETROLEUM CO 1973**
> A property originally included a house and an adjacent commercial garage. The house was conveyed to E along with an 11-foot strip of frontage. E and her successors covenanted to build a wall to divide the house and garage but never did so. In 1955 the garage was leased to J for eight years; the lease purported to include the 11-foot frontage. In 1959 the freehold of the garage was conveyed to B subject to J's lease and repeating the error as to the frontage. B was registered as owner of the garage and frontage. This title was transferred to the defendants in 1964. In 1968, E conveyed the house to the plaintiff and the apparent double ownership of the frontage came to light. The plaintiffs sought rectification of the register and claimed actual occupation by virtue of J often having parked his car on the frontage. J was E's personal representative. The plaintiff's argument was that he used the parking space in that capacity rather than as lessee of the garage.

Held

❖ (Ch D) Parking the car for an unknown time on an unidentified space was not occupation and did not amount to actual occupation for the purposes of s.70(l)(g) of the **Land Registration Act 1925**. There was no actual occupation at the time of the conveyance to the defendants. The defendants were in possession and the court refused to exercise its discretion to order rectification of the register to return the frontage to the plaintiffs. [1973] 1 W.L.R. 1071.

Commentary

The **Land Registration Act 2002** introduces the concept of alteration and makes a distinction between alteration and rectification. Schedule 4 para.1 of the Act stipulates that the rectification of the Register is an alteration that involves the correction of a mistake and prejudicially affects the title of a registered proprietor. Therefore an amendment of the Register to give effect to an interest that is overriding is no longer referred to as rectification but an alteration. This is because it does not involve the correction of a mistake but to reflect the state of the title. Schedule 4 para.2 provides for the court to have the power to order the alteration of the register to correct a mistake, to bring the register up to date or to give effect to any estate, right or interest excepted from the effect of registration. The court has to make the appropriate order unless there are exceptional circumstances which justify its not doing so (Sch.4 para.3(3)). The consequence of this is that although there is some discretion given to the court, there is a predisposition towards alteration. In *Derbyshire CC v Fallon* [2007] EWHC 1326 (Ch), the adjudicator did not order an alteration of the register because the alteration would not serve any useful purpose. Whilst the alteration would redraw the general boundary on the paper title it would not have reflected the position on the ground and hence the circumstances were exceptional enough not to order alteration.

Schedule 4 para.5 goes on to provide that the Registrar has the power to alter the Register on the grounds stipulated in para.2. The Registrar is also given power to remove superfluous entries. In *Baxter v Mannion* [2011] EWCA Civ 120 the Court of Appeal decided that Sch.4 also covered the rectification of the register where a person who was registered as the proprietor on the basis of adverse possession, was not entitled to be registered as such. It went on to stress that ensuring the Register was put back to the position it was in prior to the application for registration on the basis of adverse possession would amount to a correction of a mistake within paras 1 and 5 of Sch.4. It was clear that there was no justification to limit the "correction of a mistake" to mistakes made as a result of some official error in the course of examination of the application.

The Act protects the proprietor in possession by stipulating in Sch.4 paras 3 and 6 that rectifications cannot be made without the proprietor's consent unless there has been fraud or lack of proper care which caused or substantially caused the mistake or would for any other reason be unjust for the rectification not to be made.

The changes introduced by the **Land Registration Act 2002** are a departure from the provisions in s.82 of the **Land Registration Act 1925** and hence previous case law on this area ought to be treated with caution. However some of the previous case law may nonetheless still apply. In *Norwich and Peterborough Building Society v Steed (No.2)* [1993] Ch. 116, the court refused rectification, where the sale had been executed by a mother under her power of attorney, granted by her son. The sale was fraudulently induced by the daughter. The mother had sufficient awareness of the effect of the transfer document and the son could not rely on her alleged ignorance, having originally granted the power of attorney to the mother. In *Freer v*

Unwins Ltd [1976] Ch. 288, a restrictive covenant having previously been on the Land Charges Register did not appear on the Register because of some error when the land came into the registered system. The Register was rectified from the time of next publication and was not backdated to the time when a lease was granted over the land. The lessee thus took free of the covenant but subsequent dispositions would be subject to registration. An example of the court ordering rectification under the **Land Registration Act 2002** is *Sainsbury's Supermarkets Ltd v Olympia Homes Ltd* [2005] EWHC 1235 (Ch). It was unjust in the circumstances of the case not to order rectification.

Key Principle

A party suffering loss from an error in the register is entitled to an indemnity from the Registry.

CLARK V CHIEF LAND REGISTRAR 1994

Two judgement debtors were owners of land subject to a charge to a bank, which was registered. The plaintiffs who were judgement creditors obtained a charging order nisi against the property, which they entered as a caution in August 1990. The order was made absolute and a further caution was entered in November 1990. The second defendant advanced money to the judgement debtors secured by a charge on the land. This charge was presented for registration in December 1990. The Registry failed to give notice to the plaintiffs under s.55 of the **Land Registration Act 1925**; the creditors thus did not challenge the registration. The charge thus took effect subject to the earlier charge to the bank but not to the plaintiffs' charges.

Held

❖ (CA (Civ Div)) Sections 55 and 56 of the **Land Registration Act 1925** described the nature and effect of cautions. Lodging of a caution did not give priority to the interest upon which the caution was founded. The second defendant's charge which was registered later, took priority over the plaintiff's charging orders. An error was made by the Registrar. The plaintiffs were entitled to an indemnity. [1994] Ch. 370.

Commentary

Schedule 8 of the **Land Registration Act 2002** provides that a person is entitled to be indemnified by the Registrar if he suffers loss by reason of:

- rectification of the Register;

- a mistake whose correction would involve rectification of the Register;
- a mistake in an official search;
- a mistake in an official copy;
- a mistake in a document kept by the Registrar which is not an original and is referred to in the Register;
- the loss or destruction of a document lodged at the Registry;
- a mistake in the cautions Register; or
- a failure by the Registrar to perform his duty under s.50 of the **Land Registration Act 2002.**

This provision therefore adopts a similar approach to the issue of indemnity arising from a rectification of the Register under the **Land Registration Act 1925.** The Schedule also makes provision for the exclusion or reduction in indemnity if the loss arises from the proprietor's fraud or lack of care.

THINK POINT

In Chhokar v Chhokar [1984] Fam. Law 269, the court decided that notional or token occupation is sufficient actual occupation if she has her belongings in the property and had the intention for the purposes of claiming an interest which is overriding. In that case she was absent from the property for a short period of time—would the case be decided different if her absence from the property was of longer duration for example, if she went on a six-month round the world trip?

Land registration was intended to do away with the doctrine of notice—do you think that this is strictly the case in the context of the **Land Registration Act 2002**? Look specifically at Schs 1 and 3 of the **Land Registration Act 2002.**

Formal and Informal Methods of Acquisition of Interests in Land

3

INTRODUCTION

This chapter will focus on the three main formal and informal methods of acquiring an estate or an interest in land. These are by:

- Contract and Conveyance.
- Adverse possession.
- Doctrine of proprietary estoppel.

[A] CONTRACT AND CONVEYANCE

The first stage in a purchase of land is usually the contract of sale and thereafter this is followed by the conveyance of the estate to the purchaser. Although this is normally the case in the sale of freehold land, this is not necessarily so with a grant of a lease which sometimes involves a formal grant of the lease only.

CONTRACT FOR THE SALE OF LAND

In order for there to be a contract for the sale of land it must satisfy the elements of a valid contract under contract law, namely, an offer, acceptance, intention, capacity and consideration and more importantly there must be a final and complete agreement between the parties. Thereafter, because it is contract for the sale of land, the contract must comply with the provisions of s.2 of the **Law of Property (Miscellaneous Provisions) Act 1989**. This provides that contracts for the sale of land must be in writing, incorporate all the terms which the parties have agreed in one document (or where contracts are exchanged, in each of them), and signed by or on behalf of each party to the contract. The section further provides that the terms of the contract may be incorporated in one document, or, by reference to some other document.

Key Principle

There must be an exchange of contracts or one document containing all the terms of the agreement between the parties.

> **COMMISSION FOR THE NEW TOWNS V COOPER (GREAT BRITAIN) LTD 1995**
> The issue arose as to whether correspondence between the parties could constitute an exchange of contracts for the purposes of s.2 of the **Law of Property (Miscellaneous Provisions) Act 1989**.

Held

❖ (CA) Section 2 of the 1989 Act could not be satisfied by an offer and acceptance contained in the correspondence between the parties. Section 2 required a greater degree of formality in contracts for the sale or other disposition of an interest in land. There must either be one document recording the agreement of both parties, or, a formal exchange of contracts incorporating all the terms of the agreement, with the intention that both parties be bound by the contract once the contracts are exchanged. [1995] Ch. 259.

> **HOOPER V SHERMAN 1995**
> The court was asked to consider whether a legally valid contract to transfer the plaintiff's share in the property and mortgage liability to the defendant had come into existence by an exchange of letters.

Held

❖ (CA) An exchange of letters was sufficient to form the written contract for the sale of land for the purposes of s.2 of the **Law of Property (Miscellaneous Provisions) Act 1989**. This was because the letters dealt with the essential terms of the contract and therefore amounted to an exchange of contracts, which formed a valid agreement under s.2. The court also noted that the use of the word "without prejudice" did not prevent a contract from coming into existence. [1994] N.P.C. 153.

Commentary

The two cases are clearly in conflict but both cases can be supported in different ways. It should be noted that although the 1989 Act abolishes the doctrine of part performance in such contracts (*Yaxley v Gotts* [2000] Ch. 162 CA (Civ Div)), it does not prevent the doctrine of estoppel from applying in cases where s.2 is not complied with but the requisite elements of estoppel are present. In *Bhullar v McArdle* [1999] E.G. 84 (C.S.) Ch D, three parties had orally agreed in 1987 to swap various parcels of land. They acted upon the agreement. It was held that that there was part performance, which by the principle of mutual benefit and burden, estopped the registered owner of one parcel from preventing the appropriate changes to the Register. Similarly in *Joyce v Rigolli* [2004] EWCA Civ 79 the court held that the resolution of a boundary dispute which involved swapping several pieces of land did not need compliance with s.2 but that even if it did the agreement could be enforced on the basis of proprietary estoppel. In *Cobbe v Yeoman's Row Management Ltd* [2006] EWCA Civ 1139 the court stressed that Parliament had always intended that proprietary estoppel would still exist even after s.2 of the **Law of Property (Miscellaneous Provisions) Act 1989**.

Alternatively, a constructive trust may arise instead of reliance on proprietary estoppel. In *Representative Body for the Church in Wales v Newton* [2005] EWHC 631 (QB) where it was decided that an agreement for the sale of a business which included the assignment of a lease was void for non-compliance with s.2 of the **Law of Property (Miscellaneous Provisions) Act 1989** as it was not in writing. No constructive trust arose on the facts of the case as the sale was conditional upon the lessor's consent to the assignment which was not obtained. In contrast in *Kinane v Mackie–Conteh* [2005] EWCA Civ 45 an agreement to grant of a charge was similarly void for non-compliance with s.2 of the **Law of Property (Miscellaneous Provisions) Act 1989** but was enforceable as a constructive trust under s.2(5) of the **Law of Property (Miscellaneous Provisions) Act 1989** in the circumstances of the case. See also *Oates v Stimson* (2006) EWCA Civ 548.

It should be noted that in *Re Stealth Construction Ltd* [2011] EWHC 1305 (Ch) an exchange of emails was insufficient to comply with s.2 of the **Law of Property (Miscellaneous Provisions) Act 1989** as they did not contain all the terms of the agreement. It did not however rule out the possibility that an email exchange may be sufficient if it had contained all the terms of the contract. In addition, it was accepted that the putting of their respective names at the end of the email was a "signature" for the purposes of the section.

Key Principle

The word "signed" in s.2 of the **Law of Property (Miscellaneous Provisions) Act 1989** should be interpreted in its ordinary sense.

FIRSTPOST HOMES LTD V JOHNSON 1995

In 1993, the vendor orally agreed to sell some land to the purchaser. The purchaser prepared a letter for the vendor to sign. This letter set out the purchaser's agreement to purchase the land and had typed the purchaser's name at the top of the letter. The purchaser did not sign the letter but signed the enclosed plan. The purchaser applied for specific performance of the contract, and the personal representatives of the vendor applied to strike out the purchaser's claim.

Held

❖ (CA (Civ Div)) The purchaser's appeal would be dismissed as the letter and plan could not be regarded as a single document for the purposes of the 1989 Act. They were separate and distinct documents. Also, the typing of the purchaser's name at the top of the letter was not a signature within the meaning of s.2 of the Act. Accordingly, there was no complete contract. [1995] 1 W.L.R. 1567.

Commentary

In the case, Peter Gibson L.J. suggested that the word "signed" in s.2 of the 1989 Act should be interpreted in plain English. He further suggested, that the earlier cases on the interpretation of what amounted to a signature for the purposes of the Statute of Frauds and s.40 of the **Law of Property Act 1925** should not apply to the interpretation of the same word in s.2.

Key Principle

A lock-out agreement does not need to comply with s.2 of the **Law of Property (Miscellaneous Provisions) Act 1989**.

PITT V PHH ASSET MANAGEMENT LTD 1993
The plaintiff made an offer to purchase the defendant's property. The defendant agreed with the plaintiff that it would not consider any further offers for the property, provided contracts for the sale of the property were exchanged within two weeks. This was confirmed in writing. The defendant sold the property to a third party during this period.

Held

❖ (CA (Civ Div)) The lock-out agreement (by which the defendant agreed not to consider other offers during the operative period) was not one which needed compliance with s.2 of the **Law of Property (Miscellaneous Provisions) Act 1989**. The defendant was in breach of this agreement. [1994] 1 W.L.R. 327.

Commentary

The use of the lock-out agreement would prevent the practice of gazumping from taking place and more importantly the case emphasises that the lock-out agreement is not a contract of sale of land requiring compliance with s.2.

Key Principle

Where a contract is contained in two parts, a court may hold that there are two separate contracts, one being the main contract, which is subject to s.2 and the other, a collateral contract, which is not.

> RECORD V BELL 1991
>
> The vendor and purchaser of a property signed a contract in two parts, subject to exchange of contracts. The vendor agreed to give a warranty with regards to the state of the title. This was for the purpose of inducing the purchaser to exchange contracts. Although the contracts were exchanged, the purchaser did not complete the purchase. The vendor applied for specific performance of the contract.

Held

❖ (Ch D) The contract was enforceable as it complied with s.2 of the 1989 Act. There were two separate contracts, one being the main agreement between the parties which complied with the statutory requirements and the other, the warranty, was a collateral contract which did not require compliance with s.2. [1991] 1 W.L.R. 853.

Commentary

A similar approach was taken in *Tootal Clothing Ltd v Guinea Properties Management Ltd* (1992) 64 P. & C.R. 452 CA (Civ Div), where the plaintiff and the defendants signed two agreements. One was an agreement to grant a lease and the other was a supplemental agreement, where it was agreed that the defendant would contribute towards the costs of the shop fitting works. The defendant alleged that the supplemental agreement was invalid because of s.2 of the **Law of Property (Miscellaneous Provisions) Act 1989**. It was decided by the Court of Appeal that the supplemental agreement was not a contract in respect of a disposition of an interest in land, and therefore, once the lease had been granted, s.2 was inapplicable. However, in *Grossman v Hooper* [2001] EWCA Civ 615, the court was not in favour of the notion of collateral contracts but preferred to consider the terms upon which the property was agreed to be sold and whether those terms had been incorporated in the agreement. The issue here was whether an agreement to pay off a loan to a third party had to comply with s.2 of the 1989 Act. This was linked to an agreement for the transfer of a property from a man to a woman following the break-up of their relationship. The agreement for the payment of the debt was not part of the agreement to transfer the property and therefore did not have to be included in the agreement to transfer. Similarly in *North Eastern Properties Ltd v Coleman & Quinn Conveyancing* [2010] EWCA Civ 277 an agreement to pay a 2 per cent finder's fee in respect to 11 contracts of sale of property did not form part of the main contract but of a collateral contract and hence did not have to comply with the terms of s.2.

Key Principle

The variation of a material term in a contract for the sale or disposition of an interest in land has to comply with s.2 of the **Law of Property (Miscellaneous Provisions) Act 1989**.

McCAUSLAND V DUNCAN LAWRIE LTD 1996

Earlier court proceedings resulted in the court granting an order that the plaintiffs would purchase the property from the defendant for £210,000 with completion fixed on March 26, 1995. This settlement agreement was in compliance with s.2 of the 1989 Act. As the day fixed for completion was a Sunday, the defendants' solicitors wrote to the plaintiffs' solicitors suggesting March 24, 1995 as the completion date. The plaintiffs' solicitors agreed to it in writing. The plaintiffs were unable to complete and the defendants issued a completion notice for compliance in 10 days. The defendants then issued a rescission notice on the expiry of the completion notice. The plaintiffs applied for specific performance of the compromised agreement and the question arose as to whether compliance with s.2 was necessary with respect to the variation of the contract.

Held

❖ (CA (Civ Div)) Compliance with the formalities laid down in s.2 was necessary where there was a variation of a material term of the contract. The variation of the contract in the present case was material as it brought forward the completion date and therefore affected the time when either party may issue the notice to complete. The plaintiffs' appeal against the first instance decision would be allowed. [1997] 1 W.L.R. 38.

Commentary ....

It is therefore necessary for solicitors to consider carefully whether the term being varied is a material term. If it is, then compliance with s.2 is necessary because whenever the parties varied a material term, they were in effect entering into a new agreement. If s.2 is not complied with, the parties are relegated to their rights under the original contract.

Key Principle ....

The grant of an option to purchase land has to comply with s.2 of **the Law of Property (Miscellaneous Provisions) Act 1989**.

> SPIRO V GLENCROWN PROPERTIES LTD 1990
> The defendant was granted an option to purchase land by the plaintiff. The defendant exercised the option by notice in writing within the stipulated time. However, the defendant failed to complete the purchase. The grant of the option was signed by both the parties, but only the defendant signed the notice exercising the option to purchase.

Held ....

❖ (Ch D) For the purposes of s.2 of the 1989 Act, an option to purchase land should be regarded as being equivalent to a contract for the sale of land conditional on the purchaser's exercise of the option. The 1989 Act did not prevent the agreement creating or granting the option from being the relevant contract for the purposes of the Act. The grant of the option had to comply with s.2. Accordingly as the option did comply with s.2 the option was valid. [1991] Ch. 537.

Commentary ....

It is clear that the grant of an option to purchase land will have to comply with the formalities laid down in s.2 of the 1989 Act. The case suggests that an option to purchase can be regarded as a conditional contract, which brings it within the ambit of the section. However, the exercise of the option to purchase does not have to comply with s.2: *Armstrong & Holmes Ltd v Holmes* [1993] 1 W.L.R. 1482.

CONVEYANCE

In order for the title to the land to be validly transferred to the other party to the contract, the general rule applicable is as contained in s.52(l) of the **Law of Property Act 1925**. This provides that

> "[a]ll conveyances of land or of any interest therein are void for the purposes of conveying or creating a legal estate unless made by deed".

There are a number of exceptions to this, the most notable being s.54 of the **Law of Property Act 1925**, which removes the need for a deed in the case of a grant of lease for less than three years. In the case of registered land, there is the additional requirement that the transfer must be by registration: s.27 of the **Law of Property Act 2002**.

For the deed to be valid, it has to comply with the statutory requirements for a deed contained in s.1 of the **Law of Property (Miscellaneous Provisions) Act 1989**. Generally, the deed must be in writing, signed and delivered. As regards of what amounts to delivery, the court in *Bibby Financial Services Ltd v Magson* [2011] EWHC 2495 (QB) stated that:

> "the critical thing is that the person who has signed the deed must have separately indicated that he intends to be bound by the deed. Mere signature is not enough. Nor is it enough that what looks like a deed has been given to the person who appears to be the beneficiary of it—the issue is not whether the document has been physically handed over to the beneficiary, but whether the person whose deed it is supposed to be intended to be bound by it".

[B] ADVERSE POSSESSION

The law of adverse possession in essence allows a squatter or trespasser who has occupied land, to claim an interest or estate in the land, in cases where the owner of the land has failed to secure the eviction of the squatter or trespasser within a certain period of time. The position is that generally the claimant must have taken adverse actual possession of the land with the intent to possess the land. In unregistered land, the owner of the land is barred from claiming after 12 years from the date the right accrued: s.17 of the **Limitation Act 1980**. With respect to registered land, the position is now governed by the **Land Registration Act 2002** which introduces different rules before a claim based on adverse possession can succeed, see below.

Key Principle
Possession of land can only be adverse if it is shown that the trespasser is actually in possession of the land and there is intention to be in possession by excluding all others, including the landowner from the land.

> LITTLEDALE V LIVERPOOL COLLEGE 1899
> The defendants owned two fields in between which was a strip of land separated by hedges. This strip of land, which led from the highway to the plaintiffs' pasture, had been conveyed to the defendants with the fields. The plaintiffs had a right of way over the strip of land. More than 12 years before the commencement of the present action, the plaintiffs put up locked gates at each end of the strip. The plaintiffs commenced the action to restrain the defendants from trespassing on the strip of land.

Held
❖ (CA) The defendants had not been dispossessed of their rights to the strip of land because the act of the plaintiffs in putting up the locked gates may have been done with the intention of protecting their right of way against the public use of it. The plaintiffs had failed to demonstrate an occupation with the intention of excluding the owner as well as other people. [1900] 1 Ch. 19.

> POWELL V MCFARLANE 1977
> In 1956, the plaintiff, who was aged 14 at the time, with the help of his friends went onto the disputed land, improved the fencing, cut the brambles and cut hay for the purpose of feeding the family cow. Thereafter he allowed the family cow to graze on the disputed land until it died in 1968. Between 1956 and 1973, the plaintiff went shooting on the disputed land from time to time. Subsequently, the plaintiff started business as a contractor to fell and treat trees and had put a sign on the disputed land in a manner that could be seen from the road. The plaintiff sought a declaration that he had been in adverse possession of the disputed land within the Limitation Acts for up to 12 years.

Held
❖ (Ch D) In order to establish adverse possession the plaintiff had to prove he had the requisite intention to possess and made such an intention clear

to the world. The plaintiff's intentions at a time when he was aged 14, as interpreted primarily from his own acts, were to take various profits from the land. Such acts were equivocal in the sense that they were not necessarily referable to an intention on his part to dispossess the owner of the land and to occupy the land as his own property. The plaintiff's claim therefore failed. (1979) 38 P. & C.R. 452.

JA PYE (OXFORD) LTD V GRAHAM 2002

P was the owner of some fields adjoining G's land. P permitted G's predecessor in title to use it for specific purposes originally under a grazing licence in 1983 and by giving permission to cut hay in 1984. G's predecessor in title made subsequent requests for a renewal of these licences but P did not respond. G and his predecessor in title continued to use the land from 1986 till 1999. In 1977, a caution was lodged by G, on the basis of his adverse possession of the land. P sought to warn off the caution and commenced proceedings in 1999 to reclaim possession of the land.

Held

❖ (HL) G and his predecessors in title had made out a claim for adverse possession. It was stressed that both the fact of possession and intention to possess had to be established. However, there was no need to prove an intention to own but merely an intention to possess. G had satisfied both criteria in this case and therefore was entitled to be registered as owners of the property. [2002] UKHL 30.

Commentary

Slade J. stated in *Powell v McFarlane* that the relevant principles relating to adverse possession were:

[a] the owner of the land with paper title was deemed to be in possession and the law would, without any reluctance, ascribe possession to him or any other person claiming title through him, in the absence of contrary evidence;

[b] a claimant to possession of the land without the paper title must show both a factual possession and the requisite intention to possess;

[c] factual possession indicated a degree of appropriate physical control over the land which was dependent on the circumstances of the case, in particular the nature of the land and the manner in which the land of that nature was commonly used or enjoyed; and

[d] the requisite intention to possess involved the intention in the plaintiff's own name and on his own behalf to exclude the world at large, including the owner with the paper title so far as was reasonably

practicable and so far as the processes of the law allowed. Such an intention must be made clear to the world at large.

The approach of Slade J. in *Powell v McFarlane*, has been followed in subsequent cases such as *Buckinghamshire CC v Moran* (below), *Wilson v Martin's Executors* [1993] 1 E.G.L.R. 178 CA (Civ Div) and *Burns v Anthony*, (1997) 74 P. & C.R. D.41. This was approved by the House of Lords in *JA Pye (Oxford) Ltd v Graham*, above. In *Batt v Adams* [2001] 32 E.G. 90 Ch D, although 12 years factual possession could be proved, the necessary intent to possess was missing. This was because the squatter was a tenant and had not been aware that the land was owned by anyone other than his landlord. He was in factual possession but was under the impression that as tenant he was entitled to make use of the land and thus his possession of the land was not as a means of excluding a person with title. Similarly in *Clowes Developments (UK) Ltd v Walters* [2005] EWHC 669 (Ch) it was decided that where the occupation by the claimant was on the basis of a belief that his occupation was with the permission of the landowner, this negated an intention to possess. See also *Chaplin v Hicks Developments Ltd* [2007] EWHC 141 (Ch).

In *Lambeth LBC v Blackburn* [2001] EWCA Civ 912, the issue arose as to whether a squatter of a block of flats owned by Lambeth had the necessary intent to possess. The squatter could establish 12 years factual possession but had expected to be evicted but was prepared to negotiate with Lambeth for a lease. The Court of Appeal decided that his willingness to accept a lease did not negate the intention to possess as all that had to be established was an intention to possess to the exclusion of other people. The House of Lords in *JA Pye (Oxford) Ltd v Graham* stressed that willingness of G or his predecessors in title to pay for the use of the fields did not negate the intention to possess.

For the purposes of establishing the 12-year factual possession it has been decided that where the claimant was in occupation of land whilst negotiations took place in respect of a transfer of the interest in the land, this gave rise to an implied licence that allowed the claimant to stay on the land. Accordingly time did not begin to run during this time: *Colin Dawson Windows Ltd v King's Lynn and West Norfolk BC* [2005] EWCA Civ 9 and *Batsford Estates (1983) Co Ltd v Taylor* [2005] EWCA Civ 489.

There must also be factual possession amounting to a form of exclusive control without permission or agreement: *Wills v Wills* [2003] UKPC 84. In *Palfrey v Wilson* [2007] EWCA Civ 94, the maintenance and repair of a wall including adding a damp course and raising a wall's height could amount to factual possession. Further, in *Hare v Smith* [2010] EWCA Civ 1518 the court decided that a claim to adverse possession can still succeed even though the precise location of the boundary to the land is difficult to identify.

In *Port of London Authority v Ashmore* [2009] EWHC 954 (Ch) the court decided that in establishing adverse possession, it did not require physical possession at all times. In deciding whether there was sufficient factual possession it was important to consider the nature of the land and the way in which the land was commonly used. In that case the land in question was a river bed and hence short of building a structure on it the claimant could not be in continuous physical possession of the property. On the facts, what he had done was sufficient to establish factual possession.

Key Principle

The occupation or possession of land may be adverse even if the paper owner has no present use for the land but only a future intended use.

LEIGH V JACK 1879

A piece of land, which was owned by Leigh, was designated on the plans as being for an intended street which never materialised. Adjoining land was conveyed to Jack who operated a foundry on it and dumped materials used at his factory on this piece of land. This obstructed passage by carts on the piece of land but did not impede pedestrian access. In 1865, Jack enclosed an oblong portion on this piece of land and in 1872 he fenced in the ends of the intended street. An action was commenced in 1876 to recover possession of this piece of land.

Held

❖ (CA) The deposit of the materials by Jack on this piece of land was not adverse because as the owner had no present use of the land, this was not inconsistent with the enjoyment of the owner. (1879–80) L.R. 5 Ex. D. 264.

BUCKINGHAMSHIRE CC V MORAN 1989

Buckinghamshire CC was the owner of a plot of land. It was the council's intention that this plot of land be used for a future road diversion. Moran owned the adjoining plot of land. The Council did not fence the boundary between Moran's and its plot of land as a result of which Moran used the Council's land as part of his garden. Council employees who inspected the plot of land periodically noted that it was kept tidy. The plot of land owned by the council appeared as part of Moran's garden at all material times. Nine years after Moran started using the Council's land, the Council's solicitor wrote to him asserting the Council's title to it but no further action taken until a further nine years later when the Council commenced legal proceedings to recover possession of the plot of land.

Held

❖ (CA (Civ Div)) An owner who retains land unused because he has a future intended use of land could be dispossessed. The claimant had to establish both factual possession and an intention to possess. There was evidence in this case that Moran had acquired complete and exclusive control of the Council's plot of land and therefore his actions amounted to an unequivocal demonstration of his intention to possess the land. [1990] Ch. 623.

Commentary

In *Leigh v Jack*, Bramwell L.J. stated that,

> " ... acts must be done which are inconsistent with [the owner's] enjoyment of the soil for the purposes for which he intended to use it".

The rule usually deduced from the case is that the occupation of the land by the trespasser is not necessarily adverse if the owner with the paper title has no present use of the land but only a future intended use. Such occupation is not inconsistent with the land owner's enjoyment of it.

This rule appears to be put in doubt by *Buckinghamshire CC v Moran*. This case suggests that the fact that the owner with the paper title has no present but merely a future intended use for the land does not automatically mean that occupation of the land by the trespasser can never be adverse. It is clear from this later decision that what amounts to adverse possession of the purposes of the Limitation Acts is ultimately a question of fact. The nature of the actions, which can be regarded as evidence of adverse possession, will depend on the character and nature of the land, which is in dispute. There is an argument that after this decision, it may be easier for squatters to obtain title to abandoned property. This approach was followed in *Purbrick v Hackney LBC* [2003] EWHC 1871 (Ch).

Key Principle

In registered land, once the claimant had been registered as proprietor of the leasehold, the dispossessed leaseholder cannot purport to surrender the lease back to the lessor.

D was the registered assignee of the lessee of a 99-year lease granted in 1902. By 1968, H had acquired title to the land by adverse possession against D. H applied for and obtained registration as the proprietor of the leasehold with possessory title. The title under which D was registered as proprietor of the leasehold interest was then closed. In 1975, D purported to surrender her lease to S, who was the registered proprietor with absolute title to the freehold. S instituted legal proceedings against H, inter alia, seeking an order for the deletion of H's title from the register or alternatively, rectification of the register by reinstating D as the proprietor of the leasehold.

Held

❖ (Ch D) When D's title was closed, she was no longer able to surrender it as she had ceased to be the registered proprietor of the property. At that stage, the title to the property was vested in H and only H could surrender it. D was also not entitled to an order rectifying the register as the Registrar had registered H's interest in accordance with s.75(2) of the **Land Registration Act 1925**. [1981] 1 W.L.R. 221.

Commentary

It is clear that in the context of registered land, once the squatter acquires adverse possession of the land the Registrar, if satisfied that the requirements in s.75(2) are satisfied, is under a duty to register the squatter with possessory title of the interest. In the case of a lease, the leaseholder's interest is extinguished and therefore is not in a position to surrender the lease back to the landlord. See *Central London Commercial Estates Ltd v Kato Kagaku Ltd* [1998] 4 All E.R. 948. The position is different in the case of unregistered land. In *St Marylebone Property Co Ltd v Fairweather* [1963] A.C. 510, the House of Lords were of the view that a leaseholder who was dispossessed of his property could nonetheless surrender the lease to the lessor. The effect of which was to end the lease entitling the lessor to immediate possession of the land as against the squatter.

The **Land Registration Act 2002** introduces a new regime for adverse possession in the context of registered land. Section 96(1) of the Act states that s.15 of the **Limitation Act 1980** shall not apply in respect of a registered estate. Under the new law, the principles as to what amounts to adverse possession continues to be applicable but what has changed is the procedure for claiming adverse possession in registered land. Schedule 6 of the **Land Registration Act 2002** provides that the claimant could apply to be registered as proprietor where he has been in adverse possession for 10 years provided he can show possession up to the date of his application.

Upon receipt of the application the Registrar gives notice to the registered proprietor and certain other parties with interests in the property. If they do not respond then the claimant could be registered as proprietor. If they do respond then Sch.6 para.5 will apply. Under this the claimant can be registered as proprietor in the following situations:

- estoppel;
- some other right to the land; and
- reasonable mistakes as to the boundaries.

Where the claimant does not fall into any of the three categories then the claimant will not be registered as proprietor. If those with an interest in the land do not take action to reclaim possession within a period of two years, the claimant will be entitled to be registered as a proprietor under Sch.6, paras 6 and 7. Thus in essence 12 years' adverse possession could still give the claimant title to the property but the circumstances will be more difficult for this to arise because after the initial application under para.5, those with an interest in the property would be alerted to the claim and presumably would take action to recover the property. In the event that the claimant succeeds in establishing adverse possession under the 2002 Act, he will normally be registered with title absolute.

Key Principle

The law of adverse possession is not contrary to the **Human Rights Act 1998** in respect of cases governed by the **Land Registration Act 1925**.

OFULUE V BOSSERT 2008

The appellants (Ofulue) appealed against the decision to award the respondent on the basis of adverse possession. The appellants were the registered owners of the property in 1976. They then left for Nigeria and the property fell into a state of disrepair. The appellants entered possession of the property via a former tenant in 1981. In 1983 the first appellant visited the property and found the respondent and her father living there. He informed them that he was the owner and that they were to leave. He then left the United Kingdom and returned to Nigeria. He returned in 1987 and again asked the respondent and her father to leave and commenced possession proceedings in 1989. The respondent's father counterclaimed on the basis that he had undertaken work on the property and that the appellants had granted him a tenancy. In 1992, the respondent and her father offered to purchase the property via a "without prejudice" letter. The respondent's father died in 1996 and the possession proceedings were not continued. In 2000 and 2003 the appellants served notices to quit on the respondent and subsequently issued possession proceedings. In her defence the respondent claimed that she had acquired the property on the basis of adverse possession. At first instance it was held that the respondent and her father had been in adverse possession of the property and hence the appellants' title had been extinguished.

Held

❖ (CA (Civ Div)) Although a statement of pleadings in the first possession proceedings could amount to an acknowledgment of title, there had been no acknowledgment in the present case. The fact that the respondent was prepared to accept a lease in recognition of the appellant's claim, this did not destroy her intention to possess the property: *JA Pye (Oxford) Ltd v Graham*, above. The decision of the Grand Chamber of the European Court of Human Rights in *JA Pye (Oxford) Ltd v United Kingdom* (2008) 46 E.H.R.R. 45 that the law of adverse possession was compatible with the European Convention on Human Rights ought to be followed unless there were exceptional reasons for not doing so. There were no exceptional reasons on the facts of the case. The appeal would accordingly be dismissed. [2008] EWCA Civ 7.

Commentary

[1] It had been suggested in *JA Pye (Oxford) Ltd v Graham*, above, and in *Harrow LBC v Qazi* [2003] UKHL 43, that the concept of adverse possession was allowed within the context of the European Convention on Human Rights. *Beaulane Properties Ltd v Palmer* [2005] EWHC 817 (Ch) casts doubt on this and suggested that the pre-**Land Registration Act 2002** regime was a breach of art.1 of the First Protocol of the European Convention on Human Rights. In *Tower Hamlets LBC v Barrett* [2005] EWCA Civ 923 Neuberger L.J. suggested obiter that *Beaulane* was a well-reasoned decision.

[2] This issue was considered by the European Court of Human Rights in *JA Pye (Oxford) Ltd v United Kingdom* (2006) 43 E.H.R.R. 3. The ECHR decided by a majority decision that the law on adverse possession prior to the **Land Registration Act 2002** was in breach of art.1 of the First Protocol of the European Convention on Human Rights. This constituted interference by the government of the landowners' rights by the deprivation of their possession of the land. The Court in assessing the proportionality of the adverse possession system found that the application of the provisions of the **Limitation Act 1980** and the **Land Registration Act 1925** to deprive Pye of the ownership of its lands imposed an excessive burden and upset the fair balance between public interest and Pye's right of peaceful enjoyment of its property. The

government then appealed to the Grand Chamber of the ECHR in *JA Pye (Oxford) Ltd v United Kingdom* (2008) 46 E.H.R.R. 45. The court held that the provisions of the **Limitation Act 1980** and the **Land Registration Act 1925** did not deprive Pye of its possession but Pye had been affected by a controlled use of the land. The law of adverse possession was not in violation of the European Convention on Human Rights and hence no compensation was payable by the government to Pye. The purpose of the Limitation Act was to prevent additional litigation and not to start a compensation claim—Pye could have acted much earlier to prevent the use of his land but he had failed to do so. The decision was followed in *Agnes Ofulue v United Kingdom* [2010] ECHR 2014, where Ofulue argued that the domestic law which deprived her of her property was in contravention of art.1 of Protocol No.1 to the Convention. The court dismissed the application, inter alia, on the basis that Ofulue's claim in this respect was "manifestly ill-founded".

In light of the decisions above, the decision in *Beaulane Properties Ltd v Palmer* is no longer good law.

. . . .

[C] PROPRIETARY ESTOPPEL

The doctrine of proprietary estoppel is a flexible and equitable doctrine. There are different types of estoppel, for example promissory estoppel, estoppel by representation, etc. The difference with proprietary estoppel is that it can be used as a cause of action and hence is different from promissory estoppel which can only be used as a defence.

In order for a claim on the basis of proprietary estoppel to succeed there must generally be an assurance, reliance and a detriment. The difficulty with this doctrine is that the claimant does not essentially know that he has such rights until the court determines that such a claim would succeed and hence until there is an adjudication of the matter the claim remains in limbo.

Key Principle . . . .
For proprietary estoppel to be established, the modern position is that it is necessary to show that the assertion of strict legal rights is unconscionable.

TAYLOR FASHIONS LTD V LIVERPOOL VICTORIA TRUSTEES CO LTD; OLD & CAMPBELL LTD V LIVERPOOL VICTORIA FRIENDLY SOCIETY 1979
The second plaintiffs were the freehold owners of two properties known as Nos.21 and 22, Westover Road, Bournemouth. Title to the two properties were unregistered. The second plaintiffs granted the

predecessors in title of the first plaintiffs, a lease of 28 years of No.22, with an option to renew for a another 14 years if the lessees installed a lift in the premises. This option was not protected by registration as a Class C(iv) land charge under the **Land Charges Act 1972**. The second plaintiffs subsequently sold the freehold of Nos.21 and 22 to the defendants in 1949. At the same time, the second plaintiffs acquired a 42-year lease of No.21 subject to a break clause after 28 years if the lessees to No.22 did not exercise the option to renew.

The defendants were also the owners of the freehold of the adjoining No.20. In 1958 the lease to No.22 was assigned to the first plaintiffs, the latter installing a lift in accordance with the option, with the acquiescence of the defendants. In 1962, a 14-year lease of No.20 was granted to the second plaintiffs, also with an option to renew for a further period of 14 years should the lessees of No.22 exercise the option to renew that lease. The second plaintiffs did extensive work to Nos.20 and 21.

The first plaintiffs served a notice on the defendants in 1976 seeking to exercise the option to renew the lease to No.22. The defendants alleged that the option was void for non-registration and notice to quit was served on both the first and second plaintiffs. Both the first and second plaintiffs commenced an action seeking a declaration that the defendants were estopped from asserting their strict legal rights.

Held

❖ (Ch D) The option to renew the lease in respect of No.22 was void against the defendants for want of registration as a land charge. Thus, the first plaintiffs were not entitled to exercise the option to renew. The fact that the defendants were not aware that the option was void at the time the lift was installed was one of the factors the court would take into account. Other relevant factors present were that the defendants did not encourage the first plaintiffs in the belief that the option was valid and also, that the first plaintiffs were unable to prove that the lift had been installed by them in the belief that the option was valid. With regard to the second plaintiffs, the defendants were estopped from exercising the break clauses in the leases. This was because the defendants had encouraged the second plaintiffs to incur expenditure in undertaking extensive work on the two properties in the belief that the option was valid. [1982] Q.B. 133.

LIM TENG HUAN V ANG SWEE CHUAN 1991

The plaintiff and defendant purchased a piece of land jointly and transferred it into their fathers' names. In 1982 the defendant commenced construction of a house on the land. In 1985, the plaintiff and the defendant entered into an agreement where the plaintiff acknowledged that the construction was with his consent and agreed to give his half share in the land to the defendant in exchange for unspecified land, which the defendant expected to be allotted by the government. Upon completion of the construction of the house, the defendant went into occupation. The plaintiff, as administrator of his father's estate, commenced an action against the defendant claiming, inter alia, a declaration that he was entitled to a half share in the land. The defendant counter-claimed for a declaration that he was the sole beneficial owner of the land and for an injunction to restrain the plaintiff from entering the land or dealing with his share in it.

Held

❖ (PC (HK)) Even though the 1985 agreement was unenforceable, it provided evidence of the parties' intentions and it could be inferred that the defendant completed the construction of the house in reliance on it. Although the plaintiff had not acted unconscionably in allowing the defendant to assume that he was the sole beneficial owner of the land on payment of compensation to the plaintiff, it would be unconscionable for the plaintiff to deny that assumption. The plaintiff was therefore estopped from denying the defendant's title to the land, conditional upon payment of compensation. [1992] 1 W.L.R. 113.

Commentary

[1] This decision in *Taylor Fashions* is regarded as pivotal to the development of the doctrine of proprietary estoppel, albeit that it is only a first-instance decision. Prior to this decision, it was assumed that in order for proprietary estoppel to be established, it was necessary to satisfy the five probanda set out in *Willmott v Barber* (1880) L.R. 15 Ch. D. 96 Ch D (below). However, the *Willmott v Barber* probanda were unduly restrictive and did not apply to all different situations in which proprietary estoppel could arise. It applied to unilateral mistake cases (where one party has been mistaken as to his rights and the other party fails to take any action to rectify that mistaken belief). However, it did not apply to the imperfect gift (where a promise has been made to transfer the land from one party to another but the formalities have not been complied with) and common expectation cases (where both parties have dealt with the land giving rise to the expectation in one of the parties that he or she would have an interest in the land). Therefore, until the decision in *Taylor Fashions*, the development of the doctrine of estoppel was stifled. The requirement now is that it must be shown that it would be

unconscionable to allow the enforcement of strict legal rights. Oliver J. stated that this type of case,

> "requires a very much broader approach which is directed rather at ascertaining whether, in particular individual circumstances, it would be unconscionable for a party to be permitted to deny that which, knowingly, or unknowingly, he has allowed or encouraged another to assume to his detriment".

See also *Appleby v Cowley*, *The Times*, April 14, 1982, and *Swallow Securities v Isenberg* (1985) 274 E.G. 1028 CA (Civ Div). However, it should be noted that the *Wilmott v Barber* probanda would still apply to unilateral mistake cases.

[2] An example of the application of estoppel is *Flowermix Ltd v Site Development (Ferndown) Ltd* [2000] All E.R. (D) 522. An agreement was made to transfer six development sites. The precise dimensions of these were unclear and were unenforceable. However, the lack of precision had been understood by the parties and related to uncertainty as to planning application considerations. It was held that the necessary elements of expectation, encouragement and reliance were proven. The transferors were estopped from refusing to transfer the necessary land for the development. See also *Banner Homes Holdings Ltd (formerly Banner Homes Group Plc) v Luff Developments Ltd (No.1)* [2000] 2 All E.R. 117 CA (Civ Div).

[3] In order for a claim for proprietary estoppel to succeed there must be some estoppel and a proprietary claim. A claim based solely on unconscionability does not give rise to a claim in proprietary estoppel and may cause confusion: *Yeoman's Row Management Ltd v Cobbe* [2008] UKHL 55. This decision was followed in *Herbert v Doyle* [2010] EWCA Civ 1095.

Key Principle ....

In cases where proprietary estoppel involves the mistaken belief of the representee, the *Willmott v Barber* probanda may still be applicable.

WILLMOTT V BARBER 1880
A lease in which Barber was the lessor and Willmott the assignee thereof contained a covenant prohibiting the assignment of the lease without Barber's consent. However, both parties were unaware of this covenant and Barber upon discovering its existence, refused to grant consent to the assignment of the lease to Willmott. Willmott argued that Barber was estopped from asserting his strict legal rights because

the latter had allowed the assignment without informing Willmott of his mistake.

Held ....

❖ (Ch D) Fry J. stated that a person would be deprived of his rights if "he has acted in such a way as would make it fraudulent for him to set up those rights". Fraud in this context required that five elements be proved. These are that:

   (i)   the plaintiff must have made some mistake as to his legal rights;
  (ii) the plaintiff must have expended some money or must have done some act on the faith of his mistaken belief;
 (iii) the owner of the land must have known of his own rights which are inconsistent with that of the plaintiff;
 (iv) the owner must have known of the plaintiff's mistaken belief; and
  (v) the owner must have encouraged the plaintiff in his expenditure of money or in other acts which he has done either directly or indirectly.

On the facts of the case, it was clear that Barber was unaware of his rights and there was no evidence to suggest that he knew that Willmott had been acting in ignorance of his own rights. As such, Barber could not be prevented from asserting his strict legal rights to refuse consent to the assignment of the lease. (1880) L.R. 15 Ch. D. 96.

MATHARU V MATHARU 1994

The plaintiff was the owner of premises known as 223 Coventry Road, Ilford, which he acquired in 1968. This property subsequently became the matrimonial home to the defendant and the plaintiff's son. During the time when they stayed in the premises, the defendant's husband made extensive renovations to the premises. The defendant was under the mistaken belief that the premises belonged to the plaintiff's son. The marriage broke down in 1988 and two years later, the defendant obtained a court order excluding her husband from the premises. The husband died in 1991. The plaintiff emigrated to Canada later that year but returned a year later. The plaintiff applied for a possession order against the defendant. At first instance, the court found in the defendant's favour on the grounds that proprietary estoppel applied.

Held ....

❖ (CA (Civ Div)) In order for proprietary estoppel to arise, the *Willmott v Barber* probanda had to be satisfied. On the facts of the case, the defendant had satisfied each of those requirements, and as such, gave rise to an equity which defeated the claim by the plaintiff for possession of the premises. (1994) 68 P. & C.R. 93.

Commentary

Although the Court of Appeal in *Matharu v Matharu* applied the *Willmott v Barber* probanda, the facts clearly demonstrate that it was a case concerning the unilateral mistake of one party giving rise to proprietary estoppel. As was suggested earlier, the *Willmott v Barber* probanda are still applicable in this category of cases. However, later cases such as *Swallow Securities v Isenberg* (1985) 274 E.G. 1028 CA (Civ Div), has suggested that the *Willmott v Barber* probanda are merely guidelines, albeit that they may nonetheless be "necessary and essential guidelines". In general, the overriding criterion for the application of proprietary estoppel is now one of unconscionability. See also *Ottey v Grundy* [2003] EWCA Civ 1176.

ASSURANCE OR EXPECTATION

Key Principle

Although the overall criterion for proprietary estoppel to arise is one of unconscionability, it is still necessary to satisfy three essential elements. The first essential element is that there has been an assurance or expectation given by one party to the other.

RAMSDEN V DYSON 1865
A yearly tenant undertook building works at the property subject to the tenancy in the belief that the landlord would eventually grant him a new lease of 60 years. Upon the landlord's refusal to grant the lease, the tenant commenced an action claiming to be entitled to such a lease.

Held

❖ (HL) On the facts of the case there was only a lease for year to year. Lord Cranworth L.C. stated that:

> "[i]f a stranger build on my land, supposing it to be his own, and I, knowing it to be mine, do not interfere, but leave him to go on, equity considers it to be dishonest in me to remain passive and afterwards to interfere and take profit. But if a stranger build knowingly upon my land, there is no principle in equity which prevents me from insisting on having back my land, with all the

additional value which the occupier has ... added to it". (1866) L.R. 1 H.L. 129.

INWARDS V BAKER 1965

In 1932, a father encouraged his son to build a bungalow on the father's land, which the son did, and paid about half the cost. The son built most of the bungalow. At the time of the father's death in 1951, the son was still living in the bungalow. He continued to live there until 1963 when the trustees of the land sued for possession, claiming that he was a licensee. Judgment was given in favour of the trustees and the son appealed.

Held

❖ (CA) The trustees would not be entitled to possession of the land. This was because the son had relied on the assurances by his father which had given rise to the expectation that he could live in the bungalow for the rest of his life. [1965] 2 Q.B. 29.

THORNER V MAJOR 2009

The claimant worked on the farm of his cousin P for nearly 30 years without any payment. There were no real direct conversations between the two men. Over the years the claimant was under the impression from P's oblique remarks that the claimant was to inherit the farm. P made a will in which he had left the farm to the claimant but due to change he wished to make to the will, he revoked the will but failed to execute a fresh will. On P's death the farm vested in the hands of his personal representatives who intended to distribute P's assets under the intestacy rules. The claimant claimed he was entitled to the farm as he had relied on P's representations and he had suffered detriment as a result of it as he did not look for alternative work.

Held

❖ (HL) The assurances received by the claimant were sufficiently clear and that it was intended that the claimant would rely on them and as such the claimant was entitled to the farm. Further the property which the claimant was to receive was sufficiently certain. [2009] UKHL 18.

Commentary

In order for the doctrine of proprietary estoppel to arise, it is clear that three elements need to be satisfied. The first of these elements is that there must have been an assurance or representation made by the representor giving rise to an expectation in the representee that some benefit would accrue as a result of his detrimental reliance on the representation or assurance. However, it should be noted that whilst it is useful to consider proprietary estoppel as three elements, Walker L.J. in *Gillett v Holt* [2001] Ch. 210 stressed that it

> "cannot be treated as subdivided into ... watertight compartments ... the fundamental principle ... is ... to prevent unconscionable conduct [which] permeates all the elements of the doctrine".

In *Thorner v Major*, above, Lord Neuberger explained what was needed to establish "assurance". His Lordship stated that,

> "there must be some sort of an assurance which is 'clear and unequivocal' before it can be relied on to found an estoppel. However, that proposition must be read as subject to three qualifications. First, it does not detract from the normal principle, ... that the effect of words or actions must be assessed in their context ... Secondly, it would be quite wrong to be unrealistically rigorous when applying the 'clear and unambiguous' test. The court should not search for ambiguity or uncertainty, but should assess the question of clarity and certainty practically and sensibly, as well as contextually ... Thirdly, there may be cases where the statement relied on to found an estoppel could amount to an assurance which could reasonably be understood as having more than one possible meaning. In such a case, if the facts otherwise satisfy all the requirements of an estoppel, it seems to me that, at least normally, the ambiguity should not deprive a person who reasonably relied on the assurance of all relief: it may well be right, however, that he should be accorded relief on the basis of the interpretation least beneficial to him".

RELIANCE

Key Principle
Secondly, it must be established that there has been reliance by one party upon the assurance given by the other party.

PASCOE V TURNER 1979
Turner moved into Pascoe's house originally as his housekeeper but they subsequently cohabited together. Pascoe had purchased the

house in which they were living in. Pascoe subsequently left Turner for another woman but at the time had told her that the property belonged to her. Turner stayed on in the house in reliance of this assurance and spent money on repairs and improvements to the property.

Held

❖ (CA (Civ Div)) The doctrine of proprietary estoppel applied in this case. This was because Turner had spent money on the house, in reliance on the assurance given by Pascoe that the house was hers. In the circumstances of the case, it was appropriate to order a transfer of the fee simple to Turner rather than to merely give her a licence to remain in the house. This was because a licence would not give her protection against a purchaser with no notice and Pascoe's determined efforts to evict her. [1979] 1 W.L.R. 431.

Commentary

The question as to whether reliance can be established is a question of fact dependent on the circumstances of the case. It is necessary to establish that there has been reliance, because it is reliance that provides the causal link between the assurance and the detriment, thereby satisfying the overriding criteria of unconscionability. Thus for instance, in *Taylor Fashions Ltd v Victoria Trustees Co Ltd*, the first plaintiff failed in their claim, inter alia, because they couldn't prove that they had relied on the assurance by installing the lift. The evidence was that they would have installed it even if they were aware that the option was void. In *Ottey v Grundy* [2003] EWCA Civ 1176 it was suggested that the burden of proof would be on the representor to prove that there had been no reliance.

On the relationship between reliance and assurance, the Privy Council in *Henry v Henry* [2010] UKPC 3 explained that:

> "[A]s to the relationship between reliance and detriment in the context of the doctrine of proprietary estoppel, just as the inquiry as to reliance falls to be made in the context of the nature and quality of the particular assurances which are said to form the basis of the estoppel, so the inquiry as to detriment falls to be made in the context of the nature and quality of the particular conduct or course of conduct adopted by the claimant in reliance on those assurances. Thus, notwithstanding that reliance and detriment may, in the abstract, be regarded as different concepts, in applying the principles of proprietary estoppel they are often intertwined".

On the facts of the case the claimant succeeded in his claim based on proprietary estoppel and was given a half share of the owner's undivided half share in the property as he was able to establish that he had acted to his detriment.

Key Principle

Reliance can be inferred from the circumstances of case, where it can be shown that there has been an assurance made, and there is conduct by the other party from which such an inference can be drawn.

> ### GREASLEY V COOKE 1980
>
> In 1938, Cooke was employed as a maid in Greasley's home. From 1948 she started cohabiting with one of Greasley's sons and lived with him until his death in 1971. Cooke received wages as a maid only until 1948 when Greasley died. After the latter's death, she continued living in the home performing the duties of a housekeeper for the rest of the family. After the death of the son with whom she was cohabiting, Cooke was served with a notice to quit. She refused to leave the home and possession proceedings were commenced against her. She alleged that the family was estopped from asserting their legal rights as the son with whom she had been living with and another of Greasley's sons had assured her that she could remain in the home for as long as she wished, rent-free.

Held

❖ (CA (Civ Div)) Where assurances had been made, there is a rebuttable presumption that the plaintiff acted in reliance on those assurances and the burden of proof is on the person against whom the estoppel is sought to provide evidence to the contrary. This was satisfied in this case, which therefore gave rise to an equity in favour of the plaintiff. [1980] 1 W.L.R. 1306.

Commentary

In *Wayling v Jones* (1995) 69 P. & C.R. 170, the Court of Appeal stressed that it was necessary to establish a link between the assurances and the detriment. However, it was only necessary to show that the assurances were an inducement for the other party's conduct, not that they were the sole inducement. Once it was established that the assurances were made, reliance could be inferred if there was conduct from which such an inference could be drawn.

Key Principle ....

The doctrine of proprietary estoppel is not restricted to acts done in reliance on a belief relating to existing rights, but can also be based on the belief that future rights would be granted.

> RE BASHAM 1986
>
> From a young age, the plaintiff had helped out in her mother and stepfather's business, for which she was never paid but had under- stood that she would be entitled to her stepfather's property when he died. In 1947, the plaintiff's husband had considered moving to a job, which entitled them to a tied cottage. However, the stepfather per- suaded them not to, as he would help them acquire another suitable property. Subsequently, the stepfather purchased a tenanted property with money provided principally by the plaintiff's mother. The plaintiff's mother died in 1976 and her stepfather moved into this property which had been vacated by the tenants. The plaintiff lived near her stepfather. Both she and her husband helped the stepfather by looking after him, and doing various things around the property including laying the carpet and looking after the garden. She was told by her stepfather that she would not lose anything by doing these things. A few days prior to his death, her stepfather indicated that he wanted to have a will made which would leave his money to the plaintiff's son and the plaintiff was to have the property. The stepfather died intestate.

Held ....

❖ (Ch D) The doctrine of proprietary estoppel also applied in cases where the acts of reliance on the assurance given by the representor, was in the belief that future rights would be acquired. It was not limited to cases where the belief was that existing rights would be granted. As the plaintiff was able to establish that she had acted to her detriment in reliance on her belief, encouraged by her stepfather, that she would be entitled to his estate, she was absolutely and beneficially entitled to his estate, including the house. [1986] 1 W.L.R. 1498.

> SCOTTISH & NEWCASTLE PLC V LANCASHIRE MORTGAGE CORP LTD 2007
>
> A mortgagor was an owner of a club which had a mortgage to Scottish & Newcastle. He was also the owner of a house which was subject to a number of debts. The mortgagor arranged a loan from Lancashire Mortgage Corp which was secured on the house and used the money to pay off the debts on the house and to reduce the debts owed to Scottish & Newcastle. Notwithstanding the reduction of the debt Scottish & Newcastle asked for increased security by having a

mortgage on the house. The title to the house was registered and priority in the case of competing mortgages is dependent on the date of their respective entries on the register. Although the mortgage was granted to Lancashire Mortgage Corp a day before the mortgage was granted to Scottish & Newcastle, the registration of the charge in favour of Scottish & Newcastle took place before Lancashire Mortgage Corp. The mortgagor defaulted on the mortgage and the house was sold. However the proceeds of sale were insufficient to pay off both loans. The question was whether Scottish & Newcastle was estopped from asserting its priority?

Held

❖ (CA (Civ Div)) The conduct of Scottish & Newcastle was sufficient to give rise to a claim in proprietary estoppel. As Scottish & Newcastle was aware that Lancashire Mortgage Corp had expected to have priority over Scottish & Newcastle it permitted Lancashire Mortgage Corp to make the loan and had benefited from it. [2007] EWCA Civ 684.

Commentary

[1] *Re Basham* makes it clear that it is unnecessary for the representee to have relied on a belief that existing rights would be given but can be based on the belief that future rights would accrue. This approach has been followed in *Durant v Heritage* [1994] E.G. 134 (C.S.) and *Gillett v Holt*, below.

[2] In *Scottish & Newcastle Plc v Lancashire Mortgage Corp Ltd*, the court described the action of Scottish & Newcastle as more passive acquiescence "rather than positive representations, encourage or promise" (at 47). However this was sufficient to give rise to a claim in proprietary estoppel. The concern that this decision may undermine the statutory provisions in the **Land Registration Act 2002** as to the priority which is dependent on the registration was avoided by the Court of Appeal in deciding that Scottish & Newcastle took priority but held the proceeds of sale on a constructive trust to pay off the Lancashire Mortgage Corp loan before being entitled to claim its share.

Key Principle

For the principle in *Re Basham* to apply there is no need for the representor to have made an irrevocable promise.

GILLETT V HOLT 2000

The Gillett family had a close personal and business relationship with Holt for over 36 years. Holt had promised Gillett that he would leave his land and related farm business to him in his will. When Holt was 80 years old he formed a close personal relationship with a Mr Wood. Holt changed his will and excluded Gillett totally. Mr Gillett alleged that he was entitled to a substantial part of Holt's estate by virtue of proprietary estoppel. He alleged that he had accepted a lower salary in Holt's company to which he devoted his whole working life and had therefore suffered detriment. At first instance it was decided that Gillett's claim would fail as there was no evidence of an irrevocable promise by Holt to leave his estate to Gillett. Gillett appealed.

Held ....
❖ (CA (Civ Div)) There was no need for the promise to be irrevocable as it was not the promise that resulted in equity's intervention but the detrimental reliance by the representee that made the promise irrevocable. As there was evidence of detrimental reliance, the appeal would be allowed. [2001] Ch. 210.

Commentary ....
The first instance decision follows the earlier decision of *Taylor v Dickens* [1998] 1 F.L.R. 806, where it was suggested that there must be evidence that the representator made an irrevocable promise to leave the property to the representee. The Court of Appeal in *Gillett v Holt* stated that criticisms of *Taylor v Dickens* were well founded.

DETRIMENT

Key Principle ....
The third essential element to be satisfied in order for proprietary estoppel to arise is that the representee acted to his or her detriment in reliance on the assurance given by the representor.

DILLWYN V LLEWELYN 1862

A father gave his son possession of a piece of land and signed a memorandum stating that the land was being given to his son as a gift. The attempted gift of the land to the son was invalid, as the proper formalities for such transfer of land had not been complied with. The father consented and encouraged the son to build a house on the land at his own costs and expense. On the father's death, it was discovered that the father only left the son a life interest in the land.

Held

❖ (QB) The son was entitled to ask for a transfer of the fee simple of the land. This was because the son had acted in reliance on the representations made by the father to his detriment, by the expenditure incurred in building the house. (1862) 4 De G.F. & J. 517.

Commentary

Whilst reliance can be inferred from the circumstances of the case, it has been made clear in *Gillett v Holt*, above, that detriment had to be proved and cannot be inferred. The detrimental act or reliance can be expenditure incurred by the claimant. However, it can include detriment other than expenditure. For example, in *Jones v Jones* [1977] 1 W.L.R. 438 CA (Civ Div), the claimant had given up his home and job and did various work on the property, in reliance on the assurance given by his father. In *Greasley v Cooke*, above, the detriment suffered involved the carrying on of house-keeping duties without any wages. It was stressed in *Gillett v Holt* that detriment is not a technical or broad concept but had to be assessed in the context of the broad enquiry on whether there was unconscionability.

REMEDIES

Key Principle

The court has a discretion to grant the appropriate remedy once it is satisfied that proprietary estoppel has been established. The modern approach is that the court will grant such remedy as will be necessary to enable the plaintiff to receive the minimum equity to satisfy the estoppel rather than to make good the expectation.

PASCOE V TURNER 1979
(as above)

Held

❖ (CA (Civ Div)) In deciding the appropriate remedy, the court should grant the minimum equity in order to do justice to Turner. On the facts of the case, it was appropriate to order a transfer of the fee simple estate in the house to her. Cumming Bruce L.J. stated that "the equity to which the facts in this case give rise can only be satisfied by compelling the plaintiff to give effect to his promise and her expectations. He has so acted that he must now perfect the gift". [1979] 1 W.L.R. 431.

MATHARU V MATHARU 1994
(as above)

Held

❖ (CA (Civ Div)) On the facts, the equity was satisfied by granting the defendant a licence to remain in the property for life, or such other shorter period as she may decide. Roche L.J. decided that the defendant did not acquire a beneficial interest in the premises by virtue of the estoppel. (1994) 68 P. & C.R. 93.

CRABB V ARUN DC 1976
Crabb negotiated with the Council for a right of way. No final agreement between the parties was reached. The Council fenced around its land with gates at appropriate points, one to allow for this right of way (point B) and the other to allow Crabb access over a right of way which he already had (point A). Before any agreement could be reached, and after Crabb had sold part of his land together with the right of access at point A, the Council removed the gate at point B and fenced the gap. The Council refused to grant an easement leaving Crabb with land-locked land. Crabb claimed that the Council was estopped from denying him a right of access at point 13 and a right of way along the road leading to this point.

Held

❖ (CA (Civ Div)) It would be inequitable to refuse to grant Crabb an easement of way. The court was of the view that in deciding the appropriate remedy, it was unhindered in principle. However, there was a propensity to recognise the expenditure incurred by plaintiff or other detriment suffered rather than to make good the expectation encouraged. The equity could be satisfied here by granting Crabb an easement without any payment to the Council. [1976] Ch. 179.

Commentary

The original approach of the courts, with respect to the appropriate remedy in any given case, was to grant such remedy which would realise the expectation of the plaintiff. The court adopted this approach in *Dillwyn v Llewelyn* (1862) 4 De G.F. & J. 517, where the appropriate remedy to meet the expectation of the plaintiff, was to order a transfer of the property to the plaintiff. However, the modern approach is for the court to grant such remedy as would enable the plaintiff to receive the minimum equity to satisfy the estoppel—see *Henry v Henry* [2010] UKPC 3 and *Redstone Mortgages Plc v Welch* [2009] 36 E.G. 98. In *Pascoe v Turner*, above, the court decided that the equity would be satisfied only with a transfer of the fee simple of the property. In contrast in *Matharu v Matharu*, above, the appropriate remedy was to grant the plaintiff a licence to remain in the property for the rest of her life. Whilst in *Stallion v Albert Stallion Holdings (Great Britain) Ltd* [2009] EWHC 1950 (Ch) the court granted the claimant a right to reside at the property rent free for the rest of her life but without exclusive possession as being the minimum equity required to do justice.

The Court of Appeal in *Jennings v Rice* [2002] EWCA Civ 159 has suggested that the expectation based remedy may be appropriate where the parties have reached a mutual understanding as to what the claimant was to receive and that the minimum necessary to ensure equity between the parties would be the correct approach where the claimant's expectations are not clear or certain or would be disproportionate to the detriment suffered as in that case. Hence it will depend on the circumstances of each case. In *Mcguane v Welch* [2008] EWCA Civ 785, the Court of Appeal decided that the judge at first instance should not have felt compelled to order a transfer of a lease but that he should have taken a broader view as to the nature and extent of the equity arising from the estoppel and how the equity could be satisfied.

In deciding the appropriate remedy to grant, it must be noted that the court can grant different types of remedies. Two of these remedies have just been discussed. The other types of remedies available include damages (*Baker v Baker* [1993] 2 F.L.R. 247); the grant of a perpetual licence (*Plimmer v Wellington Corp* (1883–84) L.R. 9 App. Cas. 699; the grant of an easement (*ER Ives Investments Ltd v High* [1967] 2 Q.B. 379 and *Crabb v Arun District Council*) or the grant of a lease as seen in *Taylor Fashions Ltd v Liverpool Victoria Trustees Ltd*, above. This list is not exhaustive but is intended to demonstrate the various remedies, which the court can use in order to decide how the equity can be satisfied.

DISTINCTION BETWEEN CONSTRUCTIVE TRUSTS AND PROPRIETARY ESTOPPEL

In a number of cases, the courts have commented on the similarity between the concepts of constructive trusts with that of proprietary estoppel—see *Grant v Edwards* [1986] Ch. 638 and *Stokes v Anderson* [1991] 1 F.L.R. 391.

However other cases have suggested otherwise and that they are separate especially with reference to the remedies (in the case of proprietary estoppel the remedy is one of the minimum award in order to do justice whilst the constructive trust remedy is to provide the claimants with their entitlement)— *Lalani v Crump Holdings Ltd* [2007] EWHC 47 (Ch) and *Stack v Dowden* [2007] UKHL 17.

This issue has been recently considered by the House of Lords in *Thorner v Major*, above. Lord Scott stated that:

> "[T]here are many cases in which the representations relied on relate to the acquisition by the representee of an immediate, or more or less immediate, interest in the property in question. In these cases a proprietary estoppel is the obvious remedy ... There are many other examples of decided cases where representations acted on by the representee have led to the representor being estopped from denying that the representee had the proprietary interest in the representor's land that the representation had suggested. Constructive trust, in my opinion, has nothing to offer to cases of this sort. But cases where the relevant representation has related to inheritance prospects seem to me difficult, for the reasons I have given, to square with the principles of proprietary estoppel ... I find them made easier to understand as constructive trust cases. The possibility of a remedial constructive trust over property, created by the common intention or understanding of the parties regarding the property on the basis of which the Claimant has acted to his detriment, has been recognised and, of course, the present case [is a] good example [and], are, to my mind, more comfortably viewed as constructive trust cases."

His lordship went on to argue that it would be preferable to keep proprietary estoppel and constructive trust as remedies which are distinct and separate and to confine proprietary estoppel to situations where the representation, regardless of whether they are express or implied, which the claimant has relied on is " ... unconditional". Where the representations are in respect of some future benefits which is qualified on account of unforeseen future events they are better to be dealt with through the principles of the "remedial constructive trusts".

Key Principle

In deciding what is necessary in order to satisfy the minimum equity, there is a need to maintain proportionality between the parties so that a just result can be reached.

> SLEDMORE V DALBY 1996
>
> The plaintiff and her husband bought a house jointly in 1962. In 1965, the defendant moved into the house when he married their daughter. Rent was paid until 1976 when the defendant's wife became ill and he became unemployed. The plaintiff's husband made representations to the defendant that the latter and his wife would be left the house on the death of the plaintiff and himself. Later, the plaintiff's husband transferred his share in the house to the plaintiff. The plaintiff's husband died in 1980 and the defendant's wife died in 1983. The defendant continued to live in the house rent-free. In 1990, the plaintiff gave the defendant notice to quit and possession proceedings were commenced. By that time the defendant lived there only two nights a week and was in employment. However, the defendant's daughter, who was 27, continued to live in the house.

Held

❖ (CA (Civ Div)) That although an estoppel had arisen in the defendant's favour, the minimum necessary to do justice was to grant the order for possession, taking into account the present circumstances of the case. (1996) 72 P. & C.R. 196.

Commentary

Hobhouse L.J. stated that:

> "[I]t is always necessary to ask what is the assumption made by the party asserting the estoppel for which the party affected is to be treated as responsible. There is also the need for proportionality. The end result must be a just one, having regard to the assumptions made by the party asserting the estoppel and the detriment he has experienced ... the effect of any equity had long since been exhausted and no injustice had been done to [the defendant]".

This has been followed in *Jennings v Rice* [2002] EWCA Civ 159 where the claimant was awarded compensation of £200,000 instead of a transfer of the house on the basis that the latter would have been a disproportionate remedy.

THINK POINT

Consider the application of the **Land Registration Act 2002** on the area of adverse possession. To what extent does it make it more difficult for a claim based on adverse possession to succeed?

Think about the decision of the Grand Chamber of the ECHR in *JA Pye (Oxford) Ltd v United Kingdom* (2008) 46 E.H.R.R. 45—do you think their distinction between possession and control of the use of the land in respect of the law on adverse possession is correct?

What is the difference between "meeting the expectation" and the "minimum necessary to meet the equity" in the context of remedies in proprietary estoppel? Do you consider that the latter is fair and equitable to the claimant?

Co-ownership

4

INTRODUCTION

Whenever two or more persons acquire ownership of land, a trust of land, which gives the legal owners the power to sell and to postpone the sale of the property, is imposed by the **Trusts of Land and Appointment of Trustees Act 1996**. This will be considered in detail in the next chapter.

In co-ownership, the legal title is always held as a joint tenancy and can never be severed: ss.l(6), 34 and 36(2) of the **Law of Property Act 1925**. However, the beneficial ownership is held by the beneficial co-owners either as joint tenants or tenants in common. In a joint tenancy, the co-owners own the whole land and there are no shares in the land regardless of their individual contribution to the purchase price. For a joint tenancy to exist, the four unities of possession, time, title and interest, must be present. The doctrine of survivorship which means that on the death of one of the co-owners, his or her interest vests in the remaining co-owners, applies in the case of a joint tenancy. In contrast, with a tenancy in common, only the unity of possession needs to be satisfied. Each co-owner holds an undivided share in the property namely that the co-owners have a share in the property but there is usually no physical delineation of the property. In a beneficial tenancy in common, the doctrine of survivorship does not apply and on the death of a co- owner his or her share will go to his estate.

Where there is a beneficial joint tenancy it is possible to sever this and convert it into a beneficial tenancy in common either in part or the whole, depending on the method of severance, discussed below. There are four methods of severance:

- by notice in writing in accordance with s.36 of the **Law of Property Act 1925**;
- by an act of a co-owner operating on his or her own share;
- by mutual agreement;
- by mutual conduct.

If severance takes place, equity applies the equitable maxim "equality is equity" and the co-owner gets an equal and proportionate share to the rest— for example, if there are four co-owners and one of them severs the beneficial joint tenancy, he or she will obtain a quarter share as a tenant in common—*Kernott v Jones* [2010] EWCA Civ 578.

Once severed it is not possible to convert the beneficial tenancy in common back to the beneficial joint tenancy without a re-conveyance of the property. The co-ownership can be ended in the following three ways:

- partition;
- sale of the property;
- union of interests in one of the co-owners.

BENEFICIAL JOINT TENANCY OR TENANCY IN COMMON?

Key Principle

Co-owners who contributed to the purchase price in unequal shares are presumed to hold the property as beneficial tenants in common.

> **BULL V BULL 1955**
> The plaintiff and his mother jointly purchased a house as a home for the two of them. The property was conveyed into the plaintiff's name as he had contributed a larger proportion of the purchase price. The plaintiff subsequently got married and differences occurred between the mother and the plaintiff's wife. The plaintiff gave his mother notice to quit and applied to court for possession of the house.

Held

❖ (CA) The plaintiff and the mother were equitable tenants in common as they had contributed to the purchase price in unequal shares. Both the parties were entitled to possession of the house and neither was entitled to evict the other. [1955] 1 Q.B. 234.

> **STACK V DOWDEN 2007**
> Miss D and Mr S bought a house as their family home for £190,000 out of which Miss D had provided £58,000 from her savings and £67,000 from the sale of a property which she had owned. The balance of the purchase price was by way of a mortgage. The house was purchased in their joint names but contained no declaration of trust. By the time they had purchased the house Miss D and Mr S had been living together for 18 years and had four children. Their relationship subsequently broke down and S obtained a declaration that the house was held for them as beneficial tenants in common in equal shares with an order for the sale of the property. D appealed against the order.

Held

❖ (HL) The starting point as to the beneficial ownership where there is legal joint tenancy is a beneficial joint tenancy. The onus was on the claimant to show that the parties had intended to hold the beneficial ownership as tenants in common and would be dependent on the facts of the case. In this case there was clear evidence that although they had cohabited for a long time they had kept their financial affairs separate, which strongly indicated that they did not intend the house to be held as joint tenants. Accordingly, they held the beneficial ownership as tenants in common and therefore Miss D was entitled to a higher share from the house. [2007] UKHL 17.

Commentary

In the case of married couples or the family home, the court will presume that even though their contribution to the purchase price was unequal, a joint tenancy can be inferred. In reaching its conclusion the court would adopt a constructive trust approach to their ownership as opposed to a resulting trust approach—per Baroness Hale in *Abbott v Abbott* [2008] 2 L.R.C. 511. The latter would point towards a beneficial tenancy in common as the co-owners would have specific shares in the property. However, as is clear from *Stack v Dowden*, this is dependent on the facts and circumstances of each case. In that case, the claimant was able to prove that they did not intend the property to be held as beneficial joint tenants. This was applied in *Fowler v Barron* [2008] EWCA Civ 377 where the attempt to rebut the presumption of joint beneficial ownership failed. The Court of Appeal stressed that as the parties were registered as legal joint tenants this resulted in the presumption of beneficial joint tenancy arising. The party seeking to rebut this must provide evidence of an intention that the beneficial interest was to be held in another way and in doing so the court would have regard to the parties' whole course of conduct in respect of the property. See also *Kernott v Jones* [2010] EWCA Civ 578.

Further, it is presumed that mortgagees will hold the beneficial interest as tenants in common. In *Re Jackson* (1887) L.R. 34 Ch. D. 732, J, by his will, left all his real and personal estate to three sisters. His estate consisted mainly of land, the greater part of which was sold after his death. The proceeds of sale were used to invest on the security of mortgages of real estate with the three sisters being the mortgagees. They were described in the deeds as joint tenants. The court decided that notwithstanding the description of the mortgagees as joint tenants, the mortgagees were in fact tenants in common.

In *Chopra v Bindra* [2009] EWCA Civ 203 property was held by co-owners under a declaration of trust which created an express trust for sale and declared that they held their respective beneficial interests as tenants in common. However cl.4 of the deed provided that upon the death of either co-owner before sale, the survivor became entitled to the entirety of the proceeds of sale absolutely. The court decided that the correct interpretation was that the parties clearly intended that it should belong to both during their joint lives and to the survivor absolutely upon the death of the first to die. Hence, although the deed provided for a tenancy in common, the express terms of the trust meant that upon the death of one it had the same effect as if it was a beneficial joint tenant.

Key Principle

Business or commercial partners who purchase property or acquire a lease of business premises together, are normally presumed to have purchased the property or acquired the lease as beneficial tenants in common.

LAKE V CRADDOCK 1732

Five individuals purchased some waterlogged land from the Commissioners of Sewers. The property was conveyed to them as legal joint tenants. They intended to drain the land and sell it for a profit.

Held

❖ (Ct of Chancery) The parties held the property as tenants in common in equity as they had contributed to the purchase price in unequal shares and the doctrine of survivorship was inconsistent with the commercial enterprise undertaken by the parties. (1732) 3 P. Wms. 158.

MALAYAN CREDIT LTD V JACK CHIA-MPH LTD 1986

The defendant had a tenancy of the seventh floor of a building, which it occupied, for business purposes. It was agreed that the plaintiff and the defendant, which were separate companies, and ran separate businesses, would share the premises and a lease would be granted to them both. The lessor granted a lease of the seventh floor and car park spaces to the defendant and plaintiff as joint tenants at law. A dispute arose between the parties with regard to the area of occupation.

Held

❖ (PC (Sing)) The situations where equity would presume that joint tenants at law held the beneficial interest as tenants in common were not limited to cases of payment of purchase price in unequal shares, or the purchase of partnership property. It included lessees taking a lease of business premises for their own separate purposes. On the facts of the case, an inference could be drawn that the plaintiff and defendant held the lease as beneficial tenants in common in unequal shares. Upon a sale of the lease, the proceeds would be divided in accordance with their respective shares. [1986] A.C. 549.

Commentary

In the absence of any express agreement between the co-owners the court will apply these presumptions in order to decide if they held the beneficial title as beneficial joint tenants or tenants in common. However, the presumptions can be rebutted by evidence to the contrary as demonstrated in *Bathurst v Scarborow* [2004] EWCA Civ 411. In that case it was clear that the partners intended to hold the property as joint tenants, as such the court gave effect to their intentions. In contrast, in *Eastwood v Eastwood* [2011] EWHC 953 (Ch) the court decided that there was insufficient evidence to rebut the presumption in favour of the co-owners holding the partnership property as beneficial tenants in common. Where all things are equal and the presumptions do not enable the court to reach an appropriate decision, it may apply the maxim "that equity follows the law" and imply that the beneficial title is held as joint tenants.

SEVERANCE OF THE BENEFICIAL JOINT TENANCY

[a] Severance by notice in writing under s.36(2) of the Law of Property Act 1925

Key Principle

The notice in writing for the purposes of s.36(2) of the **Law of Property Act 1925**, can be given by way of legal proceedings but must evince an intention to sever immediately.

HARRIS v GODDARD 1983

Harris and his wife were joint tenants of their matrimonial home. In 1979 the marriage broke down irretrievably and Harris's wife petitioned for divorce. The petition contained a prayer for property adjustment orders. Harris was injured in a car accident before the hearing of the divorce petition and died shortly afterwards. The executors of Harris's estate sought a declaration claiming that the equitable joint tenancy between Harris and his wife had been severed prior to his death thereby creating an equitable tenancy in common in equal shares. The question arose as to whether the petition amounted to notice in writing for the purposes of s.36(2) of the **Law of Property Act 1925**.

Held

❖ (CA (Civ Div)) A notice in writing for the purposes of s.36(2) of the 1925 Act had to evince an intention to sever immediately. The prayer in the petition did no more than to ask the court to consider at some future time whether to exercise its jurisdiction under the Matrimonial Causes Act 1973. Therefore, this was not sufficient to amount to a notice in writing of the intention to sever the equitable joint tenancy. The wife was entitled to the whole of the proceeds of sale of the former matrimonial home. [1983] 1 W.L.R. 1203.

RE DRAPER'S CONVEYANCE 1969
The issue was whether, a summons (supported by an affidavit) issued by a wife under s.17 of the Married Women's Property Act 1882, seeking an order for the sale of the matrimonial home and distribution of the proceeds of sale in accordance with the parties' respective interests, was effective to sever the equitable joint tenancy.

Held

❖ (Ch D) The wife's summons under s.17, together with her affidavit in support, showed an intention inconsistent with a continued equitable joint tenancy. The summons and affidavit was sufficient to amount to a notice in writing under s.36(2) of the Law of Property Act 1925 to sever the equitable joint tenancy. [1969] 1 Ch. 486.

Commentary

The effect of these cases is that the pleadings used in legal proceedings can, in some instances, amount to sufficient notice for the purposes of s.36(2) of the Law of Property Act 1925. The overriding criteria are that the pleadings must evince an intention to sever immediately. This intention was present in the summons and affidavit in *Re Draper's Conveyance*. However, it is not clear if the summons or the affidavit by itself would have been sufficient notice for the purposes of s.36(2). Plowman J. however accepted the argument that the orders made under s.17 itself could not sever the equitable joint tenancy but that the summons and affidavit satisfied the requirement of s.36(2).

A notice to sever is effective notwithstanding a notice in the conveyance that the notice of severance was not effective unless attached to the conveyance: *Grindal v Hooper* [1999] E.G. 150 (C.S.). Further, in *Tennaro Ltd v Majorarch Ltd* [2003] EWHC 2601 (Ch) the court decided that there was no effective written notice where an oral instruction was given by one party's solicitor to the other party's solicitor's secretary who then passed a written note to the solicitor. Although this was not a case on s.36(2) of the Law of Property Act 1925, the principle should similarly apply.

In *Quigley v Masterson* [2011] EWHC 2529 (Ch) the Court held that where a joint tenant no longer had the capacity to handle his own affairs, an application by the other joint tenant to the Court of Protection to handle his affairs would amount to a notice of severance for the purposes of s.36(2) of the **Law of Property Act 1925**. The court was of the view that this was similar to the approach in *Re Draper's Conveyance*.

Key Principle
The notice in writing should be served on all the joint tenants.

> RE 88, BERKELEY ROAD, LONDON NW9 1970
> The plaintiff and the deceased were the joint tenants of a property. The deceased's solicitors sent a notice in writing to the plaintiff giving notice of the deceased's intention to sever the equitable joint tenancy. When the notice arrived at the property by recorded delivery, the plaintiff was not there and the deceased acknowledged receipt of the notice. Upon the deceased's death, the plaintiff claimed to be entitled to the property by reason of survivorship.

Held
❖ (Ch D) As the notice was validly served on the plaintiff in accordance with the **Law of Property Act 1925**, the equitable joint tenancy had been severed. [1971] Ch. 648.

> KINCH V BULLARD 1998
> A couple acquired a property as their family home. In 1994 the wife consulted solicitors to discuss her divorce and the severance of the joint tenancy. On August 3, she signed the notice to sever the beneficial interest, which was sent to the husband by post the next day. The husband had a heart attack and was hospitalised. He did not read the letter and the wife picked it up and destroyed it. The husband died and his beneficiaries claimed a share of the property.

Held
❖ (Ch D) The notice to sever was properly served in accordance with s.36 of the **Law of Property Act 1925**, notwithstanding that he never read it and the wife had torn up the notice. The husband's beneficiaries were entitled to a share of the property. [1999] 1 W.L.R. 423.

Commentary ....

It was suggested by the court in *Kinch v Bullard* that the outcome may have been different, if the husband had been notified that the notice to sever had been withdrawn. As he had not, the notice was effective to sever the joint tenancy in equity converting their interests into beneficial tenants in common. In *White v White* [2001] EWCA Civ 955, the Court of Appeal decided that a notice of severance was ineffective where it was contrary to the agreement between the joint tenants that the beneficial joint tenancy was not to be severed.

In *Quigley v Masterson* [2011] EWHC 2529 (Ch) the court held that the notice was effectively served when the daughter of the joint tenant, who had become incapable of handling his own affairs, took over his affairs under an order from the Court of Protection and had notice of the intention to sever under s.36(2) of the **Law of Property Act 1925**. Henderson J. stated that

> "all that was necessary was that she should be a person who could properly be treated as the passive recipient of a unilateral notice given to her father".

[b] Williams v Hensman methods of severance

Section 36(2) of the **Law of Property Act 1925**, in addition to providing severance of the joint tenancy in equity by notice in writing, also allows the joint tenant to "do such other acts or things as would, ... have been effectual to sever the tenancy in equity". This refers to the methods of severance laid down in *Williams v Hensman* (1861) 1 John. & H. 546.

Key Principle ....

An act of a joint tenant operating upon his own share may create a severance of that share. This would include an act of bankruptcy committed by the joint tenant.

RE DENNIS (A BANKRUPT) 1995

A husband and wife were the beneficial joint tenants of two properties. The husband committed an act of bankruptcy in September 1982. A bankruptcy petition was presented in December of that year. In February 1983, the wife died and in her will left her property to their two children. A receiving order was made in May 1983 and the husband was adjudicated a bankrupt in November 1983. The trustee in bankruptcy sought a declaration as to the beneficial ownership of the properties.

Held ....
❖ (CA (Civ Div)) The title of the trustee in bankruptcy related back to the date of the husband's act of bankruptcy. The husband's act of bankruptcy in September 1982 severed the beneficial joint tenancy. The wife's half share in the properties therefore passed under the terms of her will. [1996] Ch. 80.

Commentary ....
There are various acts by the joint tenant which would sever the equitable joint tenancy. An act of bankruptcy is one of the ways in which this occurs. Other acts sufficient to sever the beneficial joint tenancy include an alienation by a joint tenant of his beneficial interest to another either by sale, transfer or mortgage (*First National Bank Plc v Achampong* [2003] EWCA Civ 487 and *Barracks v Barracks* [2005] EWHC 3077 (Ch)), entering into a specifically enforceable contract of sale (*Brown v Raindle* (1796) 3 Ves. Jr. 256), and possibly, the commencement of litigation (although this is doubtful).

Key Principle ....
A joint tenancy in equity may be severed by mutual agreement.

BURGESS V RAWNSLEY 1975
In 1967, H and the defendant bought the house in which he was the tenant of the downstairs flat. The house was bought as joint tenants, with them contributing equally to the purchase price. H bought the house with the intention of marrying the defendant but this intention was never communicated to the defendant. The defendant never moved into the house. There was evidence of an oral agreement between H and the defendant in 1968 where the defendant had agreed to sell her share of the house to H for £750. However, the defendant refused to sell her interest in the house. H died and the plaintiff, as administratrix of H's estate, claimed, inter alia, that there the joint tenancy had been severed in equity.

Held ....
❖ (CA (Civ Div)) The beneficial joint tenancy had been severed in equity by virtue of the oral agreement in 1968, notwithstanding that the agreement was not specifically enforceable. [1975] Ch. 429.

GORE AND SNELL V CARPENTER 1990

Mr Carpenter and his wife were the beneficial joint tenants of two properties. In 1985, he instructed his solicitor to draw up a separation agreement. The draft agreement included a clause severing the joint tenancy of one of the properties. He moved out of that property and moved into the other property. Subsequently, they reached an agreement in principle regarding the transfer of the properties subject to an agreement relating to ancillary financial matters. A divorce petition was served at the end of 1986 but before the petition could be heard, Mr Carpenter died. The plaintiffs, who were executors of Mr Carpenter's will, sought declarations as to the beneficial ownership of the properties.

Held

❖ (Ch D) There was no mutual agreement between the parties that the beneficial joint tenancies for both the properties should be severed. Although an agreement in principle was reached this was subject to agreement regarding the ancillary financial matters, which had not been reached. Further, the clause in the draft agreement severing the joint tenancy of one of the properties was ineffective as it was presented as part of the overall proposal, which had not been accepted. The wife was therefore the sole beneficial owner of both the properties by operation of survivorship. (1990) 60 P. & C.R. 456.

Commentary

The beneficial joint tenancy can be severed by mutual agreement even where there is no valid and enforceable agreement provided that there was in fact an agreement between the parties that severance should occur. In *Gore and Snell v Carpenter*, the absence of an agreement as to all the terms enabled the court to reach the conclusion that there had been no severance of the beneficial joint tenancy. In contrast, in *Hunter v Babbage* [1994] 2 F.L.R. 806, a draft agreement relating to the sale and the division of the proceeds of sale between the parties who were beneficial joint tenants was drawn up but never signed. One of the parties died before the agreement could be executed. The court decided that there was severance of the joint tenancy in equity as the draft agreement was sufficient to serve as an indication of the common intention of the parties that the joint tenancy in equity should be severed. See also *Barracks v Barracks* [2005] EWHC 3077 (Ch).

In *Wallbank v Price* [2007] EWHC 3001 (Ch), the court decided that a declaration signed by both the beneficial joint tenants where it was agreed that the share of one of the parties was to be given to their child amounted to an agreement to sever the joint tenancy in equity.

Key Principle ....

There may be severance by any course of dealing sufficient to intimate that the interests of the co-owners were mutually treated as constituting a tenancy in common.

> GORE AND SNELL V CARPENTER 1990
> (as above)

Held ....

❖ (Ch D) There was no course of dealing between the parties whereby they had evinced an intention to regard the two properties as being held by them as beneficial tenants in common. In order for the course of dealing to be effective to sever the joint tenancy, there must be a common intention on the part of all the joint tenants to regard the joint tenancy in equity as having been severed, which was absent in this case.

Commentary ....

Likewise, in *McDowell v Hirschfield Lipson & Rumney* [1992] 2 F.L.R. 126, the facts of which were similar to Gore, the court decided that the negotiation and correspondence between the parties as to the sale of the former matrimonial home and the division of proceeds of sale, where no agreement was reached, was not a course of dealing in which both parties clearly evinced an intention that the joint tenancy should be severed. Ultimately, it is a question of fact whether there is a common intention or agreement between the parties to treat the beneficial joint tenancy as having been severed. It should also be noted that a unilateral declaration of an intention to sever is ineffective to sever the joint tenancy: *Nielson-Jones v Fedden* [1975] Ch. 222.

The three methods of severance considered here namely, the severance by an act of a joint tenant on his or her own share, mutual agreement and mutual conduct, are the methods of severance set out in *Williams v Hensman*. Where the act by a joint tenant does not fall within s.36(2) of the **Law of Property Act 1925** or within the *Williams v Hensman* methods, the joint tenancy is not severed in equity.

LIABILITIES BETWEEN TENANTS IN COMMON

[a] Rental obligations

Key Principle

A rental obligation may be imposed on a co-owner who is in sole occupation of the co-owned property, in order to do broad justice between the parties.

> CHHOKAR V CHHOKAR 1983
> A husband (the first respondent) and wife (the appellant) were the beneficial owners of the matrimonial home. Although the house was in the sole name of the husband, the wife had contributed to its purchase and upkeep. The husband sold the matrimonial home, without the wife's knowledge, to the second respondent at an undervalue. Completion of the purchase was arranged at a time when the wife would be away at hospital giving birth. The husband left the country and the second respondent tried to force the wife to leave the house. As the wife had been in actual occupation she had an overriding interest in the house.

Held

❖ (CA (Civ Div)) In balancing the interests of the second respondent and the wife, and taking into account the fact that the second respondent had acquired the legal title to the house by a fraudulent conspiracy and his attempts to force her out of the house, no order of sale would be made. In the circumstances of the case, the wife's interest had to prevail over the second respondent. As regards whether an occupational rent had to be paid by the wife, the relevant test was one of fairness. Here, the second respondent stood in the shoes of the husband and as the wife had not sought to exclude the husband from the house, there was nothing to indicate that it would be fair to order the wife to pay an occupational rent to the second respondent. [1984] Fam. Law 269.

> MURPHY V GOOCH 2007
> M and G had bought a 25 per cent share in a property as their family home under a shared ownership scheme with a Housing Association. Two years later the relationship broke down and M moved out. G made all the payments for the property. M sought a declaration that she was entitled to a half share as the property was held by G and her as beneficial tenants in common. In addition, the application sought a declaration that if G continued to stay in the property that he would pay her compensation for her exclusion from the property. The Court at first

instance held that G was entitled to credit for his payments for the mortgage, the mortgage policy and the rent to the Housing Association but that this should be offset against those credits up to half of all the payments in respect of occupational rent. M appealed against the order.

Held

❖ (CA (Civ Div)) The court could make an order for credit for occupation rent if it was just to do so regardless of whether the co-owner was forcibly evicted from the property. As M left the property because of the relationship breaking down this amounted to M having been constructively excluded. The court should take into consideration the **Trusts of Land and Appointment of Trustees Act 1996** and its power to order occupational rent was no longer on the basis of equitable accounting but under ss.12 to 15 of that Act. Hence M could set off the credit arising from the occupational rent against the credits which G had as a result of his payment and that there was no reason to limit it to only offsetting half of the payments. [2007] EWCA Civ 603.

Commentary

The question as to whether occupational rent is payable is now subject to s.13(1) of the **Trusts of Land and Appointment of Trustees Act 1996** which gives the trustees a statutory power to exclude or restrict the entitlement of one or more (but not all) the beneficiaries to occupy the land. Under s.13(6), the trustees can require a beneficiary in occupation to "compensate" the beneficiaries who have been so excluded or restricted in their occupation of the property. This supersedes the approach taken in *Chhokar v Chhokar*. However, it does not impose an obligation on the beneficiaries in occupation to compensate those beneficiaries who voluntarily vacate the property. In *Murphy v Gooch*, it was made clear that a co-owner who had left the property because of the breakdown of the relationship could be regarded as having been constructively excluded thereby giving rise to an obligation to pay occupation rent. This case has been followed in *Rahnema v Rahbari* [2008] 2 P. & C.R. D11, where the court similarly ordered the payment of occupation rent in order to do broad justice between the parties so that both the co-owners enjoyed the benefit of the property until it was sold. The principle of equitable accounting in terms of rental payment will continue to apply in the case of a claim by the trustee in bankruptcy of the non-occupier who has no statutory right of occupation—*French v Barcham* [2008] EWHC 1505 (Ch). See also *Re Byford* [2003] EWHC 1267 (Ch) and *Wright v Johnson* [2001] EWCA Civ 1667.

[b] Liability for repairs and improvements

Key Principle ....

A co-owner who has incurred expenditure on repairs or improvements to the co-owned property cannot claim a contribution or repayment from the other co-owners, in the absence of an express or implied agreement, or unless it was carried out pursuant to an obligation to a third party.

> **LEIGH V DICKESON 1884**
> The plaintiffs were trustees and part of the estate comprised of premises in Dover. The beneficiaries of the trust and the defendant were tenants in common of the property. They made a claim against the defendant for monies due as a result of the defendant's use and occupation of three-quarters of the premises in Dover. The defendant owned the other one-quarter of the property. The defendant counterclaimed for monies he had spent on repairs and improvements to the property.

Held ....

❖ (CA) A tenant in common was not entitled to undertake improvements or repairs to the property and claim a contribution from the other co-owners without the express or implied agreement of the other co-owners. The defendant's counterclaim would be dismissed. (1884–85) L.R. 15 Q.B.D. 60.

Commentary ....

Lindley L.J. also suggested in that case, that there was no obligation on the other co-owners to contribute to the cost of repairs even though the repairs may be necessary and proper and the other co-owners receive a benefit from it.

Key Principle ....

The co-owner who has incurred expenditure on repairs or improvements to the co-owned property has an "equity" which will allow him to make a claim against the proceeds of sale of the property where the value of the property has been increased as a result of the repairs or improvements.

> **LEIGH V DICKESON 1884**
> (as above)

❖ (CA) Cotton L.J. suggested obiter that the co-owner who expended money on repairs or improvements to the co-owned property may be able to make a claim against the proceeds of sale where the value of the property has been increased because of the repairs and improvements.

Commentary

Therefore, even though the co-owner may not be entitled to make a claim initially for a contribution towards the cost of repairs or improvements, a claim can be made against the proceeds of sale where the value of the property has been increased because of it. There are, however, practical difficulties with this principle, for example, where the property isn't sold until a long time afterwards or where the repairs or improvements do not increase the value of property.

Key Principle

The quantum of the co-owner's claim against the proceeds of sale of the property, where the value of the property has been increased as a result of the repairs or improvements, will be on the basis of either half the increase in value of the property or half of the actual expenditure, whichever is less.

RE PAVLOU (A BANKRUPT) 1991

The respondent husband and wife bought their matrimonial home in 1973. The house was transferred to them as beneficial joint tenants. The parties separated in 1983. The wife was left in sole occupation of the home, from which time she paid the mortgage instalments and costs of repairs and improvements to the house. In March 1987, a bankruptcy order was made against the husband with the result that the beneficial joint tenancy was severed. The house was held by them as beneficial tenants in common in equal shares. The husband's trustee in bankruptcy applied to the court for a declaration as to the beneficial interests in the house, an order for possession and an order for sale of the house. The wife agreed that the orders for possession and sale ought to be made but she alleged that she was entitled to be reimbursed in respect of her expenditure on the house.

Held

❖ (Ch D) In deciding the quantum of a co-owner's claim in respect of expenditure incurred for repairs and improvements to the property, there was no difference in approach between beneficial joint tenants and beneficial tenants in common. The guiding principle was that a co-owner cannot take the benefit of an increase in the value of the property without giving an allowance for what had been spent by the other co-owner. In the present case, the wife would be entitled to the lesser of half the increase in value of the property or half of the expenditure incurred. [1993] 1 W.L.R. 1046.

Commentary

Prior to *Re Pavlou*, there was some uncertainty as to whether the co-owner's claim against the proceeds of sale, in respect of the increase in value of the property as a result of the repairs or improvement, was on the basis of the proportionate share in the increase in value (see *Parker v Trigg* (1884) W.N. 27) or on the amount of expenditure incurred (see *Re Jones* [1893] 2 Ch. 461). *Re Pavlou* decides that it is the lesser of a proportionate share in the increase in value or the expenditure.

[c] Occupation and use of co-owned property by a tenant in common.

Key Principle

No action in trespass will lie against a tenant in common merely because he has exclusive possession over a part of the co-owned property, provided that he does not occupy more than his just share and proportion.

> JACOBS V SEWARD 1872
> The plaintiff and defendant were assumed to be tenants in common of some lands at Ealing. The defendant entered into possession of the land, cut the grass, put a lock on the gate and carried away the grass for stacking as hay.

Held

❖ (HL) The circumstances did not amount to ouster so as to enable the plaintiff to succeed in a claim for trespass against the defendant. (1871–72) L.R. 5 H.L. 464.

Commentary

Under s.12 of the **Trusts of Land and Appointment of Trustees Act 1996** the co-owners had the right to occupy the property where the trust provides for the occupation of the property by the co-owners or where it is available for occupation. The trustees have the power to exclude one or more (but not all) the beneficial co-owners from occupying the property and can impose such conditions on the occupation as is reasonable under s.13 of the 1996 Act. In *Rodway v Landy* [2001] EWCA Civ 471, Gibson L.J. stated that s.13 extended to giving the power to trustees to divide a building between the co-owners who were entitled to occupy the property and to require the co-owners to contribute to the costs incurred.

It is clear that no action for trespass can lie against another co-owner merely because one co-owner had exclusive possession over part of the property. The only exception is where the occupation of the co-owned property effectively ousts the other co-owner/s from occupying the property.

[d] Rents from a stranger and profits from the land.

Key Principle

Where a tenant in common makes a profit from the co-owned land by his own efforts by, for example, cultivating the land, he does not need to account for this profit to the other co-owners. In the case of rents received from strangers, there is a duty to account only if the co-owner receives more than his just share and proportion of it.

> HENDERSON V EASON 1851
>
> Henderson and Eason were tenants in common of some properties in the County of Kent. Eason died in 1839. A claim for an account was made against Eason alleging that Eason, who had the care and management of these properties, had taken more than his just share and proportion of the rents and profits accruing from these properties.

Held

❖ (Ex Chamber) Eason would only be liable to account to Henderson if he had taken more than his just share and proportion of the rents received from strangers. However, where the profits accrued as a result of his own occupation of the land, by for example, his cultivation of the land, Eason was entitled to keep all the profits. On the facts of the case, there was no evidence to indicate that Eason had in fact received more than his just share. (1851) 17 Q.B. 701.

Commentary

A distinction in this case is made between rents received from strangers and profits accruing to the co-owner because of his efforts on the land. The reason for this is that it was regarded as inappropriate that the co-owner who has done some work on the land, for example, by cultivating the land on his own, should have to share the fruits of his labour with the other co-owners. This is especially so if it is borne in mind that the co-owners would not have to bear a proportionate share of any loss suffered by the co-owner in the enterprise.

THINK POINT

Do you think there is any severance of the beneficial joint tenancy when one co-owner kills the other co-owner? Should this be severance or an imposition of a constructive trust?

In considering the decision in *Kinch v Bullard*, above, if it was the wife who died first instead of the husband do you think the estate would be allowed to claim a valid service of the notice?

Strict Settlements and Trusts of Land

Strict settlements

5

INTRODUCTION

Section 2(1) of the **Trusts of Land and Appointment of Trustees Act 1996** (TLATA 1996) provides that:

> "[N]o settlement created after the commencement of this Act is a settlement for the purposes of the Settled Land Act 1925; and no settlement shall be deemed to be made under that Act after that commencement".

After the commencement of the Act no strict settlement can be created expressly or arise unintentionally. The **TLATA 1996** provides for the creation of the trust of land in its place. However, two exceptions are permitted under the Act; first, where there is a resettlement of settlements in existence at the commencement of the Act and secondly, settlements created in the exercise of powers of appointment contained in settlements in existence at the commencement of the Act.

The law relating to strict settlements will be applicable to existing settlements but obviously its importance will diminish with time. A settlement will cease to be a settlement, where there is no longer any land or heirlooms subject to it: s.2(4) of **TLATA 1996**.

The details of the trust of land will be considered in the next section.

POWERS OF THE TENANT FOR LIFE

Key Principle
The powers of the tenant for life cannot be restricted by the terms of the settlement.

> RE ACKLOM 1928
> The terms of the settlement provided, inter alia, that the trustees were to sell the house and distribute the proceeds to charitable

organisations in the event that the tenant for life did not wish to reside or continue to reside there. The tenant for life lived in the house for a number of years before going abroad. Due to illness her return was delayed and she sold the house in 1927 as tenant for life. The trustees sought a declaration as to whether the tenant for life had an interest in the proceeds of sale or the income arising from it.

Held

❖ (Ch D) The tenant for life had not forfeited her interest under the settlement and as tenant for life, she was entitled to the income from the proceeds of sale. Section 106 of the **Settled Land Act 1925** made it clear that any provision in the will or settlement, which limited or prevented the tenant for life from exercising his or her power of sale, was void. [1929] 1 Ch. 195.

Commentary

This decision reiterates the point that once there is a settlement within the meaning of the **Settled Land Act 1925**, the tenant for life's powers under the Act cannot be limited or restricted in any way. Any provision to the contrary would be void by virtue of s.106 of the Act. The courts had adopted this view even in respect to the predecessor to s.106. See *Re Ames* [1893] 2 Ch. 479.

Key Principle

"A tenant for life ... shall, in exercising any powers under [the **Settled Land Act 1925**], have regard to the interests of all parties entitled under the settlement, and shall in relation to the exercise thereof by him, be deemed to be in the position and to have the duties and liabilities of a trustee for those parties." (Section 107 of the **Settled Land Act 1925**).

HAMPDEN V EARL OF BUCKINGHAMSHIRE 1893

The tenant for life of settled land, part of which was mortgaged and part of which was not, proposed to raise a sum of money by mortgaging the whole estate in order to pay off the existing mortgages and some pecuniary legacies. The settlement provided for the payment of life annuities. The effect of the mortgage would deprive the annuitants of all benefit from the land. The result would be that it would benefit the remaindermen to the detriment of the annuitants.

Held ....

❖ (CA) The tenant for life would be restrained from effecting the proposed mortgage as he was not paying due regard to the interest of the annuitants. [1893] 2 Ch. 531.

> **MIDDLEMAS V STEVENS 1901**
> A settlement provided, inter alia, that the interest of the tenant for life, who was a widow, would cease upon her remarriage. The tenant for life purported to grant a lease to her fiancé, in the exercise of her powers.

Held ....

❖ (Ch D) The tenant for life would be restrained by injunction from granting the lease on proof that the sole purpose for it was to enable her to live in the property after her marriage. [1901] 1 Ch. 574.

Commentary ....

By s.107 of the **Settled Land Act 1925**, the tenant for life, who has powers of disposition of the land, and is a trustee of the legal estate of the settled land, is required to have regard to the interests of the parties entitled under the settlement. Although the tenant may be legally acting within his powers, the court has the power to intervene in cases where the action or proposed action by the tenant for life fails to take into account the interests of all parties.

DISPOSITIONS OF THE SETTLED LAND

Key Principle ....

A purchaser dealing with the tenant for life in good faith shall not be bound by the terms of the trust and shall rely on the statements in the vesting deed.

> **WESTON V HENSHAW 1949**
> In 1921, a grandfather sold some land to his son who then subsequently sold it back in 1927. By his will, the grandfather settled the land upon his wife for life, then to his son for life and then to his grandson. The land was vested in the son in 1940 who then purported to mortgage it as the absolute beneficial owner. He was able to do this by suppressing all the documents relating to the settlement and the conveyance from himself to the grandfather in 1927, thereby giving the mortgagee the appearance that he was the absolute beneficial owner, by virtue of the conveyance of 1921. After the death of the son, the

grandson sought a declaration as to whether the mortgage was good against him.

Held

❖ (Ch D) The mortgage was void in accordance with s.18 of the **Settled Land Act 1925**. The mortgagee could not rely on s.110 of the 1925 Act because the section only applied to purchasers who knew that they were dealing with the tenant for life. [1950] Ch. 510.

RE MORGAN'S LEASE 1971

In 1950, a tenant for life granted a ten-year lease of four rooms to the plaintiffs and another person. In 1960, upon the expiry of the lease, a document purporting to be a lease granted a term of the same property to the plaintiffs for another seven years. The lease contained an option to renew for another seven years on the same terms but without the option to renew. The tenant for life died in 1962. In 1967, the plaintiffs gave a notice in writing in accordance with the terms of the lease exercising the option to renew the lease. The new landlords of the property refused to comply with the notice.

Held

❖ (Ch D) The plaintiffs who had acted in good faith within the meaning of s.110 of the **Settled Land Act 1925,** were entitled to an order for specific performance of the terms of the contract. Section 110 was applicable whether or not the plaintiffs knew or did not know that they were dealing with a tenant for life provided they were acting in good faith. [1972] Ch. 1.

Commentary

In *Re Morgan's Lease*, the court doubted whether *Weston v Henshaw* was correct. The two decisions are clearly in conflict but the approach taken in *Re Morgan's Lease* is favoured by commentators such as Maudsley (36 M.L.R. 25 at 28). The Court of Appeal in *Bevan v Johnston* [1990] 28 E.G. 113 had the opportunity to examine this issue. However, the court failed to consider either of the two decisions and the effect of s.110 of the **Settled Land Act 1925,** although implicitly, the Court of Appeal seems to have followed the reasoning in *Weston v Henshaw*. The issue remains unresolved.

VARIATION OF THE SETTLEMENT

Key Principle

> "Any transaction affecting or concerning the settled land, or any part thereof, ... which in the opinion of the court would be for the benefit of settled land, or any part thereof, or the persons interested under the settlement, may, under an order of the court, be effected by the tenant for life, if it is one which could have been validly effected by an absolute owner." (Section 64 of the **Settled Land Act 1925**).

HAMBRO V DUKE OF MARLBOROUGH 1994

In 1705, Queen Anne gave property to the first Duke of Marlborough. In 1706, an Act of Parliament was passed which provided that the titles of the first Duke and the estates should, in the event of the failure of his male issue, pass to his daughters and their male issue in tail male severally in succession with remainders over and that neither the first duke nor any other person

> "to whom the premises shall come or descend ... shall have any power ... to hinder, bar or disinherit any person ... to or upon whom the ... premises are hereby invested or limited, from holding or enjoying the same ... ".

The first defendant was the tenant in tail in possession, with the powers of a tenant for life. The second defendant was the first defendant's son and the tenant in tail in remainder who was considered to be incapable of managing the estates properly. The plaintiffs, who were the trustees of the settlement, sought the court's approval, under s.64 of the **Settled Land Act 1925**, for a scheme under which the first defendant was to execute a conveyance of the estates to the trustees of a new trust to be held on a trust for sale, upon trust to pay the income from the estates to the first defendant for life and subject thereto, on a protective trust for the second defendant and thereafter upon the trusts of the existing parliamentary settlement.

Held

❖ (Ch D) The conveyance by the first defendant was a transaction within the meaning of s.64 of the 1925 Act. Under that statutory provision, the court had jurisdiction to authorise the first defendant to execute the conveyance without the consent of the second defendant, even though it varied the beneficial interest under the Act of 1706. [1994] Ch. 158.

Commentary
This case illustrates the contemporary approach of the courts with regard to the interpretation of the word "transaction" within s.64 of the **Settled Land Act 1925**.

TRUSTS OF LAND

Introduction

The **TLATA 1996** abolished the dual system of strict settlements and trusts for sale. It replaced them with the trust of land. One of the important distinctions between the trusts for sale and the trusts of land is that, in the case of the trust for sale, the trustees for sale have a mandatory obligation to sell with the power to postpone sale. However, in the case of the trust of land, the trustees of the land have the power to sell and the power to postpone sale.

The **TLATA 1996** retains the mechanism of overreaching for trusts of land by way of amendment to ss.2 and 27 of the **Law of Property Act 1925**. As long as the purchaser pays the purchase price to two trustees or a trust corporation, the interest of the beneficiaries will be overreached. It is not an absolute requirement that capital money arises from a disposition in order for beneficial interests to be overreached: *State Bank of India v Sood* [1997] Ch. 276 CA (Civ Div).

Under s.6(1), the trustees are given the powers of an absolute owner. More specifically, the Act further makes provision to give the trustees the following specific powers:

- to purchase land (s.6(3));
- to delegate functions to the beneficiaries (s.9(1));
- to partition the land (s.7));
- to convey the land to the beneficiaries and the power to compel the beneficiaries to accept the transfer (s.6(2)).

The exercise of the trustees' powers can be made subject to a person's consent. However, the court can waive the obligation of the trustee to obtain consent under s.4. This overcomes the problem illustrated in earlier cases such as *Re Inns* [1947] Ch. 576. In addition, the trustees have the obligation to consult the beneficiaries who are of full age and beneficially entitled to an interest in possession in the land and so far as consistent with the general interest of the trust, give effect to the wishes of the beneficiaries or their majority in the exercise of any function in relation to the trust land—s.11(1).

Section 12 **TLATA 1996** gives the beneficiaries a right to occupy the property, where the purpose of the trust includes making the property available for occupation for the beneficiaries, and, if they are of full age and beneficially entitled to an interest in possession. The right to occupy is only for beneficiaries and not to third parties who have no interest in the property: *Omotajo v Omotajo* [2008] All E.R. (D) 156.

COURT'S POWERS UNDER SECTIONS 14 AND 15 OF THE TLATA 1996

The court has a discretionary power to make various orders under s.14 of the 1996 Act on the application of a trustee or any person who has an interest in property subject to a trust of land. Apart from making an order relieving the trustees from the obligation to obtain the consent of any person in connection with the exercise of any of their powers, the court may make any order relating to the exercise by the trustees of any of their functions or declaring the nature or extent of a person's interest in property subject to a trust. It can also prevent the trustees from disposing or otherwise dealing with the property including the exercise or the prevention of the exercise of the trustees' powers.

In exercising its discretion, the court is directed by s.15 of the **TLATA 1996** to have regard to the intentions of the person or persons (if any) who created the trust (s.15(1)(a)); the purposes for which the property subject to the trust is held (s.15(1)(b)); the welfare of any minor who occupies or might reasonably be expected to occupy any land subject to the trust as his home (s.15(1)(c)); and the interests of any secured creditor of any beneficiary (s.15(1)(d)).

Key Principle
Earlier authorities on s.30 of the **Law of Property Act 1925** should be treated with caution in applying ss.14 and 15 of the **TLATA 1996**.

MORTGAGE CORP LTD V SHAIRE 2000
S and H, a wife and husband, bought a house in their joint names with the assistance of a mortgage loan from Abbey National Bank. H subsequently left the house but continued to contribute to the mortgage payments. S's new partner F moved into the house. S and H then transferred the house to S and F. The terms of the trust, on which they

held the legal title, were not specified. S and F mortgaged the house to a Chase Manhattan Bank in order to redeem the first mortgage. F paid the instalments on the new mortgage loan. He later died insolvent. It was subsequently found that he had forged S's signature to obtain mortgage loans from First National Bank and the Mortgage Corporation. The last loan was used to pay off the loans from Chase Manhattan Bank and First National Bank. F had retained the balance of the money. S lived in the house with her son and wished to remain there. The Mortgage Corporation wished to realise their interest in the house.

Held

❖ (Ch D) S had a 75 per cent beneficial interest in the house, based upon the absence of a declared trust and the evidence as to circumstances of the transfer from S and H to S and F. The Mortgage Corporation's mortgage was not binding on S. The mortgage bound F's estate, which being effectively insolvent, meant that the Mortgage Corporation had a 25 per cent beneficial interest in the house. The judge refused an order of sale, provided arrangements could be made whereby S was able to repair and insure the house and enable the Bank to recover a proper return on their interest in the house. [2001] Ch. 743.

Commentary

There were concerns that the decision would cause problems with professional lenders given the approach of the court in its interpretation of the relevant statutory provisions. A more conservative approach was taken in *Bank of Ireland Home Mortgages Ltd v Bell* [2001] 2 F.L.R. 809. On similar facts to *Shaire*, the Court of Appeal granted an order for sale in favour of the mortgagees. This was on the basis that as the marriage had broken up and the child was not too far from the age of majority, the need to use the property as a family home was no longer a relevant consideration and hence an order for sale would be appropriate. The Court of Appeal suggested that the court at first instance had failed to consider that with the interest accruing; the debt to the mortgagee had grown substantially and was more than the value of the house and increasing daily. To delay the sale would be unfair to the bank as it would not be able to recoup the full amount outstanding from the mortgagors. Similarly, in *Forrester Ketley & Co v Brent* [2009] EWHC 3441 (Ch), the court granted an order for sale in favour of creditors. The court considered the interests of the owners but was of the view that their interests could not outweigh the interests of the creditors.

One important aspect of *Shaire* is the court's attitude as to how its powers under **TLATA 1996** should be applied. Neuberger J. suggested that s.15 had made a clear change to the law and that the balance in determining whether an order of sale should be granted, was in favour of families over mortgagees. Thus, in the light of this change in the law the earlier authorities on s.30 of the **Law of Property Act 1925** should be treated with caution. It might be added that cases on s.30 may still be useful to the extent that they support the approach identified in this case.

In *TSB Bank Plc v Marshall* [1998] 2 F.L.R. 769, applying ss.14 and 15 of **TLATA 1996**, it was held that the collateral purpose of providing a home for children could not be extended to cover adult children, in the absence of clear words of intention. It is possible to infer a preference for banks' interest over that of the family but in this case there was no possible way for the bank to recover the debt other than by an order for sale. Neuberger J. in *Mortgage Corporation Ltd v Shaire* disagreed with the view espoused in *TSB Bank Plc v Marshall* which suggested that the old case law remained relevant.

Key Principle

Where the purpose of the trust is still continuing, the court will be reluctant to order a sale of the property.

RE BUCHANAN-WOLLASTON'S CONVEYANCE 1939

Four individuals who owned properties near or adjoining each other, combined and purchased a piece of land for the purpose of keeping it as open land so as to maintain their sea views. It was agreed that any transaction in relation to the land must be with the majority agreement of the parties. The plaintiff sold his property and wished to sell the co-owned land and divide the proceeds of sale.

Held

❖ (CA) As the collateral purpose (the primary purpose being the trust for sale) of the acquisition of the co-owned land (the maintenance of the sea views) was still continuing and subsisting, no order of sale would be made. [1939] Ch. 738.

BARCLAYS BANK PLC V HENDRICKS 1995

A wife appealed against the grant of an order, obtained by a creditor, for the sale of the matrimonial home under s.30 of the **Law of Property Act 1925**. The husband had already moved out of the matrimonial home and had moved into another property belonging to the wife. She argued that the sale of the property should be deferred until the children had reached the age of 18 or had finished full time education and that she did not want to move to the other property.

Held

The collateral purpose of joint occupation of the property as a matrimonial home had ended when the husband moved out of the home. As the wife had failed to show any exceptional circumstances why her interest should prevail against the creditor, especially since she had another property in the area, the order made under s.30 would be upheld. [1996] 1 F.L.R. 258.

Commentary

The collateral (or primary) purpose will be one of the important factors, which the court will have to take into account when deciding whether to exercise its jurisdiction under s.14. The court is in fact directed by s.15 to take this factor into account when considering an application made under s.14. It should be noted that the reference to the term collateral purpose in these cases was because the trust for sale was applicable and as such the primary purpose had to be the sale of the property with any other purpose being merely a collateral purpose.

Where the purpose for the acquisition of the property, which is subject to the trust, is for the provision of a matrimonial or family home and the marriage irretrievably breaks down, an application should be made under the Matrimonial Causes legislation. In *Miller Smith v Miller Smith* [2009] EWCA Civ 1297 Wilson L.J. suggested that

" ... it is much more desirable that an issue ... about the sale of the home should be resolved within an application for ancillary relief ... it is hard to conceive that an order for sale would reflect a proper exercise of discretion".

See *Jones v Challenger* [1961] 1 Q.B. 176, *Williams v Williams* [1976] Ch. 278.

The primary purpose to the trust cannot be overridden by passing the beneficial interest of one party to another who was kept out of enjoyment of the property: *Abbey National Plc v Moss* [1994] 1 F.L.R. 307.

Key Principle

Any party with an interest in the property, including a mortgagee can make an application under s.14 of the **TLATA 1996**.

EDWARDS V BANK OF SCOTLAND PLC 2010
The claimant claimed against his wife and the bank arising out of the execution of a charge over a property as security for an advance of £637,500. He alleged that his wife forged his signature on the charge to

the bank and therefore he was not liable on the charge. The bank responded by seeking an order for possession and sale of the property on two alternative bases: either pursuant to its rights as legal chargee on the basis that Mr and Mrs Edwards had both executed the relevant deed or, pursuant to its rights as equitable chargee and in reliance on s.14 **TLATA 1996**.

Held

❖ (Ch D) The Bank had locus standi to make an application under s.14 **TLATA 1996** on the basis of its rights as equitable chargee in respect of the charge signed by the wife. In considering the factors in s.15 **TLATA**, the Bank as a creditor has a substantial interest which is of significance. In the circumstances the court would make an order for the possession and sale of the property deferred for four months in light of the correspondence between the parties. [2010] EWHC 652 (Ch).

Commentary

This case makes it clear that s.14 **TLATA 1996** allows a broad range of persons with an interest in the property to seek an order from the court. In considering the exercise of the discretion, the court was of the view that the interests of the creditor was such that order for possession and sale should be made. Although there was mention of a grandchild living at the property, the court was not able to consider its interest under s.15 **TLATA** as no evidence was submitted to substantiate this.

A similar conclusion was reached in *C Putnam & Sons v Taylor* [2009] EWHC 317 (Ch) where the court granted an order for sale in favour of the applicant creditor who had a charging order over the property which was held by the first and second respondents. The court was satisfied that there would be sufficient equity after the sale and payment to the applicant for the respondents to rehouse and that it was not appropriate to keep the applicant from recovering the monies owing indefinitely.

Key Principle

Instead of making an order for the sale of the property subject to the trust, it may be appropriate to order payment of compensation by one co-owner to the other.

DENNIS V MCDONALD 1981

In 1970, the plaintiff and defendant bought a house as their family home, with each contributing equally towards the purchase price part of which consisted of a mortgage. The house was conveyed into their names as tenants in common in equal shares. In 1974, the plaintiff left the house taking their five children with her. The defendant remained in occupation and later that year three of the older children returned to live with him. Mortgage payments were made by the defendant and the mortgage loan was fully repaid by March 1980. The plaintiff applied under s.30 of the **Law of Property Act 1925** for an order for sale of the house. At first instance it was decided that where the home was still needed in order to provide a home for the family, it was inappropriate to grant an order for sale of the property under s.30 of the 1925 Act. That as the actions of the defendant amounted to an ouster, the plaintiff, as a tenant in common, was entitled to occupational rent. The defendant appealed and the plaintiff cross-appealed against these orders.

Held

❖ (CA (Civ Div)) A tenant in common who had been excluded from occupation of the property was entitled to compensation. Since the defendant occupied the property by virtue of his beneficial interest, the proper way to assess the occupational rent payable was that the defendant ought to pay the plaintiff one half of such sum as would be regarded as fair rent under the Rent Act 1977. [1982] Fam. 63.

Commentary

Where the court reaches the conclusion that an order for sale is inappropriate, and one co-owner is in occupation whilst the other is not, the court may order that the co-owner in occupation pays occupational rent to the other. Under s.13(6) of the **Trusts of Land and Appointment of Trustees Act 1996**, the trustees can require a beneficiary in occupation to "compensate" the beneficiaries who have been so excluded or restricted in their occupation of the property. See *Murphy v Gooch* [2007] EWCA Civ 603 discussed in Ch.4.

THE TRUSTEE IN BANKRUPTCY AND THE TRUST OF LAND

Key Principle

Where a spouse having a beneficial interest in the property becomes bankrupt, the interests of the creditors usually prevail over the interests of the other spouse in the absence of exceptional circumstances, in relation to the question as to whether an order for possession and sale of the property ought to be made.

Re Citro (A Bankrupt) 1990

In 1985 two brothers were adjudicated bankrupt. They both had a half share of the beneficial interests in their respective matrimonial homes. The trustee in bankruptcy of their joint and separate estates applied to the court for a declaration as to their respective beneficial share in the matrimonial homes and orders for possession and sale of the homes under s.30 of the **Law of Property Act 1925.** The judge at first instance granted orders for possession and sale but postponed them until the youngest child in each case turned 16 years of age.

Held

❖ (CA (Civ Div)) The orders for possession and sale would be postponed only for six months. Unless there were exceptional circumstances, which were more than the ordinary consequences of debt and improvidence, the interests of the children and their spouse could not prevail over the interests of the creditors. On the facts of the case, although the circumstances of their spouses and children were distressing, they could not be described as exceptional, therefore there was no justification for a substantial postponement of the orders for possession and sale. [1991] Ch. 142.

Commentary

In the earlier case of *Re Holliday* [1981] Ch. 405, the Court of Appeal granted an order for the sale of the family home, under s.30 of the **Law of Property Act 1925,** on the application of the trustee in bankruptcy. However, the court postponed the order until the second child of the family reached the age of 17. The postponement was substantial in that case. In *Re Citro*, the Court of Appeal regarded *Re Holliday* as an exceptional case with one special feature, in that the postponement of the order for sale would not have caused any great hardship to the creditors. The Court of Appeal also stated that the series of bankruptcy decisions, including cases such as *Re Densham (A Bankrupt)* [1975] 1 W.L.R. 1519 and *Re Bailey (A Bankrupt)* [1977] 1 W.L.R. 278, have usually held that the interests of the creditors would prevail against the spouse and the children and a sale within a relatively short period of time would be ordered.

In *Bank of Baroda v Dhillon* [1998] F.L.R. 524, it was held that the existence of a right of actual occupation did not preclude an order of sale under s.30 Law of Property Act 1925.

THINK POINT

In exercising its jurisdiction under s.14 of the **Trusts of Land and Appointment of Trustees Act 1996**, the court is directed to have regard to the factors contained in s.15. Do you think that the court should consider factors other than those contained in s.15? See *Rodway v Landy* [2001] EWCA Civ 471—a case in respect of an order for the partition of a property.

Where all the four factors in s.15 of the **Trusts of Land and Appointment of Trustees Act 1996** are present in a case how would a court reach a decision as to whether it should make the relevant order under s.14?

Leases

....
INTRODUCTION

For a valid lease to be created, generally the commencement date and duration must be certain, the parties to the lease must have the capacity to enter into the lease, the tenant must have exclusive possession of the premises, the demised premises must be certain and the term granted should be shorter than what the grantor possesses. Although normally the lease is usually granted at a rent, this need not be strictly complied with as s.205 of the **Law of Property Act 1925** defines a term of years absolute as meaning a term which takes effect either in possession or in reversion, "whether at a rent or not ... ". This suggests that a lease need not be granted for a rent although it would be unusual for a rent not to be imposed.

A lease can be legal or equitable. For a lease to be legal it must be created by deed (s.52 of the **Law of Property Act 1925**) unless it is for a period of less than three years taking effect in possession at the best rent without taking a fine which does not need to be by deed (s.54(2) of the **Law of Property Act 1925**). In *Fitzkriston LLP v Panayi* [2008] EWCA Civ 283 the court held that a lease was not created as the evidence should that the rent was not at the best rent for the property.

In addition, in registered land, in order for the lease to be legal, where the lease is more than seven years then it also has to be completed by registration in order to be legal (s.27 of the **Land Registration Act 2002**). If it is less than seven years it does not have to be registered (subject to a number of exceptions) and will take effect as interest which is overriding (Schs 1 and 3 of the **Land Registration Act 2002**). In all other cases the lease takes effect in equity—for example a contract to grant a lease of more than three years where no deed is executed then the lease is equitable in nature.

In essence the lease is the document by which the estate consisting of the term of years is granted but in common usage, the lease is often referred to as the estate itself.

ESSENTIAL ELEMENTS OF LEASES

Key Principle
A valid lease must be for a fixed duration.

> ### PRUDENTIAL ASSURANCE CO LTD V LONDON RESIDUARY BODY 1992
> In 1930 a strip of land adjacent to a road was sold to the council and then leased back "until the ... land is required by the council for the purposes of the widening of ... " the road. The successors to the council who had no interest in widening the road sold the land to the other defendants. They in turn issued a notice determining the lease. The plaintiffs who were assignees of the lease sought a declaration that the lease could only be determined upon the land being required for road widening.

Held
❖ (HL) A lease has to be of a fixed duration. The original agreement was for an uncertain period and was thus void. The land was, however, held on a yearly tenancy by virtue of possession and payment of rent. Service of six months' notice was sufficient to determine a yearly tenancy. [1992] 2 A.C. 386.

Commentary
This confirms the principle in *Lace v Chantler* [1944] K.B. 368 CA, where it was held that an agreement for a lease for the duration of the war was uncertain and did not create a good leasehold interest. It overrules *Ashburn Anstalt v WJ Arnold & Co* [1989] Ch. 1 CA (Civ Div) which seemed to depart from the principle in *Lace v Chantler* in recognising a lease that was for an indefinite duration could be regarded as certain because both parties had the power to end it. It also overrules *Re Midland Railway Co's Agreement* [1971] Ch. 725 CA (Civ Div) in the sense that all leases must comply with the certainty rule and periodic leases are not exempt from the rule. It does not deny though that a periodic lease is for a fixed duration, if each period, and consequently each period of determination, is certain. In *Re Midland Railway Co's Agreement*, a term allowing for determination of the lease when the lessors required the land for their undertaking did not void the lease as it was not inconsistent with the existing periodic lease. The decision in *Prudential Assurance Co Ltd v London Residuary Body* was recently applied in *Mexfield Housing Co-operative Ltd v Berrisford* [2010] EWCA Civ 811, where an attempt to grant a lease for so long as the tenant paid rent and was not in breach of any of the covenants was void for uncertainty.

In *Harrow London Borough v Qazi* [2003] UKHL 43 the House of Lords considered whether the right to take possession of property upon the expiry of a lease was contrary to art.8 of the **European Convention on Human Rights**. The House of Lords held that art.8 was not contravened as the article did not confer a right to a home but a right to respect of a person's home.

Key Principle

A valid lease must confer on the lessee exclusive possession of the property.

> STREET V MOUNTFORD 1985
>
> An agreement granted the right to occupy two rooms subject to 14 days' notice to quit. It was titled a "licence agreement". The occupant signed a declaration to the effect that she understood that the agreement did not create a lease protected by the Rent Acts. Thereafter she and her husband moved in. A declaration was sought as to whether the agreement was a lease or a licence.

Held

❖ (HL) There was a grant of a term at a rent with exclusive possession. There was therefore a valid lease. Calling the agreement a licence was immaterial if there was in fact exclusive possession. [1985] A.C. 809.

Commentary

[1] The decision was important in restraining landlords from seeking to avoid the protection granted to lessees by the Rent Acts. The case disapproved *Somma v Hazelhurst* [1978] 1 W.L.R. 1014 CA (Civ Div), where emphasis was given to the stated intention of the parties. There, two separate agreements were made with a couple to occupy a bedsit with a reservation that the landlord or nominee could also move in. Despite the unlikely match between the agreement and the reality the court held there to be no lease. Since *Street v Mountford*, courts have been more astute to identify sham terms which neither party intend to rely on and should thus be ignored in determining whether factual exclusive possession has been granted. *AG Securities v Vaughan* and *Antoniades v Villiers* [1990] 1 A.C. 417 HL are good examples of the application of the principle. The two actions were heard together. *In AG Securities v Vaughan* four separate agreements were made at different times with different occupants to share a house. There was no joint tenancy with collective exclusive possession as they had different agreements on different terms. There was also no individual exclusive possession of identified rooms as the licensees did in fact move rooms. In *Antoniades v Villiers* separate but identical agreements were made with a couple asserting that no exclusive

possession was granted and that the licensor or nominee could use the premises from time to time. The House of Lords found the latter provision was a pretence designed to evade the Rent Act. It had been intended for there to be exclusive possession so a valid lease did exist.

[2] In *Westminster City Council v Clarke* [1992] 2 A.C. 288 HL the House of Lords held that the council had not granted exclusive possession to the occupant of a room in a hostel for the homeless. The council had denied exclusive possession by genuine terms such as the right to change the accommodation without notice. Exclusive occupation was also inconsistent with the purpose for which the Council had provided housing in the hostel. See also *Mansfield DC v Langridge* [2007] EWHC 3152 (QB).

In *Mehta v Royal Bank of Scotland Plc* (2000) 32 H.L.R. 45 QBD, the court held that there was a lease of a room in a hotel as the plaintiff had exclusive possession of the room. In *Uratemp Ventures Ltd v Collins* [2001] UKHL 43, the House of Lords held that long term occupation of a hotel room was on the facts held under a lease. The room was part of a property over which the occupant had exclusive possession. It had to be determined whether the room was part of larger shared premises or was a separate dwelling. It was held to be the latter and therefore held under a lease not a licence. In *National Car Parks Ltd v Trinity Development Co (Banbury) Ltd* [2001] EWCA Civ 1686 , it was held that an agreement to operate a car park on certain premises was in the nature of a licence not a lease. This was because there was on the facts no exclusive possession. A similar conclusion was reached in *Cameron Ltd v Rolls-Royce Plc* [2007] EWHC 546 (Ch).

In *Clear Channel UK Ltd v Manchester City Council* [2005] EWCA Civ 1304, two draft agreements had been made in relation to a number of plots of land for the erection of advertising hoardings. In one case there was an annual tenancy brought about by the erection of hoardings and the payment of rent. The land covered by the agreement was certain and the draft showed a clear intention to grant a tenancy. By contrast it was held that in relation to the other plots there were only licences to enter the premises in relation to the hoardings. The draft agreements did not clarify the premises to be covered nor did they indicate any intention to grant exclusive possession over the premises.

Key Principle

A tenancy can arise even though the occupant had a limited interest in the property.

The respondent Trust was granted a licence by the Lambeth LBC of a property used to house homeless people. The appellant signed an agreement with the respondent to occupy a flat in the property and claimed that he had been given a tenancy notwithstanding that the respondent had only a limited interest in the property.

Held

❖ (HL) The facts of the case were such that the defendant had been given exclusive possession of the flat even though the language used was more appropriate to a licence. It was irrelevant that the respondent would be in breach of the licence from Lambeth LBC. The character of the landlord was likewise irrelevant so long as on a true construction of the agreement, a lease/tenancy had been granted. [2000] 1 A.C. 406.

Commentary

The Court of Appeal originally decided that no lease had been granted because the intention was merely to grant a licence. However, in the House of Lords their Lordships held that on the facts of the case there was a lease rather than a licence. What the document was called did not matter so long as it was clear that the intention was to grant exclusive possession. It was not irrelevant that the lessor only had a limited interest in the property, i.e. that it only had a licence itself. It is established law that in such cases the "lessor" is taken to have granted a lease. One other important point to note is that the court stressed that the character of the lessor was irrelevant—that the lessor was a trust set up to help house homeless people did not matter. It is clear that their Lordships were reluctant to allow public policy to apply in this case. It is submitted that in cases such as this, public policy should have applied allowing organisations, like the respondent, to have the flexibility to carry out what they are supposed to do.

CREATION OF LEASES

Key Principle

An agreement for a lease can be given effect in equity.

The plaintiff and defendant agreed to a lease of a mill for seven years. The terms were to be those as stipulated in another lease. They included a term that rent was payable in advance on demand for a full year and any amount outstanding at the time of the demand. The plaintiff went into possession but paid rent quarterly in arrears. The defendant demanded a full year's advance rent plus the amount outstanding since the last payment and put in a distress. The plaintiff claimed that the distress was unlawful.

Held

❖ (CA) Since the Judicature Acts, the court could in equity give effect to the agreement for a lease upon its intended terms. The court was not bound to recognise it only as a lease from year to year by payment of rent. If under the intended terms yearly rent was payable in advance on demand and demand was made then the distress was lawful. (1882) L.R. 21 Ch. D. 9.

Commentary

If the lease had only been recognised at law as a yearly periodic one (and not a seven-year lease because of the lack of a deed) the rent would have been payable in arrears. *Parker v Taswell* (1858) 44 E.R. 1106 Ct of Chancery had already decided that equity could give effect to the intended terms of a lease. The importance of *Walsh v Lonsdale* is that it applies the Judicature Acts' principle that where there is a conflict between law and equity then equity should prevail. However, giving effect with an equitable remedy is still discretionary and subject to general equitable principles. In *Coatsworth v Johnson* (1886) 55 L.J. Q.B. 220, the court refused specific performance of the agreed lease because the tenant was in breach of one of its covenants.

In *Mexfield Housing Co-operative Ltd v Berrisford* [2010] EWCA Civ 811 where the purported lease was void for uncertainty, the exclusive possession coupled with monthly payments gave rise to a periodic tenancy terminable by notice to quit.

COVENANTS IN LEASES

Key Principle

There is implied into every lease a covenant of quiet enjoyment.

MCCALL V ABELESZ 1975

The plaintiff had a lease of part of a house. The defendants were the new landlords. They allowed for the gas, water and electricity to be left unconnected for a year and a half. The plaintiff had refused the landlord's offer of alternative accommodation. The plaintiff brought an action for harassment under the Rent Act.

Held ....

❖ (CA (Civ Div)) The **Rent Act 1965** provisions as to harassment were penal but did not create a new cause of action. They also did not destroy existing civil remedies. [1976] Q.B. 585.

Commentary ....

[1] A claim for harassment can fall within the ambit of an action for breach of the landlord's implied covenant of quiet enjoyment. A physical interference or interruption of enjoyment can constitute breach.

[2] Quiet enjoyment covers a variety of different situations. In *Sampson v Hodson-Pressinger* [1981] 3 All E.R. 710 CA (Civ Div), it covered noise of footsteps from the flat above because the properties were not constructed properly. However, in *Southwark LBC v Mills* [2001] 1 A.C. 1 HL, distinguishing *Sampson v Hodson-Pressinger*, it was held that a breach of this covenant required a substantial interference with the tenant's lawful occupation of the property. This could include a regular excessive noise. The covenant however only covered prospective acts and not acts done prior to the grant of the tenancy. As such, as the breach in this case was as a result of the lack of sound proofing during the building of the properties, there was no breach of the covenant of quiet enjoyment. A similar approach was taken in *Jackson v JH Watson Property Investments Ltd* [2008] N.P.C. 1 in respect of defective walls and its effect on the repairing covenant.

[3] In *Nynehead Developments Ltd v RH Fibreboard Containers* [1999] 1 E.G.L.R. 7 Ch D, the tenant claimed that the failure of the landlord to prevent other tenants from obstructing the tenant's right of way and right to park constituted repudiation of the lease. It was held that the landlord had not refused to carry out all his obligations. The landlord had, however, committed breaches of the express covenant of quiet enjoyment and implied covenant not to derogate from grant. Those breaches did not deprive the tenant of the substantial benefit of the lease. The appropriate remedy, therefore, was damages not termination. In contrast in *Hunte v E Bottomley & Sons Ltd* [2007] EWCA Civ 1168 where the lessor blocked one side of the access road to a right of way which had been granted to the claimant this amounted to a breach of the covenant of quiet enjoyment and derogation from grant. In another dispute concerning a right of way in a lease, it was held that the test was whether the right could be substantially and practically exercised as conveniently as before: *B&Q Plc v Liverpool and Lancashire Properties Ltd* (2001) 81 P. & C.R. 20.

Key Principle

There is an implied term in leases that the lessor shall not derogate from grant.

> ### HARMER V JUMBIL (NIGERIA) TIN AREAS LTD 1920
>
> The plaintiff was granted a lease of land for the purpose of storing explosives. The statutory licence provided that if buildings were erected within a certain distance the licence would be revoked. The defendants acquired a lease of neighbouring land from the same freeholder for the purpose of working minerals and to erect buildings for that purpose but not in such a way as to interfere with the explosives store. The plaintiffs brought an action to restrain use of the mine and use of connected sheds.

Held

❖ (CA) The acts of the defendant could be imputed to the freeholder. Those acts were in derogation from the plaintiff's lease. It must be implied on the part of the freeholder not to do anything which would break the conditions under which the plaintiff held their explosives licence. [1921] 1 Ch. 200.

Commentary

A breach of the covenant of quiet enjoyment will often also be a breach of the covenant against derogation though this will not be true in all cases. In *Scottish Widows Plc v Stewart* [2006] EWCA Civ 999 the lessee's guarantor claimed breach of both covenants. The lessee's company owned a business repairing high performance prestige cars. After granting a 15-year lease on industrial premises to the lessee the lessor installed speed bumps which it was claimed damaged cars and ruined the lessee's business. The lessee's company went into liquidation and the lease was forfeited. The landlord sued for loss of rent and the lessee's guarantor sued for breach of quiet enjoyment and non-derogation. It was held that the lessee had suffered loss as a result of the installation of the speed bumps though in the case the damages payable were off set against the guarantor's guarantee in relation to payment of rent upon liquidation.

Key Principle

There is an implied term in leases that the property be fit for human habitation at the commencement of the lease.

A house was let. Upon taking possession the lessees found that it was infested with bugs.

Held

❖ (Ex Ct) It is an implied condition in letting furnished property that it shall be reasonably fit for human habitation. Where it is not, the lessee may quit without notice. (1843) 152 E.R. 693.

Commentary

This covenant gives the lessee the right to walk away from the lease at the time of its intended commencement without paying further rent and thereby gives the lessee a defence should the lessor seek to enforce the lease. Section 8(1) of the **Landlord and Tenant Act 1985** imposes a statutory covenant that premises be, and are kept fit for habitation. This, however, only applies to extremely low-rent property and does not apply unless the renovation can be done at reasonable expense.

Key Principle

There are statutorily implied covenants of repair by the lessor in some leases though these are interpreted restrictively.

QUICK V TAFF ELY BC1985

The plaintiff was a tenant of a council flat. Severe condensation caused decoration, woodwork, furniture and bedding to rot. The condensation was caused by poor insulation and heating. The plaintiff brought an action for breach of the landlord's covenant to keep in repair, the structure and exterior of the house.

Held

❖ (CA (Civ Div)) Liability under the implied covenant did not arise where there is a lack of amenity or inefficiency. It arises where there is a physical condition that requires repair. There was no damage or disrepair to the structure or exterior. The Council was not, therefore, liable for damage caused by condensation. [1986] Q.B. 809.

Commentary

The equivalent statutorily implied covenant of repair in short leases, s.11(1) of the **Landlord and Tenant Act 1985** as amended by s.116(1) of the **Housing Act 1988**, has also been restrictively interpreted. The standard of repair required is not objective but takes into account location, standard and life of the property. See *Newham LBC v Patel* (1978) 13 B.L.R. 77 CA (Civ Div).

In *Gibson Investments Ltd v Chesterton Plc (No.2)* [2003] EWHC 1255 (Ch), the nature of a covenant to repair was considered. In this case it was accepted that it was the tenant's obligation. The dispute arose as to which of three possible work schemes was sufficient to effect repair. The problem lay in corroding steel substructures, which caused cracking of external brick and stonework. The first scheme which essentially involved filling in the cracks was held not to be acceptable because even when the work was completed the underlying steel frame would still be in a state of disrepair and would continue to rust and cause cracking. Thus repair seems to go beyond merely curing the visible defect.

Whereas a landlord's liability under s.11 above requires that the landlord has notice, this is not the case in relation to defective premises. A landlord's liability under s.4 of the **Defective Premises Act 1972** to maintain premises free of dangerous defects was a duty of reasonable care in all the circumstances. It was not dependent on actual or constructive notice being given to the landlord. The case of *Sykes v Harry* [2001] EWCA Civ 167, related to injuries suffered by a tenant following a gas explosion resulting from failings in servicing gas appliances. The landlord was found to have failed in his duty to take such care as was reasonable.

A lessee cannot set off liability for service charges against damages resulting from the lessor's breach of repairing obligation where it was the very failure to pay service charges previously which made it impossible for the lessor to carry out his repair covenants. *Bluestorm Ltd v Portvale Holdings Ltd* [2004] EWCA Civ 289.

There are situations where there will be covenants by lessees to maintain premises in good repair. In one such case *Irontrain Investments Ltd v Ansari* [2005] EWCA Civ 1681, the lessee was responsible for leaks which damaged premises below rented out by the lessor to others. It was held by the Court of Appeal that the lessor could recover damages for damage caused including loss of rent from the occupants living in the premises below.

The scope of s.11 of the **Landlord and Tenant Act 1985** was at question in *Niazi Services Ltd v Van der Loo* [2004] EWCA Civ 53. The dispute related in part to water supply to the sub-tenant. The Court of Appeal held that a lessor's liability for repairs under s.11 only applied to installations owned or controlled by the landlord and within the premises of the landlord. In the present case the water supply installations in question were not within the lessor's control.

Key Principle

There is an implied contractual duty of care to keep common parts in reasonable repair and usability.

> ### LIVERPOOL CITY COUNCIL V IRWIN 1976
> Lessees of a ninth and tenth floor maisonette withheld their rent in protest at the condition of the block of flats. The lifts did not work, the staircases were unlit and the conditions appalling as a result of vandalism. The lessees' agreement did not specify terms as to repairing obligations of the common parts. The Council sought re-possession for non-payment of rent. The lessees counter-claimed that, inter alia, the Council owed a duty of care to keep the common parts in repair and properly lit.

Held

❖ (HL) In the absence of specific terms in the lease, there was an obligation upon landlords to take reasonable care to keep means of access in reasonable repair and usability. This is subject to the responsibilities of what reasonable lessees would do for themselves. The Council had made considerable effort and expense to deal with the problems caused by repeated vandalism. They were held not to be in breach of their obligation. The obligation applies to private and public landlords. [1977] A.C. 239.

Commentary

[1] The obligation is not absolute but covers what is necessary in the circumstances. The obligation can be read narrowly to impose a minimal requirement that access to rented premises be kept as safe as is in the power of the landlord to make it. It could be read more widely to impose a duty on landlords to give effect to an agreement. If courts set a very high standard they could thereby impose a heavy burden on councils and thus taxpayers. The case indicates that there are expectations of lessees and that there is a limit to the expense that councils can be expected to make in dealing with vandalism.

[2] In *Cavalier v Pope* [1906] A.C. 428 it was held that a landlord was not liable for injury caused by defects at the commencement of a lease of unfurnished premises. The lessee's wife who was injured could not claim, as she was not a party to the contract. Nowadays, a landlord could be liable for injury caused by defects under legislation such as the Occupiers Liability Act 1957, Defective Premises Act 1972, Contracts (Rights of Third Parties) Act 1999 as well as in negligence. In *Alker v Collingwood Housing Association* [2007] EWCA Civ 343 , the Court of Appeal decided that under s.4 of the **Defective**

Premises Act 1972, the landlord's liability arose only where the defect had caused any injury or damage as a result of a failure to repair or maintain the property.

Key Principle

There are statutorily implied terms relating to unlawful eviction which provide a civil remedy as well as criminal sanctions.

> ### TAGRO V CAFANE 1991
>
> The plaintiff leased a bedsit from the defendant. There were incidents of harassment culminating in the plaintiff being excluded by the defendant, who changed the locks. The plaintiff obtained an injunction requiring the defendant to provide a new set of keys. These were made available only after an application was made to commit the defendant for failure to observe the injunction. Upon her return to the bedsit the plaintiff found her belongings damaged, destroyed or removed and the bedsit was wrecked. The plaintiff did not resume occupation and brought an action for unlawful eviction under ss.27 and 28 of the **Housing Act 1988.**

Held

❖ (CA (Civ Div)) The act of providing keys together with the failure to restore the flat to its previous condition did not constitute reinstatement. The judge was entitled to take the plaintiff's valuation of the premises if the defendant did not adduce evidence to challenge it. [1991] 1 W.L.R. 378.

Commentary

It is arguable that a plaintiff may choose whether to accept reinstatement. The test of damages in s.28 of the **Housing Act 1988** is the difference in value between the premises with a sitting tenant or the premises with vacant possession. The plaintiff's valuation of this at £31,000 was high but accepted by the court. In addition £15,000 was awarded in respect of damage to the plaintiff's belongings. The measure of damages is clearly designed to negative any financial gain to be made from unlawfully evicting a tenant. It is somewhat odd though in the sense that the penalty is awarded to the plaintiff.

Key Principle

A number of "usual covenants" are implied into leases where not expressly provided for.

> CHESTER V BUCKINGHAM TRAVEL LTD 1980
>
> An agreement for a lease of garages was made by the parties. The plaintiff entered into occupation pending completion of the lease. The lease was made for 14 years though this was impossible to grant at the time of the agreement as the landlord was holding over under a previous head lease, awaiting grant of a new one. The plaintiff brought proceedings for specific performance of the lease. The parties could not agree the terms of the lease and the matter was referred to the judge to determine what covenants should be included as the usual covenants in a lease.

Held

❖ (Ch D)

[a] The established usual covenants in a lease are for the lessee to pay rent, pay taxes except where expressly payable by the landlord, to keep and deliver up in good repair, and to allow the lessor to enter and view the state of repair. For the lessor, the usual covenant is the covenant of quiet enjoyment.

[b] It is a question of fact to be determined by the court as to what additional usual covenants should be found in a lease. In the context of a commercial lease of garage workshops, the only additional covenants should be that the tenant:

   [i]   not alter the plan, height, elevation or appearance of the building without the landlord's consent;

   [ii] not obstruct windows or lights or knowingly permit any encroachment easements to be acquired;

   [iii] not alter the user of the premises without the landlord's consent, such consent not to be unreasonably withheld; and

   [iv] not suffer any part of the premises to be a nuisance or cause annoyance to the neighbours.

The landlord has a right of re-entry for breach of covenant. [1981] 1 W.L.R. 96.

Commentary

The nature of these additional covenants reflects the residential character of the area within which these workshops were situated. In a case concerning commercial property, *Ashworth Frazer Ltd v Gloucester City Council* [2001] UKHL 59 the landlord had withheld consent to assignment on the basis that the potential assignees use of the property would breach the terms of the lease in relation to its use. In such cases, held the House of Lords, a landlord would not be unreasonable in refusing consent.

Key Principle
The standard of repair expected in respect of a covenant to repair is an objective standard.

> CARMEL SOUTHEND LTD V STRACHAN AND HENSHAW LTD 2007
> The claimant commenced an action for damages for breach of covenant against the defendant who was a tenant of industrial premises owned by the claimant. The defendant covenanted to keep the premises and to yield up the property in good and substantial repair. When the lease expired the roof was in a state of disrepair and the claimant arranged for the roof to be over cladded. The defendant argued that a patch repair would have been cheaper.

Held
❖ (QBD) The obligation to keep in repair does not oblige the lessees to keep the premises in perfect repair. The standard of repair is an objective standard and does not depend on whether the subsequent lessee would accept the repair in the circumstances of the case. On the facts, the patch repairs which were common in the industry were appropriate given the terms of the covenant and the particular disrepair of the roof. Damages would be assessed accordingly. [2007] EWHC 1289 (TCC).

Commentary
Regardless of what the new tenant wanted in respect of the state of repair of the premises, the obligation on the departing lessee was merely to repair it to an objective standard. If there were more than one method of repair then the obligation is merely to adopt whichever method was appropriate provided the required standard was achieved.

REMEDIES FOR BREACH OF LANDLORD'S COVENANTS IN LEASES

Key Principle
Damages are intended to put the tenant in the position contracted for, not to punish the landlord.

Calabar Properties Ltd v Stitcher 1983

The defendant took an assignment of a lease of a flat from the plaintiff. Due to defects on the outside, water was coming through causing damp and damage. The plaintiff asserted that the damp was caused by condensation. The plaintiff brought an action for non-payment of rent; the defendant counter-claimed that the plaintiff was in breach of his repair obligations. In the meantime the defendant and her husband moved out due to the husband's ill health caused by the damp. The judge held that the plaintiff was in breach of repair obligations and that the damage resulted from that breach. He awarded damages for the cost of making good and redecorating the flat less one-third for betterment as well as for loss of enjoyment and the husband's ill-health. The judge refused to award damages to the defendant for rent, taxes or service charge during the period in which the premises were uninhabitable. He also refused damages for consequential loss of use during that period based on the capital value of the flat or its rental value.

Held

❖ (CA (Civ Div)) The principle in assessing damages for breach of covenant is to restore the party to the position she would have been in had there been no breach of covenant. The judge properly assessed damages as the difference between the value of the flat to the defendant in the condition it was and the value it would have had to the defendant if the plaintiff had carried out his repair obligations. The cost of alternate accommodation during the period when the flat was uninhabitable was prima facie recoverable. Damages for outgoings were not recoverable as the lease was not terminated and the monies were still payable. Damages based on diminution of capital or rental value was inappropriate, as the premises were rented as a home not a saleable asset. [1984] 1 W.L.R. 287.

Commentary

A calculation as to rental of property in repair or disrepair may be relevant in determining loss of enjoyment. A low rental cannot, however, be used to justify disrepair. In *Sturolson & Co v Mauroux* (1988) 20 H.L.R. 332 CA (Civ Div), the plaintiff argued that damages awarded for disrepair should take into account the fair rent assessment on the premises. The court held that the measure of damages should reflect the property in a condition where the landlord carried out his repair obligations.

Key Principle

Specific performance is available but the discretion to grant it should be exercised carefully.

> JEUNE V QUEENS CROSS PROPERTIES LTD 1973
> In the lease between the parties there was an obligation upon the landlord to maintain, repair and renew the structure of the property, including the external walls. A balcony at the front of the building partially collapsed. The plaintiffs sought an order requiring immediate reinstatement of the balcony.

Held

❖ (Ch D) The court had the power to make an order for a landlord to carry out a specific piece of work under a repairing obligation. The discretion to grant such an order should be exercised carefully. [1974] Ch. 97.

Commentary

[1] The breach must be clear and there must be no doubt as what is required to be done. An injunction could be given at interim hearings where there is a clear health hazard as in *Parker v Camden LBC* [1986] Ch. 162 CA (Civ Div).

[2] Although the court is reluctant to grant specific performance of a tenant's obligation to repair, it would do so in appropriate cases. In *Rainbow Estates Ltd v Tokenhold Ltd* [1999] Ch. 64, the court granted such an order against the lessee because the lease did not contain any forfeiture clause nor was there a proviso for re-entry for breach of covenant. Damages, was therefore, an inadequate remedy. The court stated that it would grant an order for specific performance where there was no injustice or oppression to the lessee.

Key Principle

The remedy of self-help is available but does not allow the tenant to breach his own covenants.

> LEE-PARKER V IZZET (NO.1) 1971
> The first defendant mortgaged properties to the plaintiff. The third and fourth defendant occupied some of these properties as tenants. They had contracts to buy the properties subject to mortgage arrangements being made. The plaintiff's mortgage had been made subject to these estate contracts. It became apparent that mortgage finance would not become available and that the first defendant now a bankrupt could

not meet his mortgage loan repayments. The plaintiff seeking to protect his position agreed to honour the estate contracts providing that completion was made within one month. Failure to meet this stipulation would lead to repudiation of the contract and action for repossession. No sale took place and the plaintiff sought to repossess. The third and fourth defendants claimed that the first defendant had promised to undertake certain repairs which had not been carried out.

Held

❖ (Ch D) The plaintiff's charge took subject to the third and fourth defendants' estate contract and rights thereunder. The contract was now repudiated and that repudiation was accepted. The third and fourth defendants could, however, recoup out of future rents the cost of repairs made by them. [1971] 1 W.L.R. 1688.

Commentary

The repairs must have come within the landlord's express or implied obligations. Expenditure had to be proper on the facts. There is no right to withhold rent where the landlord is in default of repairing obligations. The remedy of self-help takes effect as a defence to an action for arrears of rent provided that it is clear that the obligation of the landlord was not being fulfilled and that reasonable expense has been incurred by the lessee in undertaking the repairs.

In *Metropolitan Properties Ltd v Wilson* [2002] EWHC 1853 (Ch) an injunction was granted to prevent the lessee from entering the lessor's premises to carry out repairs. It was held that although in appropriate cases a lessee could exercise the remedy of self-help to enter the lessor's land to carry out repairs; in the present case self-help was not available as it was not shown that the lessor had failed to take the necessary steps to carry out the repairs. See also *Princes House Ltd v Distinctive Clubs Ltd* [2007] EWCA Civ 374.

Key Principle

In extreme cases, a receiver may be appointed.

HART V EMELKIRK LTD 1982

The freeholder owned two blocks of flats, which were let to lessees on long leases. The defendants bought the blocks. The blocks had fallen into disrepair; rent was not collected nor was any contribution towards maintenance sought. The lessees brought actions against the defendants to comply with their covenants and for damages. They also applied for an order that pending trial a surveyor should be appointed to accept rent and to manage the blocks in accordance with the landlord's obligations.

Held

❖ (Ch D) Given the state of the buildings it would be just and convenient to appoint a receiver under s.37(l) of the Supreme Court Act 1981. [1983] 1 W.L.R. 1289.

Commentary

This unusual remedy is useful where the landlord is not making repairs leaving the property at risk of progressive degradation.

REMEDIES FOR BREACHES OF COVENANTS IN LEASES BY TENANTS

[a] Forfeiture of lease

Key Principle

The breach must be irremediable in the sense that it cannot be effectively remedied.

EXPERT CLOTHING SERVICE & SALES LTD v HILLGATE HOUSE LTD 1985

The plaintiffs granted the first defendant a lease for 25 years of premises, which the defendant undertook to convert to a gym and health club. The rent fell into arrears and possession proceedings were instituted. These were settled and a consent order was made varying the terms of the lease. Under the new terms the defendants were required to notify the plaintiff of their election to convert the premises to a gym or offices. They covenanted to substantially complete the reconstruction by September 1982 and complete the work as soon as reasonably possible thereafter. The first defendant charged the premises to a bank in breach of a covenant. The plaintiffs refused to accept the rent and served notice on the defendant under s.146 of the Law of Property Act 1925 claiming breaches of covenant. The plaintiffs asserted that the breaches were irremediable. In October, the plaintiffs' solicitors who acted for the plaintiffs in relation to the variation of the lease but not the s.146 notice sent a letter requesting that the defendants seal and execute the counterpart of the varied lease. The defendants now sought a declaration that this request constituted waiver of breach of covenant.

Held

❖ (CA (Civ Div)) Breach of a positive covenant whether ongoing or singular was ordinarily capable of remedy by performance of the covenant and payment of compensation. The plaintiffs suffered no irremediable loss by the work being completed within a reasonable time thereafter. The s.146 notice was defective in not requiring the breach to be remedied. The plaintiffs were not entitled to possession. In the context of forfeiture proceedings being brought it was not reasonable to assume that the solicitor's letter in October indicated an intention on the plaintiff's behalf to treat the lease as subsisting. The plaintiffs had thus not waived their right to proceed with forfeiture. [1986] Ch. 340.

Commentary

[1] The case usefully serves to show that the purpose of the s.146 notice is to achieve a remedy for a breach insofar as it is possible, rather than to achieve forfeiture.

[2] The lessor must have intended to forfeit the lease—a failure to serve the s.146 notice would indicate a lack of intention to forfeit the lease: *Charville Estates Ltd v Unipart Group Ltd* [1997] E.G.C.S. 36. Constructive re-entry by the lessor when he was unaware that a right to forfeit had arisen did not give rise to an intention to forfeit: *Cromwell Developments Ltd v Godfrey* (1999) 78 P. & C.R. 197.

[3] The obligation to specify the breach did not require the lessor to give precise details of each and every breach so long as it is served on someone with the knowledge of the situation complained of: *Adagio Properties Ltd v Ansari* [1998] 2 E.G.L.R. 69 CA (Civ Div). However, the Court of Appeal in *Akici v LR Butlin Ltd* [2005] EWCA Civ 1296 took a strict approach to the precision required of s.146 notices. In the case the lease contained covenants not to assign, underlet, part with possession or share possession. A pizza company of which the lessee became sole director started to trade from the premises. The lessor issued a s.146 notice claiming breach of the covenants not to assign sub-let or part with possession. It was held that the lessor had not parted with possession but shared it. As the s.146 notice did not specify this, it was not effective in seeking to have the lessee remedy the wrong.

[4] In the case of a breach of covenant to repair, the Leasehold Property (Repairs) Act 1938 gives the tenant the right to serve a counter notice on the landlord within 28 days of the receipt of a s.146 notice. The counter notice prevents the landlord from proceeding with the forfeiture unless leave of court is obtained. In *Smith v Spaul* [2002] EWCA Civ 1830, the Court of Appeal held that a mortgagee is not to be regarded as a tenant for the purposes of the Leasehold Property (Repairs) Act 1938.

[5] In the case of forfeiture for non-payment of rent, it used to be the rule that a formal demand on the day the rent fell due had to be made. This could be excluded by agreement or by s.210 of the Common Law Procedure Act 1852. Under the Tribunals, Courts and Enforcement Act 2007 (not yet in force at time of writing), this will amend s.210 and provides that where the rent is in arrears for at least six months and the landlord cannot use the commercial rent arrears recovery procedure, see below, the need to make a formal demand is excluded. Hence, in a claim for rent arrears in residential leases, if the rent is in arrears for six months, then the lessor does not need to make a formal demand.

Key Principle

Negative covenants are generally regarded as being irremediable.

SCALA HOUSE AND DISTRICT PROPERTY CO v FORBES 1973
In a lease of restaurant premises the lessees covenanted not to assign, sub-let or part with possession of the premises without the landlord's consent. The lease was assigned to the first defendant with consent. He intended to enter into an agreement with the second and third defendants to manage the restaurant but in fact created a sub-tenancy. The plaintiff who had bought the reversion served a s.146 notice requiring the breach to be remedied. After only 14 days he issued a writ for possession. At first instance it was held that the breach was remediable and that 14 days was insufficient to remedy the breach so the action would be dismissed.

Held

❖ (CA (Civ Div)) Breach of a covenant not to assign, sub-let or part with possession without consent was not remediable. [1974] Q.B. 575.

Commentary

[1] Breach of the covenant not to assign without consent is regarded as the most clearly irremediable of covenants. This is because it involves a transfer of the property into the hands of someone unapproved. This is particularly troublesome as the lessee may have departed, leaving outstanding liabilities whilst the occupying assignee may unwittingly be in default or not caring whether he is or not. In particular, money remedies are not available against equitable assignees, i.e. where the assignment has not satisfied the required formalities. See however, *Bass Holdings Ltd v Morton Music Ltd* [1988] Ch. 493 CA (Civ Div).

[2] In practical terms, the danger that the property will be allowed to fall into disrepair or worse leaves the landlord little effective remedy other than to forfeit the lease. In the present case, relief against forfeiture was in fact granted. Given that the plaintiff initially regarded the breach as being remediable, this seems appropriate.

[3] However, in *Savva v Hussein* (1997) 73 P. & C.R. 150 CA (Civ Div), a breach of covenant relating to alterations was held capable of remedy and the s.146 notice should have given the lessee the opportunity to remedy the defect. As it had not, the notice was defective and forfeiture proceedings could not proceed. Traditionally, case law made a distinction that positive covenants were remediable but negative ones were not. The courts tend now not to ask whether the covenant is negative or positive but whether the breach is in fact capable of remedy.

Key Principle

Breaches, which put a stigma on the premises, are irremediable.

> RUGBY SCHOOL (GOVERNORS) V TANNAHILL 1934
> The defendant lessee used the premises for the purpose of prostitution in breach of her covenant not to use the premises for illegal or immoral purposes.

Held

❖ (CA) Ceasing to so use the premises was not a remedy. The breach was irremediable in that the stigma was present. Failure to ask for a remedy or compensation did not invalidate the notice. [1935] 1 K.B. 87.

Commentary

Whilst not a common situation it is of practical importance that the law allows for tenants causing damage to the property, in the sense of illegal or immoral use, to be fairly swiftly removed. However whether this decision will be decided in the same way under modern conditions remains to be seen. See also *Glass v Kencakes* [1966] 1 Q.B. 611.

Key Principle

The court has discretion to grant relief against forfeiture.

SHILOH SPINNERS V HARDING 1972

The plaintiffs assigned their lease in a mill to T Ltd, who made covenants as to fencing and support on their behalf and that of their successors. The plaintiffs had a right of re-entry in respect of breaches of covenant. T Ltd sold their interest in the premises to the defendants. T Ltd was absolved of any further liability in respect of the premises, under the terms of the earlier assignment to them. The plaintiffs relying on their right of re-entry sought to regain possession against the defendant.

Held

❖ (HL) There was no general power to grant relief against person's bargains. A court could however, grant relief against forfeiture in limited circumstances where the primary objective of the bargain could be attained when the case came to court and where the forfeiture provision was a means of securing the objective of the bargain. Wilful breaches would only be rarely granted. Here, the breaches were substantial and showed a disregard for the plaintiff's rights. Relief was not therefore appropriate. [1973] A.C. 691.

Commentary

[1] Relief can be given, if the purpose of the lease can be reinstated by putting right the breach, provided the landlord/tenant relationship has not been fundamentally undermined. There has been a degree of merging of the tests of remediability and relief. A breach is remediable if it can effectively be remedied. Relief will be given where forfeiture is disproportionate and some remedy is made which restores the bargain.

[2] In cases of non-payment of rent, relief against forfeiture will be granted where the arrears of rent and costs are paid. This includes all rent arrears

arising after the service of the proceedings for forfeiture: *Maryland Estates Ltd v Bar-Joseph* [1999] 1 W.L.R. 83 CA (Civ Div).

[3] It should also be noted that a right of way is an independent proprietary right.

Key Principle
The court has jurisdiction to grant relief, even after peaceable re-entry by the lessor, where such re-entry was in the absence of the enforcement of a judgment for possession of the property.

> BILLSON V RESIDENTIAL APARTMENTS LTD 1991 •
> The tenants of an unoccupied property renovated in contravention of the landlord's express reservation of a right to prior written consent before such renovations could take place. The landlord's agents peaceably re-entered the property at 06.00 hours and changed the locks. They also affixed notices stating that the lease had been forfeited. The tenants' workmen regained possession of the property by breaking in four hours later. The question arose as to whether the court had jurisdiction to grant relief.

Held
❖ (HL) The court had the jurisdiction to grant relief even after peaceable re-entry where such re-entry occurred without the enforcement of a judgment for the possession of the property. [1992] 1 A.C. 494.

Commentary
The case makes it clear that the court's jurisdiction to grant relief ends where the lessor re-enters the premises in execution of a "final, unappealed and fully executed" judgment for the possession of the property. Up until that time, the court retains the discretion to grant relief against forfeiture of the lease. It should be noted that both the Court of Appeal and the House of Lords in this case were unhappy with the method in which recovery of the possession of the property was sought.

Key Principle
Waiver of breach defeats an action for forfeiture.

SEGAL SECURITIES LTD V THOSEBY 1962

By a lease the lessee covenanted to use the premises as a "private residence in the occupation of one household only". The lessee took in non-paying "guests" and a paying "guest". The landlord served a s.146 notice requiring remedy within 28 days. Between service of that notice and its expiry the landlord sent a demand for rent in a letter headed "without prejudice".

The letter went on to say that the demand was without prejudice to the service of notice or any breach of covenant. The lessee sent a cheque in payment but it was returned. The landlord issued a writ for possession.

Held ....

❖ (QBD) The lessee was in breach of covenant. The landlord had, however, waived that breach. A demand for rent is as good as acceptance of rent. An acceptance and demand cannot be without prejudice. Where rent is payable in advance, demand or acceptance constitutes waiver only in respect of past and on-going breaches known at the time. [1963] 1 Q.B. 887.

Commentary ....

The applicable principle is that a landlord cannot forfeit if he has done an act indicating that the landlord tenant relationship is still in existence. To receive rent indicates an intention to remain a landlord. Waiver does not indicate approval of the breach and other remedies may still be available. An interesting case is *Van Haarlam v Kasner Charitable Trust* [1992] 64 P. & C.R. 214, where the landlord was held to have waived the lessee's breach of covenant not to use the premises for illegal activities. The tenant was arrested and subsequently convicted of espionage. The landlord's acceptance of rent after the arrest was held to have affirmed the lease. The case illustrates the importance of waiver in that it prevents a subsequent action for forfeiture even when the lessee was convicted. The presumption of innocence seems not to apply in the context of breach of covenant.

In *Greenwood Reversions Ltd v World Environment Foundation Ltd* [2008] EWCA Civ 47 the Court of Appeal decided that a letter from the lessor's solicitors to the lessee and copied to the assignee of the lease which specified the rent arrears and stated that if payment was not received forfeiture proceedings would be commenced did not amount to a waiver. It did not constitute a demand for rent but merely stating that the lease would not be allowed to continue if the rent was not paid. Thomas L.J. stated that it is for

> "the court to consider objectively whether in all the circumstances the act relied on as constituting waiver is so unequivocal

that when considered objectively it could only be regarded as being consistent with the lease continuing".

It has been decided by the Court of Appeal in *Seahive Investments Ltd v Osibanjo* [2008] EWCA Civ 1282 that the processing of a cheque given by the tenant to the landlord is not conclusive in determining whether the payment was accepted as rent. The processing is evidence of a payment to the landlord. However for there to be waiver of forfeiture there must be evidence to show that the landlord accepted this as rent. In this case, part of the sum realised by the processing of the cheque was accepted for the purpose of discharging a bankruptcy debt rather than rent and the balance was repaid to the tenant. Hence, there was no waiver.

[b] Other remedies

Instead of applying for forfeiture of the lease, the lessor can opt for the normal common law or equitable remedies against the lessee for breaches of covenants in the lease. See *Fuller v Happy Shopper Markets Ltd* [2001] 1 W.L.R. 1681 as to the remedy of distress. Under the **Tribunals, Courts and Enforcement Act 2007** which received Royal Assent in July 2007, the remedy of distress is abolished (not yet in force at the time of writing). This Act provides a new procedure for commercial rent arrears recovery—hence it applies only to commercial leases and is not exercisable unless rent has been due and payable and exceeds a prescribed amount and a 14-days' notice has been served on the lessee. The lessor can then appoint an enforcement agent who will have three months to take control of the tenant's property or goods. This can be either securing them on the premises or removal from the premises or securing them elsewhere or in the alternative entering a controlled goods agreement with the lessee. In the latter situation the lessee can keep the goods but must agree that they are under the control of the enforcement agent. The enforcement agent can then sell the goods by auction for the best price reasonably obtainable to pay the debt and then pay any surplus to the tenant.

TRANSFER OF OBLIGATIONS IN LEASES

Key Principle

At common law, subject to contrary agreement, a tenant remained liable to the landlord after he assigned his interest.

CENTROVINCIAL ESTATES PLC V BULK STORAGE LTD 1983
A lease was granted for 21 years at a rent of £17,000 per annum. The rent was to be reviewed after 14 years in December 1978. In July 1978 the defendant assigned the remainder of his term. The plaintiff who was assignee of the reversion agreed with the assignee of the lease for the rent to be raised to £44,000. There was a default of rent and the plaintiff sought to recover from the defendant.

Held

❖ (Ch D) The rent agreement was properly made within the rent review clause of the lease. The assignee was not an agent of the lessee. The relationship between a landlord and an assignee was sui generis. An assignee owned the leasehold estate and could part with, alter its terms or deal with it, as he wished, to the extent consistent with being estate owner. The assignee could use the estate just as the original lessee could have done. By privity of contract a lessee remains liable after assignment. The lessee is liable for the lease even as altered because the lease allowed for alteration. The original lessee was liable for the rent as revised. (1983) 46 P. & C.R. 393.

Commentary

This principle is altered by s.5 of the Landlord and Tenant (Covenants) Act 1995 whereby the landlord cannot sue the original lessee in relation to breaches by the assignee. The landlord may require a guarantee from the original lessee in relation to the first assignee by s.16 but cannot be required to guarantee any future assignees. By s.18 the original lessee cannot be liable for variations in the lease. Before this legislation, courts were often reluctant to enforce the tenant's on-going liability. See *City of London Corp v Fell* [1993] Q.B. 589 and *RPH Ltd v Mirror Group Newspapers Ltd and Mirror Group Holdings Plc* [1992] B.C.C. 972.

The converse of the common law position as to lessees is that a landlord remains liable to a tenant after he assigns his interest unless there is contrary expression. For example, landlords' covenants are often expressed to bind the owner of the reversion for the time being. Under this Act, landlords can apply for release from covenants.

Key Principle

At common law the benefit and burden of covenants passes to an assignee in respect of covenants, which touch and concern the land.

A lessee covenanted for himself, his executors and administrators that he, his executors or assignees would build a wall on part of the land.

Held

❖ (Ct of QB) The covenant would not bind the lessee's assignees. (1583) 5 Co. Rep. 16a.

Commentary

The covenant must relate to the land. Even if assignees are named the covenant must touch and concern the land. The covenant must not be personal or collateral to the agreement. What touches and concerns is usually easily recognised, e.g. an obligation to pay rent. It can, however, be problematic as to whether an option touches and concerns. See *Beesly v Hallwood Estates Ltd* [1960] 1 W.L.R. 549. In relation to landlords the principle is confirmed in statute by ss.141 and 142 of the **Law of Property Act 1925** whereby the benefit and burden of covenants runs to an assignee of the reversion. The **Landlord and Tenant (Covenants) Act 1995** provides by s.2 that all terms of new leases pass upon assignment. Whilst the 1995 Act generally provides that the benefit and burden of covenants passes to assignees, personal covenants are excluded from this. In *First Penthouse Ltd v Channel Hotels and Properties (UK) Ltd* [2003] EWHC 2713 (Ch) it was held that a covenant to pay a commission to a third party was a personal covenant. The Court held that the personal nature of a covenant need not be explicitly expressed but could be implicit in the words used to convey the parties' intentions.

Key Principle

At common law the benefit and burden of covenants runs to an assignee of the lease where there is privity of estate.

PURCHASE V LICHFIELD BREWERY CO 1914

A lessee purported to assign the remainder of his lease. No deed was executed.

Held

❖ (KBD) There was no privity of estate nor privity of contract between the landlord and the assignees. The assignees were not liable, therefore, to pay rent. [1915] 1 K.B. 184.

Commentary

Privity of contract could, in common law, justify the on-going liability of tenants. It also meant that assignees not being party to the contract would not be liable. The concept of privity of estate was developed to hold assignees of the lease liable. Privity of estate depends on the assignee being privy to the same estate as the original lessee. Here although the original lease was legal, the assignment was not. Assignments are required by s.52 of the **Law of Property Act 1925** to be made by deed. Sub-lessees are different from assignees in that they take less than the full remainder of the term or less than the entire premises, they are similar in that they do not have privity of estate. Equitable assignees and sub-lessees cannot be liable for money remedies in relation to breach of covenant. The landlord may seek forfeiture of the original lease. If forfeited, all rights claimed under that lease collapse. Injunctions may be granted to restrain further breach of negative covenants. See *Tulk v Moxhay* (1848) 41 E.R. 1143 Ch D, above.

The rules as to transfer of lessees' liabilities and the availability of remedies have often left landlords in a very difficult position. For example, if the tenant assigns without permission and the assignment is not in writing, the assignee breaches terms which he may not know exist or much less care. If the landlord has no right of re-entry or has somehow waived the right then forfeiture is unavailable. The equitable assignee is immune from money remedies. The original lessee may have disappeared. It is not surprising that the courts have occasionally tried to enforce covenants more fully against assignees of leases. See *Boyer v Warbey* [1953] 1 Q.B. 234 where it was held that the distinction between assignments by deed or hand should not determine the transfer of obligations. The **Landlord and Tenant (Covenants) Act 1995** makes considerable changes to the law. The old law is still important as the Act only applies to new leases except in claims for arrears of rent where the Act applies to both existing and new leases.

Key Principle

Under the **Landlord and Tenants (Covenants) Act 1995**, a guarantor who has given a guarantee with respect to a tenant's performance of the covenants in lease cannot be required to give a guarantee in respect of the tenant's assignees.

GOOD HARVEST PARTNERSHIP LLP V CENTAUR SERVICES LTD 2010
The defendant, who was the guarantor of the original tenant of a lease of a commercial premises entered into an "authorised guarantee agreement" which guaranteed the obligations of the first assignee of

the tenant. The claimant commenced an action against the defendant for the recovery of rent due. The defendant defended the application, inter alia, on the basis that the guarantee was void under **s.25 of the Landlord and Tenant (Covenants) Act 1995.**

Held

❖ (Ch) The claimant's claim would be dismissed as the **Landlord and Tenant (Covenants) Act 1995** prevented a guarantor who had given a guarantee in respect of a tenant's leasehold obligations from having to give a further guarantee upon the assignment of the lease. If the guarantor was required to do so, this would in effect defeat the purposes of the Act contrary to s.25. Section 24 of the Act was intended to release the guarantor from its obligations. Accordingly, the defendant could not be required to guarantee the assignee's obligations and thus had a complete defence to the claimant's claim. [2010] EWHC 330 (Ch).

Commentary

This case has caused some controversy in the area of commercial leases but is of importance to commercial landlords as very often the tenant is a subsidiary of a holding company and the latter is often asked to guarantee the tenant's compliance with the obligations under the lease. At times the lease may then be assigned to another subsidiary and as a result of this decision the holding company cannot be required to guarantee this subsequent assignee. An argument that this was a new obligation as opposed to a continuation of an old obligation was not accepted by the court. The court stressed that the effect of the Act was that it precluded the tenants and its guarantors from having to provide additional guarantees on an assignment other than by way of an authorised guarantee agreement.

This case received qualified approval of the Court of Appeal in *K/S Victoria Street v House of Fraser (Stores Management) Ltd* [2011] EWCA Civ 904. Whilst the Court accepted that a guarantor cannot be required to guarantee the assignee of the tenant and especially not to ask the guarantor to guarantee future assignees in advance, there was an exception. The Court was of the view that the tenant assignor could be asked to guarantee the assignee's compliance with its obligations under an Authorised Guarantee Agreement and as a result of this the tenant assignor's guarantor could be required to guarantee the tenant's obligations (instead of the assignee's obligations) under the Authorised Guarantee Agreement in which case it would not fall foul of the Act. Lord Neuberger M.R. stated:

"while the guarantor of an assignor cannot normally validly guarantee the liability of the assignee, it can validly do so by being party to a valid AGA".

This would comply with s.16 of the Act.

. . . .

HUMAN RIGHTS ACT 1998

Key Principle
English Law is not necessarily incompatible with art.8 of the European Convention for the Protection of Human Rights and Fundamental Freedoms 1950 in respect of a public authority landlord seeking possession of a property of the determination of a tenancy.

> HARROW LBC v QAZI 2003
> The respondent and his wife as joint tenants had a secured tenancy from the appellant. His wife subsequently left the property and served a notice to quit. This brought the tenancy to an end. The respondent refused to leave the property and the appellant sought possession of the property. The respondent argued that the appellant had contravened art.8a of the **European Convention for the Protection of Human Rights and Fundamental Freedoms 1950** (Sch.1 to the **Human Rights Act 1998**). Further, the appellant's action was not justified under art.8(2) of the convention and as such contravened art.8. The House of Lords was asked to consider whether it was unlawful for a public authority landlord to recover possession by a procedure which led to automatic possession when the tenancy was determined by operation of law.

Held
❖ (HL) The law which allowed the appellant to take possession of a tenancy which had been determined as a result of a notice to quit by a joint tenant was not in contravention of art.8(1). On the facts of the case the appellants' right to possession was not qualified in English law and once the property was recovered would allow the appellant to re-let it to those in need of housing. The appeal would be allowed. [2003] UKHL 43.

Commentary
[1] This decision indicates the increasing importance of the **Human Rights Act 1998** in land law.

[2] However it should be noted that the principle enunciated in this case is only limited to public authority landlords. Lord Bingham stated that:

> "but nothing I have said in this opinion should be understood as applying to any landlord or owner which is not a public authority".

[3] In contrast in *Connors v United Kingdom* (2005) 40 E.H.R.R. 9, the European Court of Human Rights held that the eviction of the applicant and his family from a local authority gipsy site which they were licensed to occupy provided they did not cause a nuisance contravened art.8 because it had not been attended by the requisite procedural safeguards. More recently in *Lambeth LBC v Kay* and *Price v Leeds City Council* [2006] UKHL 10, by a majority decision of the House of Lords, decided that courts in dealing with a defence under art.8 to a claim to possession by a public authority landlord can assume that English law strikes a fair balance and is compatible with the occupier's rights under the convention. Their Lordships recognised that there may be some exceptions of which *Connors v United Kingdom*, above, may be one where it may be appropriate for the occupier to challenge the possession under art.8. The decision in *Lambeth LBC v Kay* was affirmed by the Law Lords in *Birmingham City Council v Doherty* [2008] UKHL 57.

THINK POINT

What factors would the court consider in deciding whether the breach of covenant giving rise to a s.146 notice is capable of remedy? Consider *Savva v Hussein* (1997) 73 P. & C.R. 150.

What do you think are the issues arising from a tenant using the remedy of self-help in order to deal with repairs which the landlord has an obligation to undertake?

What do you consider are the limits to the principle suggested in *Liverpool City Council v Irwin* [1977] A.C. 239 in respect of the landlord's obligation in the upkeep of the property?

Licences

7

INTRODUCTION

A licence is generally an express or implied permission to enter onto the land of another, either to carry out an act, or, to extract something from the land. Although it appears similar to rights in land such as easements and profits, the essential difference is that easements and profits are rights in land whilst licences are merely permissions to be on the land. As such, licences are generally revocable at will. However, in some instances, they come close to being similar to proprietary rights. For example, a licence coupled with an interest is not revocable whilst the interest is still subsisting.

Licences fall into four categories:

- bare licences;
- contractual licences;
- licences coupled with an interest; and
- licences coupled with an equity.

BARE LICENCE

Key Principle

A bare licence is a mere permission to use another's land without further obligation on either side.

> **HOLDEN V WHITE 1982**
> A milkman using a right of way to deliver milk was injured when he stepped on a broken manhole.

Held

❖ (CA (Civ Div)) The landowner owed no duty of care to a person exercising such a right. [1982] Q.B. 679.

Commentary

A bare licence is implied to allow people to walk up to a landowner's front door. This can extend to persons making deliveries or election canvassers as in *Evans v Forsyth* (1979) 90 D.L.R. 3d 155. The licence is given without consideration and involves no further liabilities.

Key Principle
A bare licence, not being an interest in land, is revocable at the will of the licensor.

> **WOOD V LEADBITTER 1845**
> The plaintiff bought a ticket for the enclosure at the Doncaster races. The defendant ordered him to leave. The plaintiff refused and was forcibly removed.

Held
❖ (Ex Ct) Notwithstanding that a ticket had been bought it was still lawful for the licensor to revoke the licence without returning the fee and without giving reasons. Having been ordered to leave, the plaintiff was no longer at the place with permission or licence of the defendant. The eviction was therefore not an assault. (1845) 13 M. & W. 838.

Commentary
The traditional view has been that a licence is revocable at will. The earlier cases did not appear to distinguish between bare and contractual licences. As this case was decided prior to the Judicature Acts 1873 and 1875, it would probably now be regarded as a case concerning a contractual licence. Subsequent case law has suggested there is an implied term in the contract that the licence will not be revoked until the contract has been performed but would be dependent on the wording of the licence (see contractual licences, below).

Key Principle
When a bare licence is revoked, sufficient time must be allowed for the licensee to leave.

> **ROBSON V HALLETT 1967**
> Three police officers came up to the defendant's front door. One was allowed to enter. The defendant's father then asked him to leave. He began to leave but was attacked by the first defendant before he exited. The other two officers came to his rescue. The first defendant assaulted both of them. The second defendant assaulted one of them.

On appeal against conviction the defendants argued that the police officers were not acting in the course of their duty.

Held
❖ (QBD) There is an implied licence to any member of the public coming on lawful business to come up to a front door and knock on it. The officers who entered the premises under this licence (which in respect of them had not been revoked) were acting in the course of their duty when coming to the help of their colleague. When a licence is revoked which requires the licensee to act, then sufficient time must be allowed for that to happen. [1967] 2 Q.B. 939.

Commentary
The implied licence to approach a front door can be expressly denied by a notice or as in this case, be revoked at any time. However where it is revoked a reasonable time must be given to vacate or leave the premises.

LICENCE COUPLED WITH AN INTEREST

Key Principle
A licence coupled with a grant of a proprietary interest is not revocable whilst the interest subsists.

DOE, ON THE DEMISE OF HANLEY V WOOD 1819
The grantee was given by deed the right to dig for tin.

Held
❖ (KB) There was no lease of the land but a licence to dig for tin. The grantor re-entered the land lawfully within the terms of the licence. (1819) 2 B. & Ald. 724.

Commentary
Although the case is often used as authority for the principle stated above, it is unclear what the case decides. The right to use the land was in effect terminated, though per atriam, it was said that the licence to search and extract tin is irrevocable in so far as the tin ore was actually extracted. The logic behind the principle is that a proprietary interest is not revocable so it would be inconsistent to allow the revocation of a licence that facilitates the use of the proprietary right.

CONTRACTUAL LICENCE

Key Principle
A contractual licence confers no interest in land and binds only the parties to it and not the land.

> ### CLORE V THEATRICAL PROPERTIES LTD 1936
> The agreement granted rights to refreshment rooms in a theatre. It was described as a lease for the "free and exclusive use" of the rooms. However, this was limited to supply and accommodation of visitors to the theatre "and for no other purpose whatsoever". The agreement was assigned in defiance of a clause requiring consent for assignment. The owners of the theatre sought to stop the assignees from exercising their rights under the agreement.

Held
❖ (CA) The agreement was a licence not a lease and could only be enforced as between the original parties to whom there was privity of contract. [1936] 3 All E.R. 483.

> ### KING V DAVID ALLEN & SONS BILLPOSTING LTD 1916
> The defendant granted the plaintiff a licence to affix advertising posters to a building, which had not been built. The defendant leased the land to a company. It appeared as if there had been an intention to assign the licence to the new landowner but no reference to it was incorporated into the lease. The company refused the permission granted in the licence.

Held
❖ (HL) The licence conferred no interest in land. The licence bound the contracting parties and not the successor in title to the land. The licensor was liable for breach of contract having put it out of his power to honour the contract. [1916] 2 A.C. 54.

Commentary
The traditional formulation of the law is found in *Thomas v Sorrell* (1673) Vaugh. 330 where Vaughan C.J. stated that:

> "a dispensation or licence properly passeth no interest, nor alters or transfers property in anything, but only makes an action lawful, which without it had been unlawful".

Key Principle ....
Depending on its nature and terms, a contractual licence may be revocable.

WINTER GARDEN THEATRE (LONDON) LTD V MILLENNIUM PRODUCTIONS
LTD 1947
Winter Garden granted Countess Mala de la Marr a licence to use their
theatre for a period of six months for stage plays, concerts or ballets.
The licence contained an option to continue for a further period of six
months subject to an increased rent. It further stated that upon the
expiration of these two periods of six months, the Countess would have
the option of continuing with the licence on making a weekly payment
and that the Countess was to give Winter Garden one month's notice to
terminate the licence. Winter Garden continued to manage the bars and
cloakroom. Millennium Productions Ltd ("Millennium") was incorporated by the Countess and with the consent of Winter Garden, the
licence was assigned to it. In September 1945, Winter Garden served a
notice terminating the licence on Millennium. Millennium claimed that
the licence was not revocable by Winter Garden except where it had
breached the terms of the licence or alternatively that it was valid for a
reasonable period after the notice of revocation.

Held ....
❖ (HL) The licence was not one that was perpetual in nature. Once Winter
Garden gave Millennium notice to terminate the licence, Millennium had a
reasonable time to withdraw. On the facts, Millennium failed to prove that the
period given by Winter Garden was unreasonable. Accordingly, the notice of
termination given by Winter Garden was valid. [1948] A.C. 173.

Commentary ....
The traditional view was that contractual licences were generally revocable
(*Wood v Leadbitter*). However, other cases have suggested that such licences
are not revocable until the contract has been performed. In *Hurst v Picture
Theatres* [1915] 1 K.B. 1 CA, the Court of Appeal held that the plaintiff was
entitled to damages, having been forcibly removed from a cinema before the
film had ended. It has been said that the reason for this is that there is an
implied term in the contract that the licence will not be revoked until the
contract has been performed. This was the approach taken by Megarry J. in
Hounslow LBC v Twickenham Garden Developments Ltd [1971] Ch. 233 Ch D.
The decision of the House of Lords in *Winter Garden* makes it clear that
whether such a term is implied into a contractual licence is ultimately a

question of interpretation of the terms of the licence. Where a contractual licence is found to exist, the equitable remedies of specific performance or injunction may be available: *Verrall v Great Yarmouth BC* [1981] Q.B. 202 CA (Civ Div). In *Sandhu v Farooqui* [2003] EWCA Civ 531 the court held that where a licence was granted in contemplation of a sale there would be an implied term that the licence would be revoked when notice of intent not to complete the sale was made. Such notice need not necessarily be done formally in writing but must be sufficiently communicated.

Key Principle

In some situations the court may be prepared to infer the existence of a contractual licence.

> **TANNER V TANNER 1975**
> A woman gave up a protected tenancy in order to move into her lover's home and to care for the children of the relationship.

Held

❖ (CA (Civ Div)) A contractual licence was inferred in her favour, which gave her the right to stay in the property for so long as the children were of school age and the accommodation was reasonably required. [1975] 1 W.L.R. 1346.

Commentary

A similar approach was taken in *Chandler v Kerley* [1978] 1 W.L.R. 693 CA (Civ Div) where a contractual licence was inferred. On the facts of that case, the court held that the licence could be terminated only on giving reasonable notice. However, in *Mexfield Housing Co-operative Ltd v Berrisford* [2010] EWCA Civ 811, the Court of Appeal decided that where a purported lease was deemed to be void for lack of certainty of its term, it could not be construed as taking effect as a contractual licence.

LICENCE COUPLED WITH AN EQUITY

Key Principle

A licence coupled with an equity may be enforceable against a third party.

> **ERRINGTON V ERRINGTON & WOODS 1951**
> A father bought a house in his own name. He promised his son and daughter-in-law that if they paid the loan instalments they could live in

the house and when the final payment was made he would transfer the title to them. The father died and left all his property including the house to his widow. The son left the house to live with his mother. The daughter-in-law continued to live in the house and paid the loan instalments. The mother brought an action for possession against the daughter-in-law.

Held

❖ (CA) The son and daughter-in-law were licensees under a personal contract entitled to remain in the house so long as they paid the instalments. Lord Denning went further in characterising the right as an equitable one, which would develop into an equitable interest once the mortgage loan was repaid. [1952] 1 K.B. 290.

Commentary

[1] The ground for making the contractual licence of occupation irrevocable is that equitable jurisdiction should intervene to prevent a breach of contract. The principle in *Wood v Leadbitter* can be dealt with by arguing that before the fusion of courts of equity and common law, injunctive relief would not have been available or on the facts an injunction would not be practically feasible. Here, Lord Denning found cause to invoke the jurisdiction in what is called a licence coupled with an equity. This can be seen as analogous to a licence coupled with an interest where the licence cannot be revoked whilst the interest subsists. The argument goes that a licence should not be revoked where it is coupled with an equity. The equity could be found in an implied term not to revoke or in a putative beneficial interest or in an estoppel-type argument that detriment and reliance should prevent revocation. Much of the problem with this case is that it is not clear if there is a single agreed equity that is being relied on.

[2] The case does not need to decide whether there is a need to transfer title once the instalments are paid. Lord Denning took the view that once paid there would be a beneficial interest in the house in favour of the son and daughter-in-law. How the equity not to revoke transforms into an equitable interest in the property is not apparent, given the shaky basis for the equity against revocation itself. It could be argued on proprietary estoppel or constructive trust grounds though which or either is not clear.

[3] The problematic aspect of this case is the impact it has on the third party. It was established law that a licence is contractual and thus binding on the parties only. The so-called equity is used as the ground for making the licence irrevocably binding on a third party, the widow.

Key Principle

A spouse does not have a proprietary interest in the matrimonial home simply by virtue of being a spouse.

> ### NATIONAL PROVINCIAL BANK V AINSWORTH 1965
>
> The husband left his wife. The matrimonial home was charged to a bank, which was owed £6,000. The husband incorporated his business and transferred the home and business premises to the company. The liability for the loan now lay with the company rather than the husband personally. The loan was defaulted on and the bank gained a repossession order. The wife sought rescission of the repossession order.

Held

❖ (HL) The rights of the deserted wife were personal. They were not proprietary rights, which could bind a transferee, irrespective of whether the rights preceded those of the transferee or not. A wife's rights to occupy a matrimonial home arising from family law do not confer proprietary rights. [1965] A.C. 1175.

Commentary

The Court of Appeal in *National Provincial Bank v Hastings Car Mart* [1964] Ch. 128, on similar facts, held that a husband was presumed to have given authority to a wife to remain in the matrimonial home. Thus, the deserted wife's right to remain was a licence coupled with an equity binding on a transferee.

Key Principle

A contractual licence has been held to be an equitable interest that the court may protect.

> ### BINIONS V EVANS 1972
>
> The defendant's husband previously occupied a cottage in return for service. When the husband died the trustees agreed to permit the widow "to reside in and occupy" the cottage as "tenant at will ... for the remainder of her life". The trustees sold the estate to the plaintiffs incorporating a clause in the conveyance to protect the widow's occupation. The plaintiff sought possession.

LICENCES

Held ....

❖ (CA (Civ Div)) The terms of the agreement were inconsistent and did not create a tenancy at will but did according to Lord Denning create a contractual licence resulting in an equity binding on the plaintiff. The owner held the estate on constructive trust to permit the defendant to remain during her life for as long as she wished. [1972] Ch. 359.

Commentary ....

This case represents the height of the enforcement of contractual licences. It, like many other cases, breaks the principle that a contractual licence is revocable and such breach is actionable in contract only. It goes against the principle of privity of contract that a contract should bind the parties only. By saying that the equity binds a third party, it gives the contract a proprietary character it should not have. Moreover, it defies principles of registration of proprietary interests. Here, a just result has been achieved at the expense of a tortuous and unnecessary interpretation of the authorities. It would have been easier to infer a tenancy, because of the parties were estopped by their knowledge of the special clause in the conveyance from claiming a failure to register. In *Midland Bank Plc v Farmpride Hatcheries Ltd* (1980) 260 E.G. 493 the court appeared to accept without question that a contractual licence was fully capable of binding a purchaser of the land provided he had notice of the licence. Fortunately, this must be obiter, as the purchaser was found to have no notice. However, the **Contracts (Rights of Third Parties) Act 1999** would render all this unnecessary as a third party can enforce a contract made for his or her benefit.

Key Principle ....

An agreement for a licence can be construed as a tenancy, which then does bind the land. A licence can alternatively be binding under a constructive trust.

ASHBURN ANSTALT V WJ ARNOLD & CO 1989

The defendant sold his lease on a shop. The agreement provided that he could remain in the property as licensee for six months. The purchaser agreed to offer the defendant a new lease of a shop once the premises were redeveloped. Before the six months were up the plaintiff bought the freehold. Though the purchase was subject to the defendant's agreement the plaintiff sought to repossess. At first instance it was held that the defendant's agreement constituted a binding licence.

Held ....
❖ (CA (Civ Div)) Though expressed to be a licence, the agreement in fact, constituted a tenancy. The plaintiff was therefore bound. The defendant had an overriding interest of actual occupation based on the proprietary interest in the tenancy. This did not entitle the defendant to prevent redevelopment of the property but did give him the right to an offer of a lease of a shop if the premises were so redeveloped. If the agreement was a licence it could not be binding as a licence, but could be enforced if there was evidence that the conscience of the owner should be affected with a constructive trust making it inequitable to revoke the licence. [1989] Ch. 1.

Commentary ....
The case reaffirms the principle that a licence is not a proprietary right but offers a better ground for giving effect to the licence by constraining the owner rather than making the licence binding on the land. See Ch.6, Leases, for cases on the test for the distinction between leases and licences.

The case is important for the dicta of Fox L.J. with regard to the decision in *Errington v Errington & Woods*. Fox L.J. stated that:

> "[t]he far reaching statement of principle in Errington was not supported by authority, not necessary for the decision of the case and per incuriam in the sense that it was made without reference to authorities which, if they would not have compelled, would surely have persuaded the court to adopt a different ratio ... the Errington rule ... was neither practically necessary nor theoretically convincing".

Although the comments in *Ashburn Anstalt v WJ Arnold & Co* are merely persuasive, this has been followed in *Habermann v Koehler* (1997) 73 P. & C.R. 515 CA (Civ Div) which referred to the decision as one which governs contractual licences. It was also followed in *Lloyd v Dugdale* [2001] EWCA Civ 1754.

THINK POINT

Do you think it is important for the court to recognise that licences with an equity is binding on third parties? Consider the extent to which the remedy for the claimant could be under the doctrine of proprietary estoppel. Examine the cases of *Dillwyn v Llewellyn* (1862) 4 De G.F. & J. 571, *Inwards v Baker* [1965] 2 Q.B. 29 and *Pascoe v Turner* [1979] 1 W.L.R. 431.

Is it possible for contractual licences and proprietary estoppel to overlap where the same facts may give rise to a claim arising in contract as well as proprietary estoppel?

Mortgages

....
INTRODUCTION

In *Santley v Wilde* [1899] 2 Ch. 474 CA, Lindley L.J. defined a mortgage as "a transaction under which land or chattels are given as security for the payment of a debt ... ". This makes clear that a mortgage is merely the security for the repayment of the land and not the loan itself. The manner in which mortgages are created in English law means that the mortgagee is given an estate in land (ss.85, 86 and 87 of the **Law of Property Act 1925**) either a lease or a sublease (depending on whether the mortgaged land is freehold or lease-hold) or by the mortgagor granting a charge over the land that gave the mortgagee the same rights as if a lease or a sublease has been granted. As a consequence of this, the mortgagee has a right to possess the land although in practice this is often postponed until the mortgagor defaults. Once all the monies due have been repaid, the lease or sublease will terminate—the "cesser on redemption".

In registered land, the method of creating a legal mortgage is through the use of the registered charge and it is only through registration (and not merely completion by deed under s.52 of the **Law of Property Act 1925**) that it is legal in nature (ss.4 and 27 of the **Land Registration Act 2002**). Where it has not been registered then the mortgage is equitable in nature. In the context of unregistered land, the creation of a mortgage or charge will trigger first registration of both the estate and the mortgage itself (s.4(1)(g) of the **Land Registration Act 2002**).

....
CREATION OF MORTGAGES

Key Principle ....
Equitable mortgages cannot be created by informal deposit of title deeds.

> **UNITED BANK OF KUWAIT PLC V SAHIB 1996**
> In 1992 the plaintiff obtained a charging order absolute over Sahib's interest in property which he jointly owned with his wife. This was to secure a judgment that the plaintiff had obtained against Sahib. However, it was subsequently discovered that in 1990, Sahib's

solicitors had written to the third defendant confirming that they were holding the land certificate for that property to the third defendant's order as security for monies advanced to Sahib. The plaintiff sought a declaration that the third defendant did not hold any equitable mortgage over the property or that if it did, that such mortgage or charge did not take priority over the plaintiff's charging order. The judge found in the plaintiff's favour and the third defendant appealed.

Held

❖ (CA (Civ Div)) Section 2 of the **Law of Property (Miscellaneous Provisions) Act 1989** abolished the rule that a mortgage or charge could be created by the deposit to title deeds. The deposit of title deeds took effect as a contract to create a mortgage, which fell within the ambit of s.2. Since there was no written document in this case, no mortgage or charge had been created and therefore the appeal would be dismissed. [1997] Ch. 107.

Commentary

This has clarified the application of s.2 of the **Law of Property (Miscellaneous Provisions) Act 1989**. With the possible exceptions of constructive/resulting/implied trusts and the doctrine of estoppel, all contracts for the sale and other disposition of an interest in land must be in writing: *Kinane v Mackie-Conteh* [2005] EWCA Civ 45.

THE EQUITY OF REDEMPTION

Key Principle

There must be no clogs or fetters on the equity of redemption—any attempt to exclude the equitable right to redeem will be void.

SAMUEL V JARRAH TIMBER AND WOOD PAVING CORP LTD 1904
A company borrowed money upon the security of their debenture stock. This was subject to the lender having the option to purchase the stock within 12 months. The loan was repayable with interest upon giving 30 days' notice on either side. Before the company gave notice of its intention to repay the loan, the lender claimed the right to purchase the stock at the agreed price.

Held

❖ (HL) The option to purchase the stock was void and the company was entitled to redeem the loan on payment of all monies outstanding. [1904] A.C. 323.

Commentary ....

The equity of redemption is the sum total of the mortgagor's equitable interest in the property and this includes the right to redeem. Equity is protective of the mortgagor's interest and thus would not generally permit anything which prevents the mortgagor from redeeming the mortgage.

In this case, the court reluctantly had to decide that the option was void. This was because although the option had been entered into by the two parties in an arms' length transaction, but, as the effect of the option was to deprive the mortgagor of his right to redeem the mortgage, the option had to be held to be void. The Earl of Halsbury L.C. suggested that if a day had intervened between the mortgage and the grant of the option, it would have been a perfectly good bargain.

In *Reeve v Lisle* [1902] A.C. 461 HL, the House of Lords decided that where there was a gap of 10 days between the mortgage and the grant of the option to purchase the mortgaged property, the option was valid because the option could be regarded as a separate and independent transaction. In contrast in *Jones v Morgan* [2001] EWCA Civ 995 a different conclusion was reached. The agreement provided that the mortgagor would release the security on certain farmland so that it could be sold in part to pay off the loan and, in addition, the mortgagee would transfer half of certain retained land to the mortgagor. The Court of Appeal held that this requirement to transfer land was a clog on the equity of redemption and the agreement was consequently void even though the agreement was contained in a later transaction. On the facts the court felt that the transaction was not a separate transaction and still related to the original mortgage.

It should be noted that that the courts have now made it clear that the "no clogs and fetters on the equity of redemption" principle only applied to mortgage transactions. In *Warnborough Ltd v Garmite Ltd* [2006] EWHC 10 (Ch), the court held that the option to purchase in that case was part of sale of the property rather than a mortgage and therefore not subject to the clogs and fetters principle.

Key Principle ....

Any provision in the mortgage, which renders the equitable right to redeem illusory, may be void.

> **FAIRCLOUGH V SWAN BREWERY CO LTD 1912**
> A mortgagor mortgaged a short lease of about 20 years as security for a loan. The loan repayments were by way of monthly instalments with the last instalment being payable about six weeks before the end of the

lease. A provision in the mortgage prevented the mortgagor from repaying the monies outstanding, other than by the agreed instalments. The mortgagor wished to redeem the mortgage early.

Held

❖ (PC (Aus)) For all practical purposes, this provision rendered the mortgage irredeemable, and therefore, the mortgagor was entitled to early redemption of the mortgage. [1912] A.C. 565.

KNIGHTSBRIDGE ESTATES TRUST LTD V BYRNE 1938
The respondents mortgaged its property to the appellants as security for a loan at a favourable interest rate. The mortgage deed provided, inter alia, that the respondents were to repay the principal with interest by way of 80 half-yearly instalments and did not allow the mortgagor the right of early redemption. The respondents sought to pay off the loan early.

Held

❖ (CA) There was no rule against unreasonable postponement of the right to redeem. On the facts, there were no provisions in the mortgage deed, which could be considered to be onerous and unreasonable. There was therefore no clog on the equity of redemption and the mortgagor was not entitled to redeem the mortgage early. [1939] Ch. 441.

Commentary

In *Knightsbridge Estates Trust Ltd v Byrne*, the court was of the view that as this was an arms' length transaction between two competent parties with expert advice, and the mortgagor had negotiated the best terms available at the time, the mortgagor should be held to its bargain. Sir Wilfred Greene stated that "equity does not reform mortgage transactions merely because they are unreasonable". However, where the terms in the mortgage render the equitable right to redeem illusory, as in *Fairclough v Swan Brewery Co*, the court may be prepared to intervene.

COLLATERAL ADVANTAGES

Key Principle

Collateral advantage clauses in mortgages are void if they are unconscionable or a clog on the equitable right to redeem.

NOAKES & CO LTD V RICE 1901

The respondent bought a lease of a public house from the appellants, who were brewers. This was with the help of a loan from the appellants, which was secured on a mortgage of the premises. The respondents covenanted, inter alia, that he and all persons deriving title under him would not, during the term of the lease, whether any money was or was not owing to the appellants under the mortgage loan, use or sell any malt liquors except that purchased from the appellants.

Held

❖ (HL) The covenant was a clog on the equitable right to redeem and as such the respondents upon payment of all monies outstanding under the mortgage, was entitled to have the property re-conveyed to him free of the collateral advantage. The collateral advantage was unenforceable after redemption of the mortgage. [1902] A.C. 24.

Key Principle

A collateral advantage may be valid and enforceable, even after the redemption of the mortgage, if it is regarded as a contract which is collateral to the mortgage.

G&C KREGLINGER V NEW PATAGONIA MEAT AND COLD STORAGE CO LTD 1913

The appellants, a firm of wool brokers, agreed to lend money to the respondents, a company carrying on the business of meat preservers. The loan was secured by way of a floating charge on the respondents' assets. It was provided in the agreement that, for a period of five years from the date of the loan, the respondents would not sell sheepskins to any person other than the appellants, so long as they were willing to purchase the sheepskins at the best price offered by any other person. The loan was paid off by the respondents three years after the loan was taken out. The appellants purported to exercise their option to purchase the sheepskins.

Held

❖ (HL) The appellants' option to buy the sheepskins from the respondents was not part of the mortgage transaction but formed a collateral contract which was entered into as a condition for the grant of the loan. In the circumstances of the case, the option was not a clog on the equitable right to redeem and because it was a separate contract from the mortgage, the option was enforceable even after the mortgage had been redeemed. The appellants were entitled to an injunction restraining the respondents from selling the sheepskins to any person other than the appellants. [1914] A.C. 25.

Commentary ....

G&C Kreglinger v New Patagonia Meat and Cold Storage Co Ltd is important because it makes it clear that if the collateral advantage is regarded as a separate contract, but one which is collateral to the mortgage, the collateral advantage is valid. More importantly, it can continue for the duration for which the advantage had been granted even after the mortgage is redeemed. Further, Lord Parker suggested that a collateral advantage would be valid provided that it was not: [a] unfair or unconscionable; [b] in the nature of a penalty clogging the equity of redemption; or [c] inconsistent with or repugnant to the contractual or equitable right to redeem. See other cases such as *Biggs v Hoddinott* [1898] 2 Ch. 307 CA.

The collateral advantage could be invalid on the basis of restraint to trade as this is regarded as being contrary to public policy. However it can be valid if it is reasonable and is in the interests of the parties. In *Esso Petroleum Co Ltd v Harper's Garage (Stourport) Ltd* [1968] A.C. 269 HL, the House of Lords decided that a solus agreement which tied the mortgagor to purchase petrol from the mortgagee for 21 years was invalid but a shorter period was upheld as valid. See also *Alec Lobb (Garages) Ltd v Total Oil Great Britain Ltd* [1985] 1 W.L.R. 173 CA (Civ Div).

....

UNCONSCIONABLE BARGAINS

Key Principle ....
The court has jurisdiction to grant relief against harsh or unconscionable terms in mortgages.

CITYLAND AND PROPERTY (HOLDINGS) LTD V DABRAH 1967
A tenant, who lived in a property for 11 years, was offered the property by the landlord for £3,500. As the tenant had only £600, it was agreed that £2,900 would be left owing on mortgage. The terms of the mortgage were that a total of £4,553 was to be repaid in 72 monthly instalments. In the event of a default the whole sum became due and payable. The landlord sought an order for the repayment of all monies outstanding, possession of the property and an order for sale. The tenant alleged that the terms of the advance were unreasonable and oppressive and that the large premium payable was harsh and unconscionable.

Held

❖ (Ch D) The premium payable amounted to an effective annual interest rate of 19 per cent. Further, the provision that upon default the whole amount would be due and payable meant that the premium would amount to 57 per cent of the sum lent. The premium was so large that it was out of all proportion to the interest rates prevailing at the time the loan was made. In the circumstances this was unreasonable. The landlord would be entitled to enforce payment of the principal sum with interest at seven per cent after taking into account the instalments already paid. [1968] Ch. 166.

> **MULTISERVICE BOOKBINDING LTD V MARDEN 1977**
> The defendant granted to the plaintiff a loan of £36,000 secured by a mortgage of the plaintiff's business premises. The terms of the mortgage provided, inter alia, that the capital was repayable by way of instalments over a 10-year period, with interest at the rate of two per cent above the prevailing bank rate. It also provided by cl.6 that the sum payable as principal or interest was to be index linked to the Swiss franc. A declaration was sought as to whether cl.6 was void.

Held

❖ (Ch D) The relevant test to decide whether a term in the contract was objectionable was whether the term was unfair and unconscionable. It was not sufficient to show that the term was unreasonable. On the facts of the case, cl.6 was not contrary to public policy. The parties were of equal bargaining power so that whilst the terms in the mortgage may be unreasonable, they were not unfair or unconscionable. The court would not intervene to relieve the plaintiffs of their obligations under the terms of the mortgage. [1979] Ch. 84.

Commentary

The plaintiff in *Multiservice Bookbinding Ltd v Marden*, may have been unfortunate because of the variation in the exchange rate between the Swiss franc and the pound sterling between the date of the mortgage (12.07 5/8 francs to a £1) and the date of redemption of the mortgage (about four francs to a £1). However, Browne Wilkinson J. was clear that in order for the clause to be held to be void, it had to be harsh and unconscionable in the circumstances of the case.

Key Principle

An extortionate credit agreement may be reopened by the court under the Consumer Credit Act 1974 (as amended by the Consumer Credit Act 2006).

WOODSTEAD FINANCE LTD V PETROU 1986

Mrs Petrou obtained a loan of £25,000 for a period of six months in order to help her husband's finances. This was secured by a mortgage of her home. Woodstead Finance Ltd imposed an interest rate equivalent to annual rate of 42.5 per cent because of the husband's bad record in repayments.

Held

❖ (CA (Civ Div)) The interest rate imposed was not extortionate in view of the husband's payment record and the risks which had been taken by the finance company. [1986] F.L.R. 158.

Commentary

Under ss.140A–140B of the **Consumer Credit Act 1974** ("CCA 1974"), as amended by the **Consumer Credit Act 2006** ("CCA 2006"), the court has the power to intervene in respect of a relationship which it deems as unfair between the individual debtor and creditor. However the court does not have the power to intervene in consumer credit agreements which are secured on land as these are regulated under the Financial Services and Markets Act 2000. Hence the **CCA 1974** is limited to second mortgages and usually within the category of sub-prime borrowers.

Under the previous law, the courts were empowered to reopen extortionate credit bargains and directed the court to have regard to the experience, age, business capacity and the degree under which the borrower was subjected to financial pressure and the degree of risk accepted by the lender in deciding whether the credit agreement is extortionate. In *Woodstead Finance Ltd v Petrou* the court was of the view that the interest rate was not extortionate given the husband's payment record. Likewise, in *Ketley v Scott* [1981] I.C.R. 241 Ch D, the borrowers, a husband and wife, obtained a loan from the plaintiff at an interest rate of 12 per cent over three months (which equated to an annual rate of 48 per cent). They subsequently applied to set aside the agreement. It was decided that an annual interest rate of 48 per cent was not to be regarded as extortionate under the 1974 Act, since on the facts of the case, the husband, because of his business experience, had known what he was doing. They had not been subjected to any financial pressure to enter into the agreement. In *Nash v Paragon Finance Plc* [2001] EWCA Civ 1466, it was held by the Court of Appeal that a bank was under an implied duty not to vary interest rates dishonestly, capriciously or unreasonably (in the Wednesbury principles sense). In the case the interest rate charges were not grossly exorbitant; they were in part justified by the financial circumstances in which the lender found itself. The amended Act replaces the requirement of extortionate credit bargain with the term "unfair" credit relationships. It remains to be seen if the court would adopt the same approach or adopt a broader remit under the amended Act.

FRAUD AND UNDUE INFLUENCE

Key Principle
There must be no fraud, undue influence or misrepresentation which induced the mortgagor to mortgage the property to the mortgagee.

> NATIONAL WESTMINSTER BANK PLC V MORGAN 1985
> A husband and wife signed a charge over their matrimonial home as security for a loan. The wife signed the charge in the presence of the bank manager who had visited the house for the purpose. The atmosphere during the visit was tense. The bank commenced possession proceedings and the wife alleged that the bank manager had exercised undue influence over her.

Held
❖ (HL) In order for a transaction to be set aside on the basis of undue influence, whether actual or presumed, it must be shown that the transaction had been wrongful in that it constituted a manifest and unfair disadvantage to the person seeking to set aside the transaction. Here, there was no evidence that the relationship between the wife and the bank had ever gone beyond that of a bank and its customer. The transaction was not disadvantageous to the wife. Accordingly, the order for possession made at first instance would be reinstated. [1985] A.C. 686.

> FIRST PLUS FINANCIAL GROUP PLC V HEWETT 2010
> The defendant was persuaded by her husband to refinance the mortgage on their family home to the claimant in order to pay off their debts. The defendant executed the charge in favour of the claimant and then discovered that her husband had been having an affair. They subsequently divorced and the defendant found it difficult to maintain the repayments to the claimant who then sought possession of the property.

Held ....

❖ (CA (Civ Div)) The charge executed by the defendant would be set aside. His concealment of his affair amounted to undue influence on his wife and as such gave rise to an obligation on the claimant to take steps necessary to militate against this. [2010] EWCA Civ 312.

Commentary ....

For a transaction to be set aside on the basis of undue influence, the nature of the conduct can include misrepresentation to the other party (*Royal Bank of Scotland Plc v Chandra* [2011] EWCA Civ 192) and the concealment of an affair of one co-owner from his co-owner spouse (*First Plus Financial Group v Hewett* [2010] EWCA Civ 312) and is not restricted to coercion or undue pressure. Briggs J. stated in *First Plus Financial Group v Hewett* that:

> " ... it would in my opinion be wrong to confine a husband's obligation of candour and fairness when proposing a risky financial transaction to his wife as confined to cases where the wife meekly follows her husband's directions without question. The purpose of an obligation of candour is that the wife should be able to make an informed decision (with or without the benefit of independent advice) properly and fairly appraised of the relevant circumstances".

Key Principle ....

A transaction can be set aside on the basis of fraud, undue influence or misrepresentation where the person who has exercised the fraud, undue influence or misrepresentation over the mortgagor or co-mortgagor is an agent of the mortgagee.

BARCLAYS BANK PLC V KENNEDY 1988

The appellant's husband was part of a group seeking to take over the business of the company that employed him. The husband agreed to guarantee the personal overdraft of the owner of the company and secure it by way of a charge on his matrimonial home. The bank required the signature of the husband and the appellant, his wife, but did not tell her until 15.00 hours, on the day she was to sign the charge. She arrived at the bank just before close of business. The bank sought to enforce the charge. The appellant alleged that her signature had been procured by the husband acting as agent for the bank.

Held

❖ (CA (Civ Div)) The bank would be liable for the undue influence of the husband, where it had been content to leave it to the husband to secure the appellant's signature, on the basis that as the charge was to her manifest disadvantage, the bank could not divest itself of vicarious liability for the husband's actions. The appeal was allowed and a retrial was ordered on the question of whether there was undue influence and misrepresentation. (1989) 58 P. & C.R. 221.

Commentary

It would in many cases be difficult, and in some cases artificial, to allege that the husband or partner was acting as an agent of the bank.

Key Principle

The mortgagee can be liable for the fraud, undue influence or misrepresentation committed by one co-mortgagor on the other co-mortgagor, where the mortgagee has constructive notice of the co-mortgagor's actions and the transaction is to the innocent co-mortgagor's manifest disadvantage.

> ### BARCLAYS BANK PLC V O'BRIEN 1994
> The husband persuaded his wife to mortgage her share of the family home as security for a business loan from the bank. The manager at the bank sent the documentation to another branch for the husband and wife to sign, with instructions to ensure that the parties were aware of the effect of the transaction and to seek independent legal advice if in doubt. The instructions were not complied with. The husband told his wife that the mortgage would be for a short duration and limited to £60,000. In fact, it was a long-term loan and the mortgage covered an unlimited liability. The bank sought an order for possession and sale of the property. The wife alleged undue influence.

Held

❖ (HL) Where a spouse or cohabitee stood as a surety for the debts of the other, which was to his or her manifest disadvantage, and the creditor was aware of the relationship between them, the surety's obligation would be invalid where the surety was induced to act by the undue influence, misrepresentation or other legal wrong of the principal debtor. The creditor is fixed with constructive notice of the principal debtor's wrongdoing unless it had taken reasonable steps to satisfy itself that the surety entered into the obligation freely. This obligation would be discharged if it had warned the surety of the extent of her liability and the risks involved and advised to seek independent legal advice. Here, in view of its failure to warn her of the risks and advise her to seek independent legal advice, the bank was fixed with constructive notice of the husband's misrepresentation. The wife could set aside the charge. [1994] 1 A.C. 180.

Commentary

[1] The House of Lords took the view that the relationship between the husband and wife fell within the category of cases where undue influence would be presumed because of the de facto relationship of trust and confidence between them. It is essential that the relationship must be one which gives rise to trust and confidence: *Hughes v Hughes* [2005] EWHC 469 (Ch). In *Thompson v Foy* [2009] EWHC 1076 (Ch) the court held that on the facts of the case, the relationship between a mother and her daughter was not one of trust and confidence, and, hence the presumption of undue influence did not arise.

[2] Although the case was decided on misrepresentation the court did seek to categorise the different types of undue influence. Class 1 (actual undue influence) consists of instances of actual undue influence where the complainant has the onus to prove that some actual influence was exercised, which caused him/her to enter into the transaction. Class 2 (presumed undue influence) consists of instances of presumed undue influence where the complainant has the onus to prove that there was a relationship of trust and confidence such that it is fair to presume that the relationship was abused in order to induce the transaction. This class was subdivided. Class 2a consists of instances where the complainant raises as a matter of law that the relationship is one which the presumption of undue influence should be made. Class 2b consists of instances where the complainant raises a matter of fact that the relationship was one where the presumption of undue influence could be fairly made.

[3] The Court of Appeal in *Royal Bank of Scotland Plc v Etridge (No.2)* [1998] 4 All E.R. 705 CA (Civ Div) has provided guidance on the nature of independent legal advice which should be expected in such transactions.

Key Principle

Banks should conduct their affairs on the principle that they are put on inquiry in every case where the relationship between the surety and the debtor is non-commercial. The creditor must in such circumstances take reasonable steps to bring home to the guarantor the risks s/he is running by standing as surety.

> **ROYAL BANK OF SCOTLAND PLC V ETRIDGE (NO.2) 2001**
> Eight appeals were co-joined to be considered by the House of Lords. Each arose from similar circumstances involving a transaction in which a wife charged her interest in a family home in favour of a bank as security for the husband's debt. In seven of the cases the Bank sought to enforce the charge made by the wife and consequently sought an order of re-possession. In these cases the wife raised the defence that the Bank was on notice that the agreement to the transaction had been procured by the husband's undue influence. The eighth case involved a claim by the wife against her solicitors who had advised her before entering into such a transaction.

Held

❖ (HL) There are two necessary elements to establish in order to reverse the burden of proof in a case where the complainant alleges that undue influence induced the agreement to a transaction which as a consequence should be set aside. Those elements are that:

(a) there should be a relationship of trust and confidence in the other party in regard to the management of the complainant's financial affairs; and

(b) there should be a transaction, which calls for an explanation.

If these are satisfied, then, failing satisfactory evidence to the contrary, the burden of proof is shifted. The court can infer that there is a prima facie case that the defendant used undue influence in the relationship to induce the transaction. Consequently, the defendant must produce evidence to counter the inference. The phrase "manifest disadvantage" should not be used to describe the second element as its interpretation has been at times narrow and/or confusing. A wife's guarantee of her husband's debts is not of itself explicable only by the exercise of undue influence in procuring agreement. Such cases may be innocent or may call for an explanation.

Where a wife proposes to charge the family home as security for the husband's debts the following principles apply:

- The Bank is put on enquiry whenever a wife offers to stand surety for her husband's debt. The rationale for this is twofold. First that such a transaction is not to the financial advantage of the wife and secondly there is a substantial risk that in procuring the wife's agreement, the husband has committed a wrong which would entitle the wife to have the transaction set aside. It is not, however, necessary that both elements of the rationale be proven in every case for the bank to be put on enquiry. It is not essential that the bank be aware that the couple are cohabiting or that the particular surety places implicit trust and confidence in the husband in relation to the wife's financial affairs. The Bank is also put on enquiry in circumstances where the wife becomes surety for a business debt where she is also a director or secretary of the company. Such cases should not be considered to be a joint loan for joint purposes.

- Where the Bank is put on enquiry it needs do no more than take reasonable steps to ensure that the practical implications of the proposed transaction have been brought home to the wife. This must be done in a meaningful way so that the wife enters into the transaction understanding its basic elements if not all of its details. This can be achieved in a private meeting with the wife. The Bank can also discharge its responsibility by relying on confirmation from the wife's solicitor that she has been advised appropriately. If the bank knows or ought to have known that the solicitor did not provide appropriate advice then the Bank has not discharged its responsibility. If the Bank has discharged its responsibilities, any defects in the detailed advice given by the solicitor to the wife may be actionable by the wife against the solicitor. In relation to such advice, the solicitor is not the agent of the Bank.

- In carrying out its responsibilities the solicitor needs to clarify the context that s/he is retained to provide confirmation to the bank that risk in the proposed transaction has been brought home to the wife. S/he also needs to make clear that if necessary s/he may be required to give evidence subsequently to confirm that the wife was not overborne by the husband and that the wife understood the implications of the transaction. The solicitor needs to explain the documents of the transaction and the practical consequences of her agreement. The seriousness of the risk must be explained. The purpose, amount and principal terms should be explained including the possibility that the loan be increased without her knowledge. The transaction should be explained in the context of the wife's wider financial circumstances. It must be made clear that the wife has a choice and it is hers alone to make. The solicitor must take instructions as to whether to proceed or seek revisions to the transaction. The solicitor may not issue a confirmation to the Bank without the wife's permission. The discussion between the wife and solicitor should be face-to-face and the husband should not be present. The solicitor may not veto the transaction by refusing to provide the Bank with confirmation. S/he should give reasoned advice as to whether the proposed transaction is in the wife's best interests or not. S/he cannot stop the wife from entering in an informed way into a disadvantageous transaction. In an extreme case where the wife is being grievously wronged by the proposed transaction, the solicitor should decline to act further. The solicitor may act for both wife and husband or Bank but must cease to act for the wife if his other duties impair the ability to act properly for the wife. The Bank should communicate directly with the wife advising of the steps to be taken with the solicitor. The Bank should get consent from the husband to divulge to the wife his financial circumstances. Without this the transaction cannot proceed. The Bank must provide this information directly to the wife or via the solicitor. Where the Bank believes that the husband has misled the wife, it should inform the solicitor. The Bank should not act on any future transaction unless the solicitor's written confirmation has been received.

Banks should now operate on the basis that they are put on enquiry in every case where the relationship between the surety and debtor is non-commercial. If the bank does not take those steps set out to discharge its responsibility, it will be deemed to have notice of any claim the guarantor may have that the transaction was procured by undue influence or misrepresentation by the debtor. [2001] UKHL 44.

Commentary

[1] Whilst the case refers to the wife being the guarantor and the husband being the debtor, it should be noted that the principles apply equally where the spouses' roles are reversed. It also applies to other relationships such as between parent and child as in *Turkey v Awadh* [2005] EWCA Civ 382 and to same sex relationships.

[2] The case represents a move away from an increasingly convoluted development of case law, which centred on fine interpretations of concepts of actual undue influence, presumed undue influence and manifest disadvantage.

[3] Previously, it was said that there was a principle that the steps, which have to be taken by the mortgagee in order to avoid constructive notice of undue influence may depend on the facts of the case, *Credit Lyonnais Bank Nederland NV v Burch* [1997] 1 All E.R. 144 CA (Civ Div). This is still true to the extent that the contents of each transaction will be different and banks and solicitors will have to advise in the context of those facts. The more detailed requirements set out in *Etridge* will of course apply. Both *Credit Lyonnais v Burch* and *Royal Bank of Scotland v Etridge (No.2)* make clear that it is not enough to simply advise the mortgagor to take legal advice. See also *Wright v*

Cherrytree Finance Ltd [2001] EWCA Civ 449. Where the mortgagor declines to take advice, the Bank runs the risk that if they proceed with the transaction they may be fixed with constructive notice.

[4] Previously it was also said that constructive notice only applies in the context where the mortgage or charge is to the manifest disadvantage of the co-mortgagor alleging undue influence: *CIBC Mortgages Plc v Pitt* [1994] 1 A.C. 200 HL. See also the Court of Appeal judgment in *Barclays Bank Plc v Coleman* [2001] Q.B. 20 CA (Civ Div), *Leggatt v National Westminster Bank Plc* [2001] 1 F.L.R. 563 CA (Civ Div) and *Barclays Bank Plc v Sumner* [1996] E.G. 65 (C.S.) Ch D. The requirement of manifest disadvantage has been reduced in the sense that it is seen to have been too narrowly interpreted. Now the question is more to do with whether the transaction needs explaining rather than whether the transaction is definitely of manifest disadvantage. This seems correct as the test serves to determine whether the Bank is put on enquiry not whether there has in fact been undue influence. In *Goode Durrant Administration v Biddulph* [1994] 2 F.L.R. 551 Ch D, the principle was that it is a question of fact whether the mortgage is to the innocent co-mortgagor's manifest disadvantage. Clearly it will still be a factor in many cases to determine the extent of the potential disadvantage when looking at the adequacy of the advice given by banks and solicitors. However, it is clear that a co-mortgagor can wilfully enter into a disadvantageous transaction. The Bank will not be fixed with constructive notice of undue influence in such a case provided the solicitor confirms the co-mortgagors understanding of the risk. The solicitor may be liable to the co-mortgagor in negligence if the advice given falls below the duty of care required.

[5] The judgment provides detailed and practical steps which banks and solicitors must take in such circumstances. The detail of the steps to be taken by banks may suggest that benefit of the doubt lays with the wife in such cases. However, the steps are in reality not burdensome and are typical of the formulaic procedures that banks and solicitors follow in many areas of land law. In the eight cases co-joined, three were decided on the basis that the banks could not be imputed with knowledge of undue influence and thus could enforce the security against the wife. In three others, the wife's appeal was allowed and the cases sent for trial. In one case, the appeal was allowed because the Bank had failed to disclose the applicable agreement. In the final case the solicitor was not found to be negligent in his enquiries and advice.

[6] In *UCB Corporate Services Ltd v Williams* [2002] EWCA Civ 555, the Court of Appeal decided that once undue influence was established it was irrelevant

that the co-mortgagor would have entered into the transaction anyway. It was also held that the Bank could not rely on the solicitor's advice to a co-mortgagor of which it was not aware at the time.

Key Principle
Confirmation by a solicitor does not of itself justify striking out a defence of undue influence.

> ### NATIONAL WESTMINSTER BANK PLC V AMIN 2002
> Parents gave a second legal charge over their home to the Bank as security for their son's debts. The Bank had requested a solicitor to deal with the formalities by ensuring that the parents were fully aware of the terms of the charge. The solicitor returned the signed charge to the Bank with confirmation that the terms had been explained to the parents. The Bank subsequently commenced possession proceedings. The defendant claimed undue influence and that the Bank had constructive notice of that undue influence on the following grounds. The Bank knew that the co-mortgagors spoke no English, the solicitor had not in fact explained the terms and that he was acting for the Bank not the co-mortgagors. The Court of Appeal rejected the defence on the ground that the confirmation was clear and did not therefore require further enquiry by the Bank.

Held
❖ (HL) The solicitor's confirmation was not of itself sufficient to strike out the defence. There was sufficient doubt as to who was retaining the solicitor to require the issue to be determined by trial. There was sufficient evidence to suggest that the solicitor could not have given the parents an explanation of the terms in a language they could understand. [2002] UKHL 9.

Commentary
The case suggests that the *Etridge (No.2)*, guidelines cannot cover every eventuality. It might be argued that the guidelines are undermined if the facts behind the solicitor's confirmation are to be re-opened by the courts for the purpose of determining whether a bank has notice or not. Moreover, it creates uncertainty in the mind of banks if they cannot rely on a solicitor's confirmation. It could also be argued that the case should have been between the co-mortgagors and the solicitor and not with the Bank. A counter argument is that the Bank should not be fixed with notice because the solicitor failed to explain the terms. Rather, the Bank is potentially on notice

where it knows that the co-mortgagors are non-English speakers and fails to get confirmation from the solicitor that the co-mortgagors have been advised in their own language. *Bank of Scotland v Hill* [2002] EWCA Civ 1081 was also decided on facts pre-dating the *Etridge (No.2)* guidelines though the court was aware of them. It was held that that the Banks' obligation was discharged, where it had been informed by the solicitor that the wife had been advised of the risks involved. On the facts, this was the case. See also *Chater v Mortgage Agency Services Number Two Ltd* [2003] EWCA Civ 490.

It should also be noted that even though a solicitor may have been present and given legal advice, this may not necessarily rebut the presumption of undue influence in every case. It would depend on the circumstances of the case and whether the solicitor's advice was the sort of advice that a competent advisor would have given: *Pesticcio v Huet* [2004] EWCA Civ 372. See also *Lloyds TSB Bank Plc v Holdgate* [2002] EWCA Civ 1543.

Key Principle

Where the undue influence, fraud or misrepresentation is established, the whole mortgage is set aside even though there may have been an agreement to be liable for a lesser amount.

TSB BANK PLC V CAMFIELD 1994

Mrs Camfield was induced by her husband's innocent misrepresentation to stand surety and charged their matrimonial home as security for a business loan. The husband had told her that the maximum liability for the loan was limited to £15,000 when in fact it was unlimited.

Held

❖ (CA (Civ Div)) The bank was fixed with constructive notice of the misrepresentations. As such the charge be set aside. The bank was not entitled to an order that the charge be partially enforceable against Mrs Camfield. The House of Lords' decision in *Barclays Bank v O'Brien* was not authority for such a proposition. [1995] 1 W.L.R. 430.

Commentary

[1] Where a mortgage is set aside because of undue influence, fraud or misrepresentation, it is an all or nothing process. The whole mortgage is set aside even though there may have been an agreement to be liable for a lesser amount. This has been followed by the Court of Appeal in *Castle Phillips Finance Co Ltd v Piddington* (1995) 70 P. & C.R. 592.

[2] Where a property is mortgaged for a dual purpose and a co-mortgagor has received a benefit from one of these purposes, although it is to her manifest disadvantage, the co-mortgagor would not have to make restitution of the benefits she had received before she can set aside the mortgage. A suggestion to the contrary by the court at first instance in *Dunbar Bank Plc v Nadeem* [1998] 3 All E.R. 876 CA (Civ Div), was rejected by the Court of Appeal.

RIGHTS AND REMEDIES OF THE MORTGAGEE

[1] To take possession

Key Principle

The mortgagee's estate in land gives it the right in law to take possession immediately upon the creation of the mortgage unless the right has been impliedly or expressly postponed until default.

> FOUR-MAIDS LTD V DUDLEY-MARSHALL (PROPERTIES) 1957
> The defendant charged its property to the plaintiff to secure repayment of £6,000. The charge provided that the principal sum would not be recalled before December 17, 1958 if the mortgagor paid the interest within seven days after the date when it became due. On the defendant's failure to pay the interest within seven days after it became due, the plaintiff served a written notice requiring repayment of the principal sum and interest immediately. The plaintiff applied for an order for possession of the property.

Held

❖ (Ch D) The mortgagee has a right to possession of the property in the absence of an express or implied agreement to the contrary. This right arises because the mortgagee has a legal term of years or its statutory equivalent. As such the plaintiff was entitled to an order for possession of the property. [1957] Ch. 317.

Commentary

[1] Harman J. at 320 stated that the

> "mortgagee may go into possession before the ink is dry on the mortgage unless there is something in the contract, express or by implication, whereby he has contracted himself out of that right".

[2] Examples of where there can be express or implied postponement of the right to possession or not, can be found in cases such as *Esso Petroleum Co Ltd v Alstonbridge Properties Ltd* [1975] 1 W.L.R. 1474 Ch D. The mortgagee has the right to an order for possession of the property notwithstanding that there are counter allegations or a claim for set off by the mortgagee, no matter how serious, sound or unsound: *Midland Bank Plc v McGrath* [1996] E.G. 61 (C.S.) CA (Civ Div), *Ashley Guarantee (formerly Gulf Guarantee Bank) v Zacaria* [1993] 1 W.L.R. 62 CA (Civ Div) and *Abbey National Plc v Tufts* [1999] 2 F.L.R. 399 CA (Civ Div).

[3] Although there has been some suggestion in *Quennell v Maltby* [1979] 1 W.L.R. 318 that the right to possession is dependent on the mortgagor's default, subsequent cases have followed the traditional rule that a right to possession is a right and not a remedy.

Key Principle

A mortgagee in possession must take reasonable care of the premises and where it is rented out it is strictly accountable for the best rent obtainable.

> **WHITE V CITY OF LONDON BREWERY CO 1889**
> The mortgagees of a public house, who took possession of the property, let it out with a restriction that the tenant should only take his supply of beer from the mortgagees.

Held

❖ (CA) The mortgagees had to account for such additional rent that it would have received if it had let the premises out without the restriction. (1889) L.R. 42 Ch. D 237.

Commentary

The court stressed that the duty includes the obligation to obtain the best rent obtainable even if this may be contrary to the interests of the mortgagee. In *Silven Properties Ltd v Royal Bank of Scotland Plc* [2003] EWCA Civ 1409 (see below), the Court of Appeal decided that the duty of the mortgagee in possession is only to take reasonable care of the property and did not include an obligation to increase the value of the property for example by obtaining planning permission.

SECTION 36 OF THE ADMINISTRATION OF JUSTICE ACT 1970 (AS AMENDED)

Key Principle

Section 36 of the Administration of Justice Act 1970, as amended by s.8 of the Administration of Justice Act 1973, authorises the court to suspend the order for possession or to postpone or adjourn the proceedings provided the mortgagor appears likely to be able to pay the sums due under the mortgage within a reasonable time.

> **TARGET HOME LOANS LTD V CLOTHIER 1992**
>
> The defendants charged their home as security for a loan. They stopped making monthly repayments in July 1990. In October 1991, the plaintiffs applied for an order for possession. This was adjourned for 56 days under s.36 of the Administration of Justice Act 1970 (as amended). The plaintiffs appealed against this decision. Upon the defendants providing a bank draft of £10,000 and evidence of a prospective sale of the property, the proceedings were adjourned for four months. The plaintiffs again appealed against this order and the defendants made a small payment but produced evidence that they had placed the property on the market and the estate agents were optimistic of an early sale.

Held

❖ (CA (Civ Div)) There was no evidence that the defendants could settle the sums due under the mortgage within a reasonable time. However, on the evidence available, the defendants would only be able to discharge the debt by a sale of the property and since an early sale would serve the interests of the parties, the court would defer the order for sale for three months. The plaintiffs would be entitled to possession if the defendants failed to settle the sums due within this time. [1994] 1 All E.R. 439.

Commentary

In deciding whether to exercise its discretion to suspend or postpone the proceedings or order under s.36 of the Administration of Justice Act 1970 as amended the court will have regard to the facts and circumstances of the case. In *Cheltenham and Gloucester Building Society v Grant* (1994) 26 H.L.R. 703 CA (Civ Div), the Court of Appeal reiterated that the discretionary power under the Administration of Justice Act 1970 could be exercised if the court was satisfied of the mortgagor's ability to pay the sums due under the mortgage within a reasonable time. In *Halifax Plc v Okin* [2007] EWCA Civ 567 the Court of Appeal held that the judge was correct in refusing to stay a warrant of possession under the **Administration of Justice Act 1970** as the circumstances were such that the mortgagor was unable to make the existing loan payments let alone the arrears. A recent example of where the court refused to exercise its discretion is *Cheval Bridging Finance Ltd v Bhasin* [2008] EWCA Civ 1613.

In *Ropaigealach v Barclays Bank Plc* [2000] Q.B. 263 CA (Civ Div), it was held that a mortgagee who was entitled to go into possession as of right could do so without an order of the court. The purpose of s.36 is to provide an opportunity to the mortgagor to seek suspension of an order for possession where a court had given an order for possession. It did not deal with cases of possession lawfully taken without a court order. This decision was followed by the court in *Horsham Properties Group Ltd v Clark* [2008] EWHC 2327 (Ch), discussed later.

Key Principle
The question of what amounts to a reasonable time for the purposes of s.36 of the **Administration of Justice Act 1970** (as amended) is dependent on the circumstances of the case.

CHELTENHAM AND GLOUCESTER BUILDING SOCIETY V NORGAN 1995
In order to assist her husband's business, the defendant charged her home as security for a loan for the business. The repayments of the loan fell into arrears and the plaintiffs obtained a possession order. This order was suspended on a number of occasions and the plaintiff reapplied for an order for possession. The defendant cross-applied for a further suspension of the order.

Held
❖ (CA (Civ Div)) In assessing what amounts to a reasonable period for the payment of mortgage arrears by the mortgagor for the purposes of s.36 of the **Administration of Justice Act 1970** (as amended), it was appropriate for the court to take into account of the whole of the remaining part of the original term of the mortgage. The case was then remitted back to the County Court. [1996] 1 W.L.R. 343.

BRISTOL & WEST BUILDING SOCIETY V ELLIS 1996
An initial order was granted where the second defendant was to pay £5,000 immediately and £200 per month thereafter. This was in addition to the interest payments to the Building Society. The possession order was suspended under the **Administration of Justice Act**

1970, on terms that she paid the £5,000 and discharged the mortgage debt by selling the property within three to five years, after the children had completed their education. The Building Society appealed on the ground that the period of repayment wasn't reasonable.

Held
❖ (CA (Civ Div)) The concept of a reasonable period was not strictly definable. Ultimately, it depended on the circumstances of the case, having regard to the delay in selling the property, which had already occurred, and the adequacy of the security. As there was insufficient evidence to show that the property could be sold at a sufficiently high price, the suspension order would be set aside and a possession order granted. (1997) 73 P. & C.R. 158.

Commentary
The effect of *Cheltenham and Gloucester Building Society v Norgan* is that the court has the discretion under the 1970 Act to capitalise the arrears of mortgage payments and spread it over the remaining term of the mortgage, provided the circumstances of the case justified it. The difficulty with the case is that it would appear to allow substantial postponement of the order or proceedings for possession. Cases prior to this always assumed that the postponement would only be for a reasonably short duration to allow the mortgagor time to pay off the arrears. In *National & Provincial Building Society v Lloyd* [1996] 1 All E.R. 630 CA (Civ Div), a case decided shortly after *Norgan*, the Court of Appeal decided that if there was evidence of a proposed sale of property which had been mortgaged to the mortgagee, that is sufficient to justify the suspension of a possession order on the basis that it was likely that any sums due would be repaid within a reasonable period of time. These cases are not in conflict as they relate to different issues. What is clear is that a reasonable period of time for the purposes of s.36 of the **Administration of Justice Act 1970** (as amended), is a question of fact dependent on the circumstances of each case. See also *Barclays Bank Plc v Alcorn*, Lawtel, April 24, 2002.

[2] Mortgagee's power of sale

Key Principle
Although the mortgagee is not a trustee of the power of sale, the mortgagee, in the exercise of its power of sale, must have regard to the interests of the mortgagor.

CUCKMERE BRICK CO V MUTUAL FINANCE 1971

The plaintiff who owned land with planning permission to erect 100 flats charged it to the defendants as security for a loan. The plaintiff later obtained planning permission to erect 35 houses. Subsequently, the defendants' power of sale became exercisable and took possession of the land. In the advertisements for sale of the land by public auction, the planning permission to erect 35 houses was mentioned but not in respect of the 100 flats. The plaintiff drew this to the defendants' attention and requested that the auction be postponed. The defendants refused.

Held

❖ (CA (Civ Div)) A mortgagee in the exercise of its power of sale owed a duty to the mortgagor to take reasonable care to obtain a proper price. The defendants were in breach of this duty in failing to adequately publicise the planning permission for the flats or in refusing to postpone the sale. [1971] Ch. 949.

Commentary

[1] Salmon L.J. suggested that a mortgagee owes both a subjective duty to act in good faith and an objective duty to take reasonable care to obtain the true market value (the other Lord Justices suggested that the duty is to obtain a proper price) of the mortgaged property at the moment that the mortgagee decides to sale. In deciding whether the mortgagee had discharged its duty when it sold the property, the court would look at the steps taken to sell the property and then decide if those steps ensured that it would obtain the best possible price: *Bishop v Blake* [2006] EWHC 831 (Ch).

Further, it has been decided in *Parker-Tweedale v Dunbar Bank Plc (No.1)* [1991] Ch. 12, that a mortgagee in the exercise of its power of sale did not owe a duty of care independent to that owed to the mortgagor, to a person with a beneficial interest in the mortgaged property even though the mortgagee may have notice of such an interest. In *Freeguard v Royal Bank of Scotland Plc*, *The Times*, April 25, 2002, it was held that the mortgagee did hold a duty of care to the legal owner of the property even though the owner was not the borrower.

[2] If the mortgagee is unaware of the existence of the planning permission affecting the mortgaged property, then no inference of breach of the duty to take reasonable care can be inferred from a failure to disclose its existence in the particulars of sale: *Palmer v Barclays Bank Ltd* (1972) 23 P & C.R. 30.

[3] In *Silven Properties Ltd v Royal Bank of Scotland Plc* [2003] EWCA Civ 1409 (see below), the Court of Appeal confirmed that there was no duty of care on the mortgagee to postpone the exercise of the power of sale until it had improved the value of the property by for example obtaining planning permission. The mortgagee's duty was restricted to taking reasonable care to obtain a sale price which reflected the possible increase in value if planning permissions had been obtained and ensuring that prospective purchasers were aware of the potential. This decision was followed in *Bell v Long* [2008] EWHC 1273 (Ch).

[4] In *Potomek Construction Ltd v Zurich Securities Ltd* [2003] EWHC 2827 (Ch) the court left open the question of whether it was appropriate to sell a property privately prior to the auction. It stated that whether it was appropriate to do so depended on the circumstances of the case, the level of interest and whether the sale price reflected its market value.

[5] Where the mortgagee is a building society then it is under an obligation to obtain the best price that can reasonably be obtained as stated in s.13 and Sch.4 of the **Building Societies Act 1986**.

Key Principle

The statutory power of sale under s.101 of the **Law of the Property Act 1925** does not contravene art.1 of the First Protocol to the **European Convention on Human Rights**.

HORSHAM PROPERTIES GROUP LTD V CLARK 2008

The defendants were registered proprietors of a property which was mortgaged as security for a loan. They defaulted on the payments and receivers were appointed under an express power in the deed and s.101 of the **Law of Property Act 1925**. The property was sold by auction and was transferred to the purchasers. The purchaser subsequently transferred the property to the claimant.

The claimant commenced an action against the defendants for trespass and argued that the defendants' rights had been overreached by the sale. The defendants claimed the power to take possession and sale without the need for a court order was in contravention of art.1 of the First Protocol and the Human Rights Act.

Held

❖ (Ch D) The exercise of the statutory power of sale under s.101 of the **Law of Property Act 1925** after the mortgagor's default did not amount to a deprivation of possession by the government contrary to art.1 of the First Protocol. On the contrary, s.101 of the **Law of Property Act 1925** was in recognition of the contractual terms and the bargain between the mortgagor and mortgagee and sought to provide a convenient power of sale outside the ambit for the need of a court order to mortgagees in the form of a conveyancing shorthand. [2008] EWHC 2327 (Ch).

Commentary

The court was of the view that the mortgagee's right to possession was as a result of the leasehold estate which had been granted by the mortgagor on the creation of the mortgage. Briggs J. went on to say that

> "any deprivation of possession constituted by the exercise by a mortgagee of its powers under section 101 of the LPA after a relevant default by the mortgagor is justified in the public interest".

Hence, the statutory power of sale did not contravene art.1 of the First Protocol.

Notwithstanding this decision, the Association of Mortgage Lenders has agreed that members of the association would seek a court order for possession or sale of residential mortgages. The Ministry of Justice Consultation Paper, *Mortgages, Power of Sale and Residential Property*, (MoJ, December 29, 2009), CP55/09 have made recommendations for a change in the law which would require a court order before the sale of residential owner-occupier mortgages.

Key Principle

The mortgagee has the discretion to decide when to sell the mortgaged property in the exercise of its power of sale.

CHINA AND SOUTH SEAS BANK LTD V TAN 1989

The appellant creditor granted a loan to a company ("the debtor") which was secured by a guarantee from the respondent. It was also secured by a mortgage of shares of the debtor company, allegedly worth twice the loan amount. The debtor failed to repay the loan and although the shares were still worth more than the loan at that time, the appellant did not dispose of the shares in the exercise of its power of sale. After the shares had become worthless, the appellant brought an action against the respondent as guarantor demanding repayment of the loan and interest.

Held

❖ (PC (HK)) The appellant creditor owed no duty to the respondent to exercise its power of sale with regards to the mortgaged shares. The appellant creditor could decide in its own interest whether and when to sell the property. The surety was therefore liable to repay the amount outstanding. [1990] 1 A.C. 536.

Commentary

In the earlier case of *Standard Chartered Bank Ltd v Walker* [1982] 1 W.L.R. 1410 CA (Civ Div), Lord Denning suggested that part of the mortgagee's duty to take reasonable care may include the duty to choose an appropriate time for the sale. However, *China and South Sea Bank Ltd v Tan* makes it clear that although there is a duty on the mortgagee to obtain the current market value, the mortgagee nonetheless has the discretion to decide if and when he should sell. This discretion extends to the marketing of the property and how its sale should be advertised (subject to the disclosure of all relevant information): *Michael v Miller* [2004] EWCA Civ 282.This was followed in *Silven Properties Ltd v Royal Bank of Scotland Plc* [2003] EWCA Civ 1409.

In *Wilson v Halifax Plc*, Lawtel, January 11, 2002, the mortgagor sold the property for £80,000 on the basis of valuations which took into account the dilapidation of the property and the absence of any planning permission. The claimant alleged a breach of duty on the grounds that considerably higher valuations could have been obtained. It was held that Halifax had not been in breach of duty. The purchasers had spent considerable amounts on repair and acquisition of adjacent property, which explained its increased value. The value of the property at the time of the sale reflected its condition and the depressed market. The open market value of the property has been obtained.

In exercising its power of sale, one of the mortgagee's motives must be the recovery of the debt otherwise it would be an improper exercise of the power of sale: *Meretz Investments NV v ACP Ltd* [2006] EWCA Civ 1193.

Key Principle

A purported sale of the mortgaged property by the mortgagee to itself or its servant is void and ineffective although the sale may be at market value.

> **MARTINSON V CLOWES 1882**
> The Building Society was the mortgagee of five houses, which it was selling under a power of sale. Before the properties were auctioned, part of it was sold by private contract. The rest of the properties were put on sale by auction. The secretary of the Building Society bid for a number of the properties, and eventually became the owner of two of the properties.

Held

❖ (Ch D) A mortgagee exercising its power of sale or its agent cannot purchase the property on its own account. Accordingly, the sale of the two properties to the secretary of the Building Society would be set aside. (1882) L.R. 21 Ch. D. 857.

Commentary

Where there is a sale of the mortgaged property to the mortgagee or its agent or servant, the sale is likely to set aside because of the potential conflict of interest. In the case of a sale of the mortgaged property to an associated person or company, the burden of proof is on the mortgagee to establish that the sale was in good faith. The mortgagee also has to ensure that it had taken reasonable precautions to obtain the best price obtainable at the time: *Tse Kwong Lam v Wong Chit Sen* [1983] 1 W.L.R. 1349 PC (HK) and *Bradford & Bingley Plc v Ross* [2005] EWCA Civ 394.

However, the court will not set aside a sale by the mortgagee unless there was bad faith or impropriety on the part of the mortgagee. Bad faith on the part of an employee of the mortgagee by using a third party to purchase the property was not sufficient as the mortgagee had no control over his actions: *Corbett v Halifax Building Society* [2002] EWCA Civ 1849.

Key Principle

> "The money which is received by the mortgagee, arising from the sale, after discharge of prior encumbrances ... shall be held by him in trust to be applied ... first, in payment of all costs, charges and expenses properly incurred by him as incident to the sale ... and secondly in discharge of the mortgage money, interest, and costs ... and the residue of the money so received shall be paid to the person entitled to the mortgaged property ... ". Section 105 of the **Law of Property Act 1925**.

Thomas had a mortgage with the Halifax Building Society. Upon default of payments, the Building Society took possession and exercised its power of sale. After the payment of the loan, interests and costs, the Building Society placed the surplus in a suspense account. The Building Society claimed it was entitled to keep the surplus on the basis that it wouldn't have arisen had it not granted the loan to Thomas.

Held

❖ (CA (Civ Div)) The mortgage was only the security for the loan and s.105 of the **Law of Property Act 1925** was clear as to the mortgagee's duty with respect to the proceeds of sale. The surplus was therefore held on trust for Thomas. [1996] Ch. 217.

Commentary

The case serves as a useful reminder that s.105 of the **Law of Property Act 1925** is clear as to the application of the proceeds of sale, and that the mortgage is merely a security for the loan.

[3] The appointment of a Receiver

Key Principle

Where a receiver is appointed as an agent of the mortgagor, the receiver's duty is to ensure the payment of the debt.

SILVEN PROPERTIES LTD V ROYAL BANK OF SCOTLAND PLC 2003

The appellant appealed against an order dismissing its claims against the receivers appointed by the respondent mortgagee. The appellant argued that the receiver had sold its properties at an undervalue because they did not seek planning permission for the properties nor find tenants for the vacant properties before the sale. The issue for the court was whether the duties of the receivers appointed as agents of the mortgagor was different to that of a mortgagee.

Held

❖ (CA (Civ Div)) In respect of the exercise of the power of sale, the receiver had the same equitable duty as a mortgagee in that it had to exercise reasonable care in the enforcement of the security. However in other respects the receiver is in a different position to the mortgagee. Although the receiver has the power to sell the mortgaged property, he has a fiduciary duty in favour of the mortgagors, the mortgagees and others interested in the equity of redemption and the primacy of the duty is to ensure that the debt is paid. The appeal would be dismissed. [2003] EWCA Civ 1409.

Commentary

The Court of Appeal stated that a receiver had broader management responsibilities than a mortgagee and could not remain passive if the conduct would damage the interests of either the mortgagee or the mortgagor. The receiver had an equitable duty to both the mortgagee and to other parties interested in the equity of redemption. It also owed a duty to mortgagor as its agent (s.109 of the **Law of Property Act 1925**) to take reasonable steps to obtain a proper price for the property and not to act in bad faith. However this duty to the mortgagor did not extend to incurring expenses in improving the property in order to obtain a higher price on the sale of the property. This followed the approach in *Medforth v Blake* [2000] Ch. 86, where the court state that the duty of care of receivers of mortgaged property went beyond good faith.

There was no obligation on receivers to run a business, which had been put into administrative receivership. However, if they did they must do so with due diligence with the primary duty of paying off interest and capital.

Horsham Properties Group Ltd v Clark, above, is a recent example of the appointment of a receiver and the subsequent sale of the mortgaged property by them.

SECTION 91(2) OF THE LAW OF PROPERTY ACT 1925

Key Principle

Where the mortgagor wishes to sell the mortgaged property but the mortgagee refuses to consent to the sale, the court has the power under s.91(2) of the **Law of Property Act 1925** to grant an order for the sale of the property.

> PALK V MORTGAGE SERVICES FUNDING PLC 1992
> The plaintiff mortgagors were unable to pay the instalments under a mortgage and secured a buyer for the mortgaged property for £283,000. The amount needed to redeem the mortgage was £358,587. The mortgagee refused to consent to the sale but obtained an order for possession of the property with a view of leasing out the property and postponing the sale until a later date. The rental income would not have been sufficient to pay the interest due under the loan. The plaintiffs applied for an order for sale under s.91(2) of the **Law of Property Act 1925**.

Held

❖ (CA (Civ Div)) The court in deciding whether to exercise its discretion under s.91(2) of the 1925 Act would have regard to the interests of the parties concerned. In the circumstances of the case, it was just and equitable to grant an order for the sale of the property notwithstanding that the proceeds of sale would not have been enough to pay off the loan. [1993] Ch. 330.

Commentary

It was made clear in this case that the court's discretion under s.91(2) of the **Law of Property Act 1925** is unfettered and that it could grant an order for sale of the mortgaged property, even in cases of "negative equity".

In *Polonski v Lloyds Bank Mortgages Ltd* [1998] 1 F.L.R. 896, the court suggested that in deciding whether it should exercise its discretion to grant an order for the sale of the property, the court can take into account non-financial matters including pressing social needs. Particularly, in cases of negative equity the court should examine the reasons for the sale of the property carefully.

Key Principle

Section 36 of the **Administration of Justice Act 1970** (as amended) cannot be used to suspend possession proceedings or orders so that an application can be made by the mortgagor for an order for sale under s.91(2) of the **Law of Property Act 1925** in cases of negative equity.

> CHELTENHAM AND GLOUCESTER PLC V KRAUSZ 1996
>
> The plaintiff mortgagee obtained a possession order against the defendant mortgagor. Subsequently, the defendant found a buyer for the property. However, the plaintiff refused consent to the sale because of negative equity and also because it believed that a higher price could be obtained for the property. The defendants made an application under s.36 of the **Administration of Justice Act 1970** to postpone the possession order as well as an order for sale of the property under s.91 of the **Law of Property Act 1925**.

Held

❖ (CA (Civ Div)) Section 36 of the **Administration of Justice Act 1970** could not be used to postpone a mortgagee's possession of the property so that the mortgagor could make an application for an order of sale under s.91 of the **Law of Property Act 1925**. This was especially so if the proceeds of such a sale was insufficient to pay off the amount due to the mortgagee. [1997] 1 W.L.R. 1558.

Commentary

The relationship between s.91 of the **Law of Property Act 1925** and s.36 of the **Administration of Justice Act 1970** (as amended) has been clarified by this case and puts a limitation on *Palk v Mortgage Services Funding Plc*, above.

MORTGAGES OF EQUITABLE INTERESTS—THE RULE IN DEARLE V HALL

Key Principle

Unless notice is given to the holders of the legal estate, mortgages of equitable interests will not have priority.

> #### DEARLE V HALL 1828
>
> Brown was given a life interest in a fund, the income which amounted to about £93 a year, by his father through the latter's will. Brown subsequently granted two annuities which were charged upon and payable out of his life interest. The first annuity amounted to £37 and was granted to William Dearle and the second amounted to £27 which was granted to Caleb Sherring. Brown then sold his life interest in the fund to Joseph Hall. Joseph Hall's solicitors made proper enquiries but had no notice of the two annuities. The solicitors gave notice to the executors of Brown's father's will of the transfer of the life interest from Brown to Joseph Hall. The executors subsequently discovered the existence of the annuities. William Dearle and Caleb Sherring claimed that their interest took priority over Joseph Hall's interest.

Held

❖ (Ch D) Joseph Hall's interest took priority over the annuities granted to William Dearle and Caleb Sherring. This was because the equitable rule that the first in time prevails did not apply in the context of the legal estate. For the annuities to bind the legal estate, notice had to be given to the holders of the legal estate, which in this case were the executors. This had not been done and therefore the annuities did not have priority over Joseph Hall's interest. (1828) 3 Russ. 1.

Commentary

[1] In summary, the rule in *Dearle v Hall* is that the mortgage of an equitable interest will have priority from the time written notice is given to the legal

owners. In *Dearle v Hall*, Joseph Hall's interest had priority over the annuities because his solicitors had given notice of the transfer of the life interest from Brown to him, to the executors of the father's estate who held the legal title to it.

[2] It should also be noted that the rule in *Dearle v Hall* appears to apply to both registered and unregistered land as well.

THINK POINT

In *Palk v Mortgage Services Funding Plc*, the Court decided that it would exercise its discretion under s.91(2) of the **Law of Property Act 1925** in making an order for the sale of the property on the application of the mortgagor even in cases of negative equity. What are the factors that compelled the court to exercise its discretion in favour of granting the order?

Consider the case of *Cheltenham and Gloucester Building Society v Norgan* in the context of the application of s.36 of the **Administration of Justice Act 1970**. What was the reaction of the mortgagees to the decision? Do you think the decision is correct in that it in effect allows the capitalisation of arrears in giving the mortgagee more time to pay?

Easements

9

INTRODUCTION

An easement is essentially a right attached to a property which gives the owner of that land a right over someone else's land without allowing the owner to take any part of its produce. There are however exceptions to this—see, for example, the rule in *Wheeldon v Burrows*, below. The land over which the easement is exercisable over is known as the servient tenement and the land which has the benefit of the easement is known as the dominant tenement. It is important to understand the difference between a grant and a reservation of an easement as the principles in respect of the acquisition of an easement is different dependent on whether it is a grant or a reservation.

The four requisite characteristics of an easement as stated in *Re Ellenborough Park* [1956] Ch. 131 are:

- there must be a dominant and servient tenement;
- an easement must "accommodate" the dominant tenement;
- the dominant and servient owners must be different persons; and
- a right over land cannot amount to an easement, unless it is capable of forming the subject matter of a grant.

In order for an easement to be binding on the subsequent owners or successors in title of the servient tenement, in addition to satisfying the requirements in *Re Ellenborough Park*, above, the easement must have been properly acquired or reserved and must be protected in the appropriate way depending on whether the easement is legal or equitable and whether it is in the context of unregistered or registered title.

Key Principle

The right to use pleasure grounds is capable of being recognised as an easement.

RE ELLENBOROUGH PARK 1955

The vendors sold plots surrounding Ellenborough Park. The conveyances granted purchasers "full enjoyment of the pleasure ground".

This enjoyment was to be held in common with other persons granted "such easements" and was subject to payment of a fair proportion of the cost of keeping the park in good order. The vendor covenanted with purchasers and successors to keep the park as a pleasure ground.

Held

❖ (CA) "Full enjoyment of the pleasure ground" was a common and clearly understood concept. The right of enjoyment accommodated the dominant tenement even if there was no absolute necessary connection between enjoyment of the park and the premises. The rights granted and obligations incurred were not repugnant to the freeholder's proprietorship or possession of the park. The right to use the pleasure ground was beneficial to the houses and was not merely a right of recreation and amusement. [1956] Ch. 131.

Commentary

The case is used as authority for the four characteristics of an easement. The court adopted as correct the formulations set out in G. C. Cheshire, *Cheshire's Modern Law of Real Property,* 7th edn (London: Butterworth & Co, 1954), p.456. The first and third requirements were not problematic here. The court held that the first was satisfied notwithstanding that enjoyment of the park could benefit people unconnected to the neighbouring premises. The court found the concept of enjoyment of the park sufficiently certain to be the subject matter of a grant. In modern terms it is clear that such a right adds to the use and value of the land and can be easily regarded as an easement. This was confirmed by the Court of Appeal in *Mulvaney v Jackson* [2002] EWCA Civ 1078, where use of a communal garden for recreational and amenity purposes was capable of existing as an easement. The case also decided that such an easement can be acquired by prescription or implied grant under s.62 of the **Law of Property Act 1925**.

THERE MUST BE A DOMINANT AND SERVIENT TENEMENT

Key Principle

There must be a dominant and servient tenement, which must be defined at the time of the grant.

LONDON & BLENHEIM ESTATES LTD V LADBROKE RETAIL PARKS LTD 1993
The plaintiff bought land together with an easement of car parking over land retained by the vendor. The schedule to the sale agreement allowed for unspecified later acquired land to be benefited by the easement.

Held

❖ (CA (Civ Div)) For an easement to exist the dominant tenement must exist and be defined at the time of grant of the easement. The easement could not therefore benefit the after-acquired land that was unknown at the time of the grant of the easement. [1994] 1 W.L.R. 31.

Commentary

An easement cannot exist "in gross", that is, without benefiting a known piece of land. Easements can be distinguished from public rights of way in that the latter are enjoyed without reference to benefited land and are hence not property rights.

THE EASEMENT MUST ACCOMMODATE THE DOMINANT TENEMENT

Key Principle

A right conferring a personal benefit does not accommodate the dominant tenement unless it also benefits the land as land.

> HILL V TUPPER 1863
> Under his lease the plaintiff claimed the sole right of letting out pleasure boats for hire upon the adjacent canal.

Held

❖ (Ex Chamber) The right did not accommodate the tenement but was a personal licence to him. (1863) 2 Hurl. & C. 121.

Commentary

The case may be differently decided now on the basis that mooring rights are valuable and would benefit any owner of the land, not just one who used them for business. The plaintiff may have had a contractual claim against the canal owners but the court was unwilling to infer a property right against a third party. Compare this with *Moody v Steggles* (1879) L.R. 12 Ch. D. 261 Ch D, where the right to place a sign for a public house on another's land was held to be capable of being an easement. Here, the benefited land had been used as a pub for more than 200 years. The court found that the land and its use had become inextricably linked so that the right was not a personal commercial benefit, but something benefiting the land itself. To accommodate the dominant tenement:

- the right should benefit the land as land;
- the land should be adjacent or close enough to identifiably benefit;

- the right should add value or use to the land; and
- the right must confer more than a personal benefit to the current owner.

In *Das v Linden Mews Ltd* [2002] EWCA Civ 590, the Court of Appeal held that there was no general principle that an easement in favour of a dominant tenement could be extended to ancillary uses which may benefit the dominant tenement. In this case it did not follow that a right of access to two houses extended to vehicular access to a separate garden plot behind the houses. An easement should benefit a particular plot of land of the dominant owner and should not be extended for purposes which may benefit any property which the dominant owner may happen to own: *Peacock v Custins* [2002] 1 W.L.R. 1815 CA (Civ Div).

DOMINANT AND SERVIENT OWNERS MUST BE DIFFERENT PERSONS

Key Principle
An easement cannot be enjoyed against a person's own land.

> KILGOUR V GADDES 1904
> The defendant claimed, as a defence to the plaintiff's trespass action, that he had acquired a prescriptive right to use the well on the plaintiff's land. Both plaintiff and defendant were tenants of the same landlord.

Held
❖ (CA) An easement could not be acquired by prescription by one tenant against another tenant of the same landlord. [1904] 1 K.B. 457.

Commentary
Such a usage could be a leasehold term or a licence but could not be an easement as the freeholder cannot enjoy a right against himself in relation to one part of his land against another. It has subsequently been held that such usage may convert to easements upon the conveyance of part of the land. See *Wheeldon v Burrows* and *Wright v Macadam*, below.

THE EASEMENT MUST FORM THE SUBJECT MATTER OF A GRANT

Key Principle

The right must be a recognised one made by a capable grantor to a capable grantee.

PHIPPS V PEARS 1964
The defendant demolished his house exposing his neighbour's flank wall to the weather. The houses had not been joined but were close enough so that the plaintiff's house had been shielded from the weather and was not otherwise protected.

Held

❖ (CA) There was no known easement to be protected from the weather. The plaintiff had no claim to stop the defendant demolishing his house exposing the plaintiff's house to the weather. [1965] 1 Q.B. 76.

Commentary

[1] In *Sedgwick Forbes Bland Payne Group v Regional Properties Co* (1981) 257 E.G. 65, it was indicated that an easement of protection may be possible in relation to a property above another.

[2] The standard recognised easements include rights of passage, water, air and light. A right to a high degree of light for the benefit of a greenhouse can be acquired: *Allen v Greenwood* [1980] Ch. 119 CA (Civ Div).

[3] Slightly anomalous but recognised easements are those of:
- Support: Had the houses in the present case been attached to each other, the plaintiff may have been able to claim an easement of support. The easement of support prevents the servient owner from demolishing his side (*Dalton v Henry Angus & Co* (1880-81) L.R. 6 App. Cas. 740 HL) but doesn't require the servient owner to maintain it so that it doesn't collapse through disrepair (see *Jones v Pritchard*, below).
- Fencing: The easement of fencing (*Crow v Wood* [1971] 1 Q.B. 77 CA (Civ Div)) obliges the servient owner to maintain fencing. This is unusual in that it falls foul of the normal requirement that the servient owner shouldn't be burdened by expense in observing an easement's obligation.
- Storage: The easement of storage could be seen as being more in the nature of a lease or licence. However, it can fall into the domain of easements provided it is defined with certainty (*Wright v Macadam*,

below), and doesn't serve to exclude the servient owner of the proper right of possession of his own land (*Copeland v Greenhalf*, below).

- Usage of facilities: The easement of using facilities could likewise be associated with other kinds of rights. However, this has been accepted in relation to using facilities such as a lavatory (*Miller v Emcer Products Ltd* [1956] Ch. 304 CA), a kitchen (*Heywood v Mallalieu* (1884) L.R. 25 Ch. D. 357 Ch D) or a post box (*Goldberg v Edwards* [1950] Ch. 247 CA). It was held in *P&S Platt Ltd v Crouch* [2003] EWCA Civ 1110 that a right to use river moorings was capable of being an easement. Even though it restricted the servient owner's use of his land it was not a sufficiently substantial interference to prevent an easement coming into existence.

Key Principle

An easement must be defined with certainty.

> ### TRAILFINDERS V RAZUKI 1988
> The plaintiff granted the defendants a lease of neighbouring land reserving the right of passage of pipes, wires and other conduits for, amongst other things, electric current. The plaintiff later sought to pass computer cables across the land.

Held

❖ (Ch D) The right reserved did not extend to entering the premises and laying computer cables, which were said to be "of an entirely novel kind". [1988] 30 E.G. 59.

Commentary

[1] Generally rights of passage must be along specific channels. Rights of air should be along specific routes such as air ducts (*Wong v Beaumont Property Trust*, below) not generally across the surface (*Harris v De Pinna* (1886) L.R. 33 Ch. D. 238 CA) or a draught across chimneys (*Bryant v Lefever* (1878–79) L.R. 4 C.P.D. 172 CA).

[2] Rights of light should be for light coming through defined apertures not a general right to light coming across the land (*Colls v Home & Colonial Stores Ltd* [1904] A.C. 179 HL).

[3] Rights of water should be through particular channels or pipes (*Race v Ward* (1855) 4 El. & Bl. 702 Ct of QB); there is no general right to water

percolating through the soil (*Palmer v Bowman* [2000] 1 W.L.R. 842 CA (Civ Div)).

[4] Rights of way should be across a given route. The extent of a right of way under an express reservation or grant is determined in light of the circumstances existing at the time of the reservation or grant: *St Edmundsbury and Ipswich Diocesan Board of Finance v Clark (No.2)* [1975] 1 W.L.R. 468 CA (Civ Div) and *Mills v Blackwell*, Lawtel, September 20, 1999. The present and reasonably foreseeable purposes should not be exceeded; the form of use can, however, change. A right of way cannot be extended to include a right to store equipment (*VT Engineering v Richard Barland & Co* (1968) 19 P. & C.R. 890 Ch D). However, its form of use can be changed from, for example, horse-drawn vehicles to motor vehicles (*Sunset Properties Pty Ltd v Johnston* [1975] 3 B.P.R. 9185).

FACTORS IN CLAIMS TO EASEMENTS

Key Principle
A grantor may not derogate from grant.

> **CABLE V BRYANT 1907**
> The plaintiff leased a stable from the defendant who subsequently put up a hoarding blocking ventilation to the stable.

Held
The defendant could not derogate from grant by making the stable unusable. A claim to an easement of air through a defined aperture was recognised notwithstanding that there was no defined airflow channel through the servient land. [1908] 1 Ch. 259.

Commentary
[1] In most cases a defined airflow channel is required (*Bryant v Lefever*, above). The court may have been willing to vary this requirement in order to emphasise the principle of non-derogation from grant.

[2] Lessors' reservations of easements are likely to be construed strictly against the lessor on the basis that to seek to extend the reservation later would be to derogate from the grant of the lease (*Trailfinders v Razuki*, above).

Key Principle

An easement should not have the effect of excluding the servient owner from possession of his property by giving the plaintiff exclusive or joint use.

> ### COPELAND V GREENHALF 1952
>
> The defendant claimed by 50 years' long use a prescriptive right to store vehicles on a strip of land which the plaintiff used for access between her house and orchard. The vehicles were stored at the strip of land's narrowest point, which was just 15 feet wide.

Held

❖ (Ch D) The right claimed would not be accepted as an easement as it would effectively give the whole beneficial use of the strip of land to the defendant. [1952] Ch. 488.

Commentary

[1] A claim to exclusive use or joint use will usually fail. In cases involving use of facilities, greater leeway seems to be afforded plaintiffs presumably on the basis that use of a lavatory (*Miller v Emcer Products Ltd*, above) or a kitchen for washing (*Heywood v Mallalieu*, above) would only be for part of a day, in the same way as passing along a right of way is a limited use of the land. The right to store coal in a garden shed (*Wright v MacAdam*, below) is perhaps more difficult to justify. In *Grigsby v Melville* [1972] 1 W.L.R. 1355 Ch D, it was held that a claim for an easement of storage in a cellar would fail as it amounted to a claim for exclusive use.

[2] It should be remembered that an easement of car parking is recognised as an easement provided it does not exclude the use and possession by the servient owner and is defined with certainty: *London & Blenheim Estates Ltd v Ladbroke Retail Parks Ltd*, above. This was confirmed in *Hair v Gillman* [2000] 48 E.G. 117 CA (Civ Div). In *Montrose Court Holdings Ltd v Shamash* [2006] EWCA Civ 251 the Court of Appeal held that the servient owner could properly set out parking regulations in respect of easements of parking enjoyed by a number of servient owners and tenants. This did not negate the existence of the right to park but merely regulated it. In *Batchelor v Marlow* [2001] EWCA Civ 1051, the Court of Appeal held that the parking of six cars on a strip of land during the day was not capable of being an easement. This was because, in the circumstances, it left the landowner with no reasonable use of his own land. This decision was doubted by two of the Law Lords in *Moncrieff v Jamieson* [2007] UKHL 42, below.

The easement of parking was considered by the House of Lords in *Moncrieff v Jamieson* [2007] UKHL 42. Although a Scottish decision, the court decided that Scottish law in this area is similar to English law. Lord Scott was in favour of recognising such an easement and stated that there should be a distinction between use and possession. A right giving the dominant owner the sole use of part of the servient tenement does not prevent it from being an easement but where the dominant owner has been given exclusive possession this would not be consistent with such a right. Further his Lordship made it clear that a right to park could be implied if it was reasonably necessary for the exercise of the right of way. The facts of this case were unusual in that the right of way over the servient land was on a slope which ended at the dominant tenement. Although the dominant owner could unload his car or off load passengers at the end of the road the dominant owner had never been given a right to park there. Their Lordships decided that the right of way came with an incidental right to park as this was necessary for the enjoyment of the dominant land. This decision was considered by the Court of Appeal in *Waterman v Boyle* [2009] EWCA Civ 115. The claimants relied on *Moncrieff v Jamieson* in claiming an incidental right to park. However as they had been given express rights to park no further rights would be implied. The additional right to park was desirable but not necessary as compared with the situation in *Moncrieff*.

[3] In *Hanina v Morland* (2000) 97(47) L.S.G. 41 CA (Civ Div) the dispute related to access from an upstairs maisonette to a flat roof over the shop below. For practical purposes the only access to the roof was through the maisonette. It was held that the tenants of the maisonette had exclusive and restrictive access to the roof. Therefore their rights to use the roof for recreational purposes arose under the tenancy and not from an easement passing under s.62 of the **Law of Property Act 1925**.

Key Principle
An easement should not involve expenditure or any positive obligation by the servient owner.

REGIS PROPERTY CO LTD V REDMAN 1956
A lease contained a covenant to supply hot water and central heating.

Held
❖ (CA) The right to this benefit was not in the nature of a property right of an easement. [1956] 2 Q.B. 612.

Commentary

[1] The easement of fencing (*Crow v Wood* [1971] 1 Q.B. 77 CA (Civ Div)) is an acknowledged exception where expense is imposed on servient owners. In *Liverpool City Council v Irwin* [1977] A.C. 239 HL, the use of stairs, lifts and rubbish chutes were held to be implied easements. Inevitably, maintenance of these would involve expense, which the court may have felt legitimate in the context of a public authority landlord. The terms of the lease were inadequate and the court used this artifice to give the lease its proper effect, though it might have been easier to phrase the obligations as implied leasehold terms rather than implied easements.

[2] An easement should not require the owner to carry out positive acts in order to respect them. This is often coincident with the tests that the servient owner should not incur expense or have to give permission. It is sometimes said that the courts will not accept new negative easements. This is perhaps an overstatement of the principle that a court will not accept new easements that exclude the servient owner from the proper possession of his property. Whether an easement is positive or negative in character does not depend on how it is phrased, but on the content of the obligation. It could be said that if the servient owner can respect an easement by doing nothing then it is a negative easement.

[3] In relation to easements of support there is a duty of care on the servient owner to avoid danger to the dominant owner's land. This duty extends to danger of landslip which ought to have been foreseen but does not extend to the danger of a catastrophic collapse which could have only been discovered by a further geological investigation: *Holbeck Hall Hotel Ltd v Scarborough BC* [2000] Q.B. 836 CA (Civ Div).

Key Principle

An easement should be in the nature of a right not a permission.

GREEN V ASHCO HORTICULTURIST, LTD 1966

The plaintiff was a lessee of a shop. The original lease was granted in 1931 and renewed in 1959. The defendant owned the freehold of the shop and other property, including a passageway from the street past a courtyard behind the shop and onto some garages. In 1963, the plaintiff claimed that he had a right of way along the passageway having used this since 1931 as sole means of access to the courtyard. He alleged that this right was being blocked. On evidence, it was found that until 1960 there had been gates between the passageway and courtyard which were only open during office hours. There had been times when the plaintiff had not been allowed to use the passageway at all. The lease also allowed the lessor unlimited power to build on the land.

Held

❖ (Ch D) The use of the passageway was by permission and not as of right and therefore could not be claimed against the freeholder as an easement. [1966] 1 W.L.R. 889.

Commentary

In *Burrows v Lang* [1901] 2 Ch. 502, a claim to take water from an artificial water source was rejected as it would depend on the servient owner giving intermittent permission by refilling the source. See also *Gardner v Hodgson's Kingston Brewery*, below.

ACQUISITION OF EASEMENTS

Key Principle

An easement can arise by necessity.

NICKERSON V BARROUGHCLOUGH 1980

The plaintiff bought a field. It was landlocked except for a lane, which ran parallel to the field and continued onto a public highway. The lane was accessed via a bridge from the plaintiff's land over a ditch. The 1906 conveyance of most of what became the plaintiff's land had a restriction that the vendor did not undertake to make up any roads nor grant any rights of way. A 1922 conveyance of a strip of land brought together what was now the plaintiff's land. The 1973 conveyance was expressed to include a right of way over the lane in so far as the vendor had power to convey it. The defendant knocked down the bridge over the ditch to the lane twice and denied the easement of a right of way.

Held

❖ (CA (Civ Div)) As a matter of public policy no transaction should without good reason be regarded as depriving access to the land conveyed. The 1906 conveyance freed the vendor from any obligation to make up roads but did not preclude an easement of necessity from arising. [1981] Ch. 426.

....

An easement of way for agricultural and sporting purposes to land beyond that conveyed in the 1922 conveyance was also held to have arisen by virtue of s.62 of the **Law of Property Act 1925**. In *Corp of London v Riggs* (1879–80) L.R. 13 Ch. D. 798 Ch D, it was held that a right of way of necessity is limited to what is necessary at the time of the grant. Thus, access to the land for agricultural purposes cannot later be extended to access for building purposes. The land must be completely landlocked for an easement of necessity to arise. It would be more difficult to claim such an easement if there is a realistic alternative access: *Adealon International Corp Proprietary Ltd v Merton LBC* [2007] EWCA Civ 362. *Sweet v Sommer* [2004] EWHC 1504 (Ch) shows that an easement of necessity of a right of way can be the subject matter of an implied reservation of an easement.

Key Principle ....
An easement can arise out of the common intention of the parties.

> ### WONG V BEAUMONT PROPERTY TRUST LTD 1964
> A lease of cellar premises for use as a restaurant was conveyed with a stipulation that the lessee would comply with health regulations. These included ventilation. The new landlords refused permission for the erection of a ventilation duct fixed to the building above which they retained.

Held ....
❖ (CA) There was an easement of necessity to erect and maintain a ventilation duct. [1965] 1 Q.B. 173.

Commentary ....
This case is often cited as supporting the principle that an easement can arise from the intention of the parties. The Court of Appeal did however characterise it as an easement of necessity. In fact, neither party realised where the air duct would subsequently have to be. It is fair to say, however, that the intended use of the premises made the easement a necessity. A more recent case is *Thorburn v Holland*, Lawtel, April 24, 2002, which related to a passage behind a row of houses. Having been assured that there was a right of vehicular access and having used it for some time the claimant was barred from using it. It was evident from dealings with the Land Registry that the previous owner of the relevant properties had widened the passage to provide access and that subsequent conveyances reserved rights of way. The

vehicular right of way was held to exist in part due to the intention of parties and in part due to necessity.

Key Principle
An easement of intention can arise if there is a common intention as to the purpose and manner of use of the land and that an easement is necessary to give effect to that use.

> **STAFFORD V LEE 1992**
> An area of woodland was conveyed, described as fronting a road but without expressly granting a right over it. The plaintiff subsequently built a dwelling on the woodland. The defendants conceded a right of way but only for purposes necessary for the reasonable enjoyment of the land as woodland.

Held
❖ (CA (Civ Div)) The question was whether the parties at the time of the conveyance intended the land to be used in a definite and particular manner, not how the land was in fact used at the time of the grant. The plans which accompanied the grant indicated that the parties intended that the land be developed for residential purposes. (1993) 65 P. & C.R. 172.

Commentary
[1] Intention is again defined in terms of what is necessary to achieve the intention of the parties as opposed to what is objectively necessary.

[2] In order to give effect to the common intention of the parties, the court would look at the circumstances under which the grant of land was made and was not dependent on the terms of the grant itself: *Davies v Bramwell* [2007] EWCA Civ 821. In that case the court decided that an easement giving a right of way in order to access a ramp in a garage would be implied in order to give effect to the common intention of the parties—which was to use the property as a garage for the repair of cars.

[3] In *Kent v Kavanagh* [2006] EWCA Civ 162, the Court of Appeal had to consider whether an easement was intended in respect of a shared pathway. The boundary between a pair of semi-detached properties ran down the middle of the shared pathway which gave access to the back of the houses. The leases in respect of the two properties were silent on the use of the pathway. The pathway was only three feet wide and therefore the path could

not be used by one owner without passing over his neighbour's half of the pathway. Accordingly, the court decided that the original parties to the leases must have intended that the use of the pathway would be shared.

Key Principle

A grant of a part of a tenement passes with it those continuous and apparent "easements" over the other part of the land which are necessary for the enjoyment of the granted land which have hitherto been in use.

> WHEELDON V BURROWS 1879
> A workshop and adjoining piece of land owned by the same vendor were put up for sale. The land was sold and the workshop retained but later sold to a different purchaser. The workshop had windows, which received light from the piece of land previously sold.

Held

❖ (CA) There was no reservation of light made when the land was sold. No right to light could therefore pass to the subsequent owner of the workshop. (1879) L.R. 12 Ch. D. 31.

Commentary

[1] The case is important for the effect it could have on converse facts. If the vendor sold the workshop first and retained the other piece of land, the purchaser would have the benefit of an easement of light. However, this was provided that its existence had been continuous, apparent and necessary for the reasonable enjoyment of the land as well as being in use at the time of the sale. This could be binding on subsequent owners of the land.

[2] There are three elements to the rule in *Wheeldon v Burrows*, namely that:
- the quasi easement must be continuous and apparent;
- necessary for the enjoyment of the land;
- in use by the owner at the time of the sale.

[3] The rule in *Wheeldon v Burrows* is problematic. The passage of the easement upon the grant of the land cannot be correct. Prior to the grant there could have been no existing prior easement because both the workshop and piece of land lay within the ownership and occupation of the same person. One of the four essential requirements for an easement is that the dominant and servient owners are different persons. The best that could have existed before the grant is what has come to be known as a "quasi-

easement". These can be converted to an easement if the conditions set out in the case are met. In *Borman v Griffith* [1930] 1 Ch. 493 Ch D it was held that an easement of a right of way could be implied into a specifically enforceable agreement for a lease under the *Wheeldon v Burrows* rule (even when the usage was regular if not continuous). In *Ward v Kirkland* [1967] Ch. 194 Ch D the claim to a right to enter neighbour's land to maintain a wall failed on the ground that there was no apparent evidence manifesting the exercise of such a right.

[4] The rule in *Wheeldon v Burrows* requires that the right must have been in use by the owner at the time of the sale. In *Kent v Kavanagh* [2006] EWCA Civ 162, the court rejected a claim for an easement under the rule in *Wheeldon v Burrows* as the dominant tenement was occupied by the tenant and not by the owner.

Key Principle

The court is unwilling to allow implied reservations of easements except in cases of necessity or common intention.

> PECKHAM V ELLISON 1998
> Two properties, owned by a local authority, were acquired by the plaintiff and the defendant's predecessor in title. The plaintiff claimed an easement of way over the defendant's land. The evidence was that the "right of way" which was being exercised prior to the sale, could only exist as a quasi-easement before the first sale to the defendant's predecessor.

Held

❖ (CA (Civ Div)) An easement giving a right of way had been impliedly reserved by the common intention of the parties in favour of the local authority. The benefit of the easement was passed to the plaintiff on the sale of the property. (1999) 31 H.L.R. 1030.

Commentary

[1] Courts are unwilling to allow implied reservations of easements except where the easement is of necessity (*Corp of London v Riggs* (1879-80) L.R. 13 Ch. D. 798 Ch D) or of common intention. To allow implied reservation in other cases would be to allow derogation from grant.

[2] For an easement to arise by implied reservation by necessity it is essential that the land must be totally landlocked. In *Adealon International Corp Proprietary Ltd v Merton LBC* [2007] EWCA Civ 362 the court held that where there was an alternative route for access over the land of third parties, it was more difficult to establish a case of necessity. In that case the court refused to allow an easement of necessity as the claimant should have expressly reserved a right of way over the land it had sold to the council.

[2] In order for an easement to be impliedly reserved by common intention, the intention, must be specific as to the precise nature and extent of the right, otherwise, no easement would be implied: *Peckham v Ellison*, above, and *Chaffe v Kingsley* (2000) 79 P. & C.R. 404 CA (Civ Div).

Key Principle
An easement can come into existence as a result of s.62 of the **Law of Property Act 1925**.

> ### WRIGHT V MACADAM 1949
> A tenant was allowed by the defendant landlord to use the garden shed for the storage of coal. After three years, in 1943 the landlord granted the plaintiffs a new one-year lease of the property plus an extra room. The plaintiffs continued to use the shed though there was never any written agreement to this effect. Four years later the landlord asked for an extra charge for the use of the shed. The plaintiffs refused and the landlord removed the shed.

Held
❖ (CA) The use of the shed was a recognised right in land. This right passed with the agreement of 1943. That agreement was a conveyance of land and by virtue of s.62 of the **Law of Property Act 1925** a conveyance is deemed to pass with it, inter alia, all rights and easements unless expressly excluded. [1949] 2 K.B. 744.

> ### HAIR V GILLMAN 2000
> The claimants were the freehold owners of No.182, High Road, South Benfleet. Their predecessors in title had built a nursery at the rear of the property, known as No.182A. The defendant was granted a lease of the nursery from 1972 and at the time was given permission to park her car on the forecourt of No.182. In 1979, the defendant purchased the freehold of No.182A. The claimants bought the freehold of No.182 and a

dispute arose as to whether the defendant could continue parking on the forecourt of No.182.

Held

❖ (CA (Civ Div)) The defendant had an easement to park her car on the forecourt of No.182. The permission to park the car given in 1972 and which was still in existence in 1979 when the defendant bought the freehold of No.182A gave rise to an easement under s.62 of the **Law of Property Act 1925**. (2000) 80 P. & C.R. 108.

Commentary

Like *Wheeldon v Burrows*, there is a logical problem that the conveyance is being used to change something into an easement which previously had been regarded as a leasehold covenant or a licence. The purpose of s.62 is not to create new land rights but was intended as a word saving device. However, there is also a similarity in the cases in that it may have been unjust to allow the landlord to effectively derogate from grant. In *Graham v Philcox* [1984] Q.B. 747 CA (Civ Div), a right of way benefited a lease of a flat. The lease was subsequently conveyed to new lessees. When that flat was enlarged with the neighbouring flat into a single residence the question arose as to whether the right of way was co-terminus with the lease. It was held that a subsequent lease was a conveyance, which by s.62 created an easement.

Key Principle

For s.62 to operate so as to convert some right into an easement there must have been diversity of ownership or occupation under which the de facto "right" was enjoyed.

LONG V GOWLETT 1923
The vendor owned two plots of land along a river. He had passed from one to the other to clear blockages from the river. The purchaser of one plot claimed this right over the purchaser of the other.

Held

❖ (Ch D) The precursor to s.62 could not pass such a right unless there had been some prior, even precarious, right over land owned or occupied by another. [1923] 2 Ch. 177.

In 1960 the Greater London Council leased a site to the first plaintiffs
for 150 years. They developed it, building maisonettes on top of
showrooms and garages. The maisonettes were not occupied. In 1972,
Camden BC made a compulsory purchase order of the lease of the
maisonettes. They documented (outside the Order itself) certain
ancillary rights such as those of support from the building below and
rights of passage of electricity water, etc. which they regarded as
passing under s.62. In 1974, the first plaintiff sub-let the maisonettes to
the second plaintiffs. The plaintiffs appealed that the ancillary rights
could not pass by virtue of s.62.

Held

❖ (HL) The ancillary rights claimed did not pass as there had not been
diversity of ownership or occupation of the quasi-dominant and quasi-
servient tenements. [1979] A.C. 144.

Commentary

[1] The notion that diversity of occupation, less than diversity of ownership, is
sufficient still leaves a problem that a usage enjoyed in a leasehold or licence
context could be converted to a right, claimed as between freeholders.

[2] In *Sovmots Investments Ltd v Secretary of State for the Environment*, in
analysing the definitions of house, appurtenance and land, the House of
Lords also found that the ancillary rights could not be claimed unless they
pre-existed with clear definition. There appears to be an underlying dispute
as to who should have effective control over the property, the developers or
the Borough Council, and to the appropriateness of the Council using compulsory purchase orders as a part of its function of providing housing.

Key Principle

To acquire an easement by prescription, the use must be "as of right"—
without force, secrecy or permission.

GARDNER V HODGSONS KINGSTON BREWERY CO LTD 1903

For more than 40 years a landowner crossed his neighbour's yard to
reach the public road from his own yard. This was done in return for an
annual payment. There was no written agreement and insufficient
evidence as to the origin of the agreement or payment.

Held

❖ (HL) The payment was for the use of the access way and that usage was thus not "as of right". Given the usage was on evidence not as of right the presumption of a lost modern grant under the Prescription Act 1832 could not be made. [1903] A.C. 229.

> LONDON TARA HOTEL LTD V KENSINGTON CLOSE HOTEL LTD 2010
> The claimant and the defendant were owners of adjoining hotels and in 1970 the owner of the defendant hotel was given a right of access over land owned by the claimant. This was under a licence with a small fee if this was demanded by the claimant. There was no evidence of any demand for the fee. The defendant hotel changed ownership a number of times and the claimant subsequently wanted to restrain the defendant from using the right of access and issued an application for an injunction.

Held

❖ (Ch D) When the original owner of the defendant used the right of way this was by way of a licence which lapsed when the hotel was sold. Thereafter the use of the right of access was without permission and therefore the current owners of the defendant hotel could claim an easement arising from prescription under the doctrine of lost modern grant. [2010] EWHC 2749 (Ch).

Commentary

Long use cannot make for a prescriptive right if there is no property right underlying the usage. In the case of *Gardner v Hodgsons Kingston Brewery* the use of an access way took the form of a licence, i.e. with permission. The traditional phrasing of the requirement is that the use must be nee vi, nee clam, nee precario, that is, not by force, not secretly, and not with permission. In contrast in *London Tara Hotel Ltd v Kensington Close Hotel Ltd* the licence came to an end when the hotel was sold at which point the use was without permission.

In *Bakewell Management Ltd v Brandwood* [2004] UKHL 14 it was held by the House of Lords that an easement of vehicular access over a common had come about by prescription with evidence of 20 years' use. Lower courts had denied the easement in part on the ground that it was an offence under s.193 of the **Law of Property Act 1925** to drive across a common without lawful authority. The House of Lords found that if the appellant had been given lawful authority an easement could have come into being. The 20 years' use was held to be evidence supporting a presumed grant of an easement in that there was a presumed grant of lawful authority. This is distinguishable said the House of Lords from cases where the use of the land is itself unlawful and cannot be made lawful by a grantor and therefore cannot be the basis for acquisition of an easement by long (unlawful) use.

Key Principle
Acquiescence does not equate to permission.

MILLS V SILVER 1991
The defendants bought a hill farm. The only vehicular access was over a track across the plaintiff's land. The previous owner had used the track openly, without force and without permission albeit not frequently between 1922 and 1981. The track was only passable in dry weather. The defendants arranged to lay a stone road to make the track passable in all weather. The plaintiff sought an injunction and damages for trespass.

Held
❖ (CA (Civ Div)) The previous use of the track had to be sufficient to warrant the implication of a lost modern grant. The use was open and toleration of its use did not rebut the presumption of a grant. The user was "as of right" known about and acquiesced to by the servient owners. [1991] Ch. 271.

Commentary
The acquiescence is in effect regarded as evidence of the grant of right rather than permission denying the right. (Compare with *Jones v Price* [1965] 2 Q.B. 618, where use of a track to drive sheep was held on evidence to be based on original and ongoing permission, rather than grant followed by use as of right. Relevant evidence included the fact that similar permission was given to others.) That the farm was otherwise landlocked may have been an underlying consideration. The defendants were however held to be trespassing in relation to improving the track. The grant of an easement allows for maintaining its usability but not improving it. The improvements increased the burden on the servient owner. By holding that there was a trespass, the court recognised the easement to the extent that it existed when the hill farm was bought. The damages paid for the trespass done in improving reflect the extra burden imposed on the servient owner. See *Trailfinders v Razuki*, above, as to extending easements. *R. (on the application of Beresford) v Sunderland City Council* [2001] EWCA Civ 1218 concerned access to common lands and whether use as of right could be defeated by implied permission. The Court of Appeal stated that mere acquiescence could not prevent use "as of right" for the purpose of prescription. Normally permission would be

express. It was held that permission could be implied and in the case it could be inferred from the owner's acts that there had been an implied permission which destroyed a claim to use as of right.

Key Principle

To acquire an easement by prescription the period of use must be 20 years without interruption.

REILLY V ORANGE 1955

In September 1934 the plaintiff granted his neighbour, the defendant, permission to use his driveway for domestic purposes. In December 1953 the plaintiff withdrew that permission and in July 1954 brought an action in court to determine the land's use. The defendant claimed an easement by prescription.

Held

❖ (CA) An easement by way of prescription required a full 20 years' use without interruption. Section 4 of the **Prescription Act 1832** deems that period to be the period next before the commencement of an action of a matter relating to the period. The defendants' claim therefore failed. [1955] 2 Q.B. 112.

Commentary

[1] Where there is an interruption, it must be acquiesced to for one year to be effective. Here, the defendant claimed that the bringing of the action was an interruption, which could not be acquiesced to for one full year before the completion of 20 years. The defendant then argued that it could not therefore be an effective interruption against him and that his claim to a prescriptive easement was good. Ingenious as this argument was, the court held that the bringing of the action was not an interruption for the purposes of the Act but a defining event against which the previous 20 year period should be calculated.

[2] In *Newnham v Willison* (1988) 56 P. & C.R. 8 DC, the plaintiff had a right of way over a driveway which merged into a track. The plaintiff argued that the turning was, from one to the other, a swept curve, the defendant said it was a sharp corner and placed a post at the junction to enforce that view. The post was placed in about March 1983, the plaintiff brought his action in June 1984. The Court of Appeal held that there had been an interruption for more than a

year in the 20 years preceding the action so that there was no prescriptive right to use the swept curve.

Key Principle

[i] To acquire a prescriptive right at common law there must be use since time immemorial. There is a presumption of this if there has been 20 years' uninterrupted use. The presumption is rebutted upon proof that the right began after 1189 or the land was in common ownership since 1189.

[ii] To acquire an easement by lost modern grant there must be 20 years' uninterrupted use. This raises a presumption of a lost modern grant, which can be rebutted by proof that the grant was impossible.

[iii] To acquire a prescriptive right under the **Prescription Act 1832** the usage must be uninterrupted in the relevant period leading up to the action.

TEHIDY MINERALS V NORMAN 1970
The defendant farmers claimed rights of common of grazing over a down owned by the plaintiff. Some of the farms had been in common ownership with the down until purchased by the defendant in 1920. In 1941, the down was requisitioned by the government. In 1954 the government granted the commoners' association, including the defendants, a licence to use the down for grazing. After de-requisition the association paid the plaintiff for permission to control grazing on the down. To assert control over the down the plaintiff erected a fence across the middle of the down. The defendants dismantled the fence and were sued for trespass. The defendants claimed that they had acquired rights of common of grazing over the down at common law, by lost modern grant and under the **Prescription Act 1832**.

Held

❖ (CA (Civ Div)) The period of requisition had displaced all other interests in the property during that period, so that the claim to rights of common of grazing over the down failed under the Prescription Act. There had not been 20 years' uninterrupted use immediately prior to the action being brought. However, it is still possible to ask if rights have been acquired by common law prescription, or the doctrine of lost modern grant.

In relation to those farms not previously in common ownership with the down there was proof of a period of 20 years' enjoyment of a profit raising a presumption of use since time immemorial. That presumption was not rebutted, so the right existed by common law prescription.

In relation to the farms in common ownership there was proof of 20 years' enjoyment from 1920 to 1941 raising a presumption of a lost modern grant. That presumption was not rebutted so the right existed by the doctrine of lost modern grant. Common law prescription would not help in relation to this land as the presumption of use since time immemorial was rebutted by the land being in common ownership before 1921. [1971] 2 Q.B. 528.

Commentary
[1] The case illustrates the inconsistency whereby a prescriptive right can be rejected by one method but accepted by another.

[2] Where the owner of the potential servient tenement was prevented by statute from disposing of land there was no one who could properly grant an easement and hence the claimant could not succeed in acquiring an easement by prescription: *Housden v Conservators of Wimbledon and Putney Commons* [2007] EWHC 1171 (Ch).

Key Principle
The doctrine of lost modern grant survives as a legal fiction that deems an easement has been created.

> BRIDLE V RUBY 1989
> In the conveyance of a plot of land, there was a reservation of an easement over a driveway but this had not been agreed and was crossed out. The successors in title used the driveway in the mistaken belief that they had the right to do so.

Held
❖ (CA Civ Div)) That the driveway was used under a mistaken belief as to the grant of an easement did not rebut the presumption of a lost modern grant. [1989] Q.B. 169.

Commentary
It had been thought that the doctrine of lost modern grant was rendered unnecessary by the **Prescription Act 1832**. The inadequacies of the Act however allowed for the doctrine's return. This case illustrates the strength of the presumption, which appears to survive even proof that there was no

grant. The legal fiction of a grant after its apparent denial prevailed because there clearly was 20 years' use.

The Law Commission published a Consultation Paper, *Easements, Covenants and Profits à Prendre* (Law Commission, March 2008), CP No.186 with a view to their reform and rationalisation. Such reforms are intended to take into account commonholds and the requirements of the **Land Registration Act 2002** and more importantly it seeks to reform the different methods of acquisition of easements. It seeks to abolish the different ways in which prescriptive easements can be acquired and to replace that with one single method of acquiring such easements.

Key Principle

"When the access and use of light to and for any dwelling house, workshop, or other building shall have been actually enjoyed therewith for the full period of 20 years without interruption, the right thereto shall be deemed absolute and indefeasible, ... unless it shall appear that the same was enjoyed by some consent or agreement ...". **Prescription Act 1832** s.3.

RHJ LTD v FT PATTEN (HOLDINGS) LTD 2008

The appellant owned an office building under a 99 year lease from 1975 which was acquired at auction in 2001. The respondents were the owners of three properties nearby—a building and two car parks. The local authority was the owner of all four properties until 1989. The appellant argued that its property had a right to light over the respondents' land which arose by prescription. The respondents argued that the appellants did not acquire this right. Clause 2 of the lease stated that:

" ... provided always that nothing herein contained shall operate to grant by way of implication or otherwise any estate right or easement not hereby expressly granted or not hereafter expressly granted by the lessor over or in respect of any land retained by or belonging to the lessor whether now held on lease from the lessor or not or over any land to be hereafter acquired by the lessor".

In paragraph (i) in the first Schedule to the lease it reserved the following right:

"the full and free right to erect build rebuild and/or alter as they may think fit at any time and from time to time any buildings or bays or projections to buildings on any land adjoining the demised property and/or on the opposite sides of the adjoining streets and access ways".

The question arose as to whether these clauses inferred consent in respect of the rights to light.

Held

The two provisions read together implied the requisite consent for the purposes of s.3 of the **Prescription Act 1832** and therefore the appellant did not acquire any rights of light over the respondents' property by way of prescription but by virtue of the agreement. It was not necessary for there to be an express agreement or consent. [2008] EWCA Civ 151.

Commentary

[1] In contrast in *Salvage Wharf Ltd v G&S Brough Ltd* [2009] EWCA Civ 21, the court in interpreting the agreement, decided that consent could not be inferred from it and hence did not trigger s.3 of the **Prescription Act 1832**. Therefore, there was no restriction in the agreement preventing the claimant from claiming prescriptive rights under the **Prescription Act 1832**.

[2] In respect of the remedies available in respect of an interference with an easement of light, note should be made of *HKRUK II (CHC) Ltd v Heaney* [2010] EWHC 2245 (Ch), where the court was prepared to grant a mandatory injunction removing a building or part thereof which was built in violation of the existing right of light. This seems to be a serious consequence for developers and in this case the matter was subsequently resolved out of court. However, in *Tamares (Vincent Square) Ltd v Fairpoint Properties (Vincent Square) Ltd* [2006] EWHC 3589 (Ch), the court refused to grant an injunction requiring the defendant to demolish part of its building which infringed the easement of light claimed by the claimant. Instead it made an award of damages in lieu of an injunction with the court stating that this infringement was such that it could be adequately compensated with damages. The court subsequently awarded the claimant 30 per cent of the anticipated profit from the development (reported at [2007] EWHC 212 (Ch)). In the residential context, in *Regan v Paul Properties Ltd* [2006] EWCA Civ 1391 the court was prepared to grant a mandatory injunction protecting the claimant's right to light. It could be argued that *HKRUK II (CHC) Ltd* and *Tamares* are both commercial developments cases whilst *Regan* is a residential dispute.

VARIATION OF EASEMENTS

Key Principle
Where the servient owner seeks to vary the use or extent of the easement the court will consider whether the dominant owner can continue to use his land in the way that was originally intended in deciding whether there has been an infringement.

> **CELSTEEL LTD V ALTON HOUSE HOLDING LTD (NO.1) 1984**
> The issue was whether a reduction of the width of a right of way from 9m to 4.14m amounted to an infringement of the right of way.

Held
❖ (Ch D) The plaintiff was entitled to enjoy the right of way which it had paid for giving it right over driveway which at the time of the purchase was 9m wide. [1985] 1 W.L.R. 204.

Commentary
Similarly in *Heslop v Bishton* [2009] EWHC 607 (Ch), where the appellant constructed a wall and pillars which was alleged to have interfered with the respondent's right of way, the court held that the appellant could not change the nature of the right of way. In the case, the appellant argued that he had offered an alternative route to the respondent. The court was of the view that this did not militate against the infringement but may affect the remedy to be awarded in respect of the breach.

Where the dominant owner seeks to vary the easement which may change the nature of its use each case will be decided on its facts. In *Greatorex v Newman* [2008] EWCA Civ 1318 the court was asked to consider whether the easement which provided a right of way

> "with or without horses, carts and carriages to pass and repass from and to the said other premises belonging to the said ... as now used by her tenant ..."

allowed customers of a public house to use the right. At the time of the grant the right of way was used by tradesmen and suppliers to the shop. The court decided that the easement did not cover the use by customers. See also *Bee v Thompson* [2009] EWCA Civ 1212 and *Davill v Pull* [2009] EWCA Civ 1309. Contrast these cases with *Risegold Ltd* v Escala *Ltd* [2008] EWCA Civ 1180 where the court provided a more flexible interpretation of the easement in question.

EXTINGUISHMENT OF EASEMENTS

Easements can be extinguished where the dominant and servient tenements come into the same ownership and occupation. During unity of possession the rights will be suspended. Easements are also extinguished by release, which can be express or implied by abandonment. Further, a radical change of use of the dominant tenement, which substantially increased the burden on the servient tenement would normally cause the loss of the easement, although it may not apply to an easement of support: *Attwood v Bovis Homes Ltd* [2001] Ch. 379.

Key Principle

Abandonment must be supported by evidence that the dominant owner and his successors do not intend to use the easement again.

> BENN V HARDINGE 1992
> A track ran along the boundary of the appellant's land connecting the entrances to two of his fields. In 1818 an enclosure order made the track into a private pathway benefiting, amongst others, the owners of the appellant's land. Neither the appellant, nor his predecessors used the track as they had alternative access. The appellant wished to use the pathway when other parts of his land became waterlogged.

Held

❖ (CA (Civ Div)) The setting out of the private carriageway necessarily created a right of way as there could have been no purpose in setting it out for the appellant's predecessor unless it was for the right to use it. The fact that no one had cause to use the track did not of itself raise a presumption of abandonment even after 175 years. (1993) 66 P. & C.R. 246.

Commentary

CDC2020 Plc v Ferreira [2005] EWCA Civ 611 illustrates the courts' reluctance to infer abandonment of easements. In the case the easement related access to garage space. The garages were subsequently demolished. Access to a different parking area was used via two ramps. It was agreed that this exceeded the original grant. The Court of Appeal declined to infer that demolition of the garages and other acts amounted to abandonment. Thus when the garages were re-built the defendants could continue to use them. The Law Commission's Consultation Paper, *Easements, Covenants and Profits à Prendre* (Law Commission, March 2008), CP No.186, seeks to reform the law in respect of extinguishment of easements.

LIABILITY TO REPAIR

Key Principle
A dominant owner is not liable for damage caused by the proper use of an easement.

> #### JONES V PRITCHARD 1908
> The defendant's house was built with a party wall connecting it to the plaintiff's house. It was agreed that the ownership be divided along a vertical plane which bisected the chimney flues serving both properties. The flues on the defendant's side became defective due to subsidence. Use of the flues then resulted in smoke escaping through cracks, entering the plaintiff's house and causing damage.

Held
❖ (Ch D) There was an implied mutual grant of right to use the flues. The defendant was not liable for damage caused by use of the easement. The use was as contemplated by the parties and was not negligent. [1908] 1 Ch. 630.

Commentary
[1] A servient owner is not bound to carry out repairs. Generally positive obligations are not consistent with easements. The servient owner could not destroy the supporting wall but could not be required to maintain it. Either party could carry out repairs on their own side and could gain reasonable access to effect repairs on the other side.

[2] In *Leakey v National Trust for Places of Historic Interest or Natural Beauty* [1980] Q.B. 485 CA (Civ Div), it was held that an occupier had a general duty in relation to hazards occurring on his land affecting his neighbour. The occupier was held liable for damage caused by the natural slippage of earth. Where damage was foreseeable the occupier should take reasonable care to avoid that damage. This case, however, says more about general occupiers' duties than it does about liabilities of servient owners. Similarly in *Bradburn v Lindsay* [1983] 2 All E.R. 408 Ch D, it was held that a landowner was liable to the neighbour caused by negligence in allowing such disrepair that a demolition order became necessary thus removing the support to the neighbour's property.

PROTECTION OF EASEMENTS

Under the Unregistered Title system, legal easements bound the world. Equitable easements created before 1926 depended on the doctrine of notice for their survival. Equitable easements created after 1925 were registrable as Class D (iii) Land Charges in the name of the estate owner whose estate is affected. By s.4 of the **Land Charges Act 1972**, an equitable easement created after 1926 if unregistered was void against a purchaser for money or money's worth of a legal estate in the land. Exceptions have been made, however, for equitable easements arising by estoppel. See *ER Ives Investment v High*, above, in Ch.2.

Under registered land, legal easements were by s.70(1)(a) of the **Land Registration Act 1925** overriding interests, which bound a purchaser without any requirement for registration. Under the **Land Registration Act 2002** legal easements and profits à prendre are interests that are capable of overriding first registration of title. However s.27 of the Act limits the types of legal easements and profits à prendre which can override a registered disposition. From October 2006 an unregistered legal easement or profit can override a registered disposition if it is obvious from a reasonable inspection of the land or is otherwise known to the person to whom the disposition is made. As a consequence of the 2002 Act only legal easements created by implied grant or reservation, by virtue of s.62 of the **Law of Property Act 1925** or those created by prescription can override a registered disposition. Other legal easements such as those created by express grant or reservation should be protected by entry on the register of a notice. Equitable easements should also be protected by entry on the register of a notice (either an agreed or unilateral notice).

PROFITS À PRENDRE

A profit is a property right related to easements. A profit is the right to take something, which is part of the land or the right to take something off the land, which is susceptible to ownership when taken. Examples of the former include peat, turf, wood gravel or sand. Examples of the latter include game or fish though not wild animals. For a relatively modern example of litigation on these unusual rights, see *Newman v Bennett* [1981] Q.B. 726 DC where it was held that a right to take grass by grazing was not just a defence to trespass but a right of pasture over the land. In exercising that right the dominant owner had to observe local byelaws. In a case concerning grazing rights, the House of Lords in *Bettison v Langton* [2001] UKHL 24, held that where grazing rights were registered under s.15 of the **Commons Registration**

Act 1965 the rights became converted into rights of grazing for a specific number of animals. As such these rights could be severed from what was previously the dominant tenement and sold as separate economic rights. Admittedly this is a somewhat obscure area of law but presumably of commercial significance to some people.

THINK POINT

Consider the various methods in which easements can be acquired. Do you think that this is necessary and more importantly is it appropriate for the right to an easement to be based on a fiction? Refer to the Law Commission Consultation Paper (No.186).

What are the differences between s.62 of the **Law of Property Act 1925** and the rule in *Wheeldon v Burrows*?

Freehold Covenants

10

INTRODUCTION

In this chapter, the reference to freehold covenant refers to restrictive covenants in freehold land. Positive covenants are generally not enforceable against the subsequent owners of the burdened land either at common law or in equity—only restrictive covenants are enforceable in equity in appropriate circumstances. The difference between a positive and restrictive covenant is that in the case of the former, it is a promise to do something or to carry out an action, which at times, may incur expenditure. In the case of the restrictive covenant, it restricts the use of the covenantor's land in a particular way, for example a covenant not to build more than one dwelling house on the land.

Between the original parties to the covenant, the covenant is enforceable on the basis of privity of contract. The original covenantor can enforce the covenant against the covenantee for breach of covenant. The problem arises where the benefited and burdened land has since been transferred after the covenant has been made. This chapter will examine the circumstances in which the restrictive covenant can be enforced against the subsequent owners of the burdened land.

Unlike easements, restrictive covenants are only equitable interests in land—it can never be legal. This is because it does not fall within the rights recognised as legal under s.1(2) of the **Law of Property Act 1925** and by virtue of s.1(3) of the **Law of Property Act 1925** it is therefore an equitable interest. In unregistered land these covenants must be protected by means of lodging a class D(ii) land charge (if created after January 1, 1926) or by the doctrine of notice if created before January 1, 1926. In the context of registered land the covenants should be protected by entry of either an agreed or unilateral notice.

WHO IS A COVENANTEE?

The covenantee is the person in whose favour the covenant has been made and is usually a party to the contract or deed containing the covenant. The covenant is enforceable against the covenantor by the covenantee because there is a privity of contract between them. However, the definition of a covenantee has been extended by s.56 of the **Law of Property Act 1925** and may, in some instances, include a person who was not party to the contract or the deed. This may also be affected by the **Contracts (Rights of Third Parties) Act 1999**. Normally, the covenantor and covenantee shall be owners of different land on the basis that one cannot enjoy a right against oneself. Exceptions to this include where a trustee holds different lands for the benefit of different beneficiaries. In *University of East London Higher Education Corp v Barking and Dagenham LBC* [2004] EWHC 2908 (Ch) it was held that where a statutory body held different tenements for different purposes the unity of possession did not destroy covenants relating to the land.

Key Principle

"A person may take an immediate or other interest in land or other property, or the benefit of any condition, right of entry, covenant or agreement over or respecting land or other property, although he may not be named as a party to the conveyance or other instrument." Section 56(1) of the **Law of Property Act 1925**.

RE ECCLESIASTICAL COMMISSIONERS FOR ENGLAND'S CONVEYANCE 1934
In 1887, the Ecclesiastical Commissioners conveyed a freehold house and land known as "West Heath House" to H. G. Gotto. H. G. Gotto covenanted to observe a number of restrictive covenants for himself, his assigns and also all future owners and tenants of the said land. As a separate covenant, he covenanted with the assigns and owners for the time being of the lands adjoining or adjacent to the land conveyed to him that he would observe these covenants. Several other plots of land adjoining or near West Heath House, which was conveyed to H. G. Gotto, had been conveyed to the respective purchasers prior to the conveyance of 1887 by the Ecclesiastical Commissioners. The owners of West Heath House sought a declaration that West Heath House conveyed to H. G. Gotto was no longer subject to the restrictive covenants or in the alternative, a determination as to which of the covenants were enforceable and by whom.

Held

❖ (Ch D) On a true construction of the covenant, the original covenantees, who were the purchasers of land which was near to or adjoining West Heath House, and the present owners of such land were entitled to enforce the covenants although the original covenantees were not parties to the conveyance of 1887. [1936] Ch. 430.

Commentary

[1] In *White v Bijou Mansions Ltd* [1938] Ch. 351 CA, the covenant made no reference to the fact that the covenant was to be for the benefit of any person other than the covenantee and his assigns. The plaintiff, who was the owner of adjoining land, was not entitled to the benefit of the covenant under s.56 of the **Law of Property Act 1925**. The plaintiff's argument that his predecessor in title was the assignee of the covenantee failed. The position was different in *Re Ecclesiastical Commissioners*, where the covenant was specifically made with the owners of the land, which had previously been sold. Therefore, the owners of these properties could enforce the covenant as they received the benefit of it by virtue of s.56 of the **Law of Property Act 1925**. This approach has been followed in *Amsprop Trading Ltd v Harris Distribution Ltd* [1997] 1 W.L.R. 1025. Neuberger J. decided that in order for a third party to take the benefit of a covenant, it must be purported to be made with him.

[2] It is arguable that provided it is clear that the covenant was made for the benefit of third parties to the contract, for example owners of adjoining land, the third party can enforce the covenant under the **Contracts (Rights of Third Parties) Act 1999**. However, s.56 of the **Law of Property Act 1925** goes further and allows the owners of the adjoining land to sue the successors in title as it is a proprietary interest. This would therefore be more effective that the 1999 Act.

FREEHOLD COVENANTS AT COMMON LAW

[1] Transmission of the benefit of the covenant

Key Principle
In order for the benefit of the covenant to pass to the covenantee's successors in title, the covenant must touch and concern the land.

SMITH V RIVER DOUGLAS CATCHMENT BOARD 1949

In 1938, the defendant covenanted with the owners of some lands which were prone to flooding, adjoining Eller Brook in Lancashire, that it would replace the then defective outfall from Low Meadows situated near the junction of Eller Brook with the River Douglas, by a new outfall. It would also widen, deepen and make good the banks of the Eller Brook and maintain the work when completed for all time. This was in consideration of the landowners contributing to the costs of the works. In 1940 one of the lands was transferred, together with the benefit of the covenant, to the first plaintiff. The land was subsequently let to the second plaintiff from 1944 on a yearly tenancy. In the autumn of 1946, the brook burst its banks and flooded the plaintiffs' land. The plaintiffs claimed for damages in tort and for breach of contract.

Held

❖ (CA) The defendant was in breach of its covenant and that such breach had resulted in the plaintiffs suffering a loss. It was clear from the covenant that it affected the land as land and demonstrated an intention that benefit of the covenant was to be attached to the land. The covenant by the defendant ran with the land, and by virtue of s.78 of the **Law of Property Act 1925**, could be enforced by the covenantee, her successors in title and persons deriving title under her, namely the second plaintiff and the first plaintiff. [1949] 2 K.B. 500.

Commentary

Tucker L.J. stated that the term "touches and concerns land" meant that the covenant in question must

> "either affect the land as regards mode of occupation, or it must be such as per se, and not merely from collateral circumstances, affect the value of the land".

On the facts of the case, this was satisfied. It was also evident that the other requirements for the running of the benefit of the covenant, namely, that the covenantee and her successors in title held the same legal estate in land, and that the covenant was intended to benefit the subsequent owners of the land, were satisfied here. The covenant was therefore enforceable by the plaintiffs.

Key Principle

The covenantee and his successors in title need not have the same legal estate in the land.

SMITH V RIVER DOUGLAS CATCHMENT BOARD 1949
(see above)

Held

❖ (CA) The second plaintiff, a tenant of the first plaintiff, was entitled to succeed in its claim for damages because s.78(l) of the **Law of Property Act 1925** had changed the common law rule requiring the covenantee and his successors in title to have the original covenantee's estate. [1949] 2 K.B. 500.

Commentary

Section 78(1) of the **Law of Property Act 1925** deems that a covenant is made with the covenantee, his successors in title and with persons deriving title under him or them. This would therefore include the second plaintiff, who was only a tenant, and therefore did not have the same legal estate as the covenantee, but because it derived title from the first plaintiff, it was entitled to claim damages as a result of the section.

[2] Transmission of the burden of the covenant

Key Principle

The burden of the covenant does not run with the land at common law.

> **AUSTERBERRY V OLDHAM CORP 1885**
> The defendants were the successor in title to land on which a road was built by its predecessor in title. The predecessor in title had covenanted with the original owner of the land, John Elliott, who was also the owner of adjoining lands, that they would build and maintain the road. The plaintiff was the successor in title to John Elliot's adjoining lands and sought to enforce the covenant against the defendant.

Held

❖ (CA) The plaintiff could not enforce the covenant against the defendant because the burden of a covenant imposing a positive obligation does not run with the land. (1885) L.R. 29 Ch. D. 750.

> **RHONE V STEPHENS 1994**
> The owner of a house divided it into two dwellings in 1960. The roof of the larger dwelling ("the house") lay above the bedroom of the smaller dwelling ("the cottage"). When he sold the cottage in 1960, he covenanted for himself and his successors in title to maintain such part of the roof of the house as lies above the cottage in wind and watertight condition. The condition of the roof deteriorated. The successors in title to the original covenantee sought to enforce the covenant against the defendant, who was the successor in title to the original covenantor.

Held

❖ (HL) Although it was clear that the defendant as successor in title was the owner of the roof, and was therefore in breach of the covenant to keep the roof in repair, the burden of that covenant did not run with the land at common law. The covenant could not therefore be enforced against the defendant. [1994] 2 A.C. 310.

Commentary

Tucker L.J. in *Austerberry v Oldham Corp* stated that:

> "I am not prepared to say that any covenant which imposes a burden upon land does run with the land, unless the covenant does, upon the true construction of the deed containing the covenant, amount to either a grant of an easement, or a rent-charge, or some estate or interest in land. A mere covenant to repair or to do something of that kind, does not seem to me, I confess, to run with the land in such a way as to bind those who may acquire it".

The approach of the Court of Appeal in *Austerberry v Oldham Corp*, has been followed by the House of Lords in *Rhone v Stephens* (above) and *Thamesmead Town Ltd v Allotey* (1998) 30 H.L.R. 1052 CA (Civ Div). The common law rule therefore is that the burden of a positive covenant does not run with the land at common law.

The rule in *Tulk v Moxhay* (see later) does not apply to positive covenants and therefore the burden of the covenant does not run in equity as well. There are however alternative methods of enforcing positive obligations, for example, as suggested by Tucker L.J., it could take the form of a rent charge, or an easement. It could also be through the grant of a covenant together with a chain of indemnity, a covenant imposed in a long lease instead of through a sale, through commonhold or through the rule in *Halsall v Brizell*, below.

Key Principle

As an exception to the general rule that the burden of a positive covenant does not run with the land at common law, the rule in *Halsall v Brizell* provides that a benefit cannot be taken under a deed without being subject to the obligations contained in it.

HALSALL V BRIZELL 1956

The vendors were the owners of 40 acres of land in Liverpool, which they sold off in 174 building plots. The vendors retained ownership of the roads, sewers, a promenade and sea wall. They entered into a deed with a number of the purchasers of the building plots declaring that the vendors held the roads, sewers, promenade and seawall on trust for the purchasers. The purchasers covenanted for themselves, their heirs, executors and assigns that they would contribute towards its maintenance and upkeep. The vendors covenanted on their own behalf, their heirs and assigns. In 1931, F purchased one of the plots of land together with a dwelling house built on it, which was conveyed to him subject to the covenants contained in the earlier deed. F subsequently let the property to five tenants.

Up until 1950, the owners of the various plots of land paid an equal sum per plot sufficient for the upkeep of the roads, sewers, promenade and sea wall. This was paid by F, and upon his death by his executors. In 1950, the owners of the other plots of land agreed that additional sums would be payable where the dwelling house on any of the plots of land had been divided into two or more flats or dwellings. F's executors refused to pay this additional amount.

Held

❖ (Ch D)

[a] Prima facie, the covenant contained in the deed was unenforceable, inter alia, because the burden of a positive covenant did not run with the land.

[b] The defendants were not entitled to take advantage of the use of the roads, and sewers contained in the original deed without being subject to the obligations contained in it. On that principle, the defendants were bound to pay the additional sums demanded. [1957] Ch. 169.

Commentary

The rule of mutual benefit and burden is seen as an exception to the principle that the burden of a positive covenant does not run with the land at common law. This is however restricted to the situation where the person subject to the burden also receives some benefit from the covenant otherwise it does not apply. In *Thamesmead Town Ltd v Allotey* (1998) 30 H.L.R. 1052 CA (Civ Div), the Court of Appeal stressed that it was necessary to relate the contributions to the benefits received.

The issue was considered in *Davies v Jones* [2009] EWCA Civ 1164 where the Court of Appeal suggested that the decisions in *Rhone v Stephens* and *Thamesmead Town Ltd v Allotey* establish a number of propositions which are as follows:

> "(1) The benefit and burden must be conferred in or by the same transaction ...
>
> (2) The receipt or enjoyment of the benefit must be relevant to the imposition of the burden in the sense that the former must be conditional on or reciprocal to the latter ...
>
> (3) The person on whom the burden is alleged to have been imposed must have or have had the opportunity of rejecting or disclaiming the benefit, not merely the right to receive the benefit... " Per Sir Andrew Morritt.

On the facts of that case, the first and second condition were not met and hence the rule in *Halsall v Brizell* did not apply.

. . . .

FREEHOLD COVENANTS IN EQUITY

Transmission of the burden of the covenant in equity

Key Principle . . . .
The burden of the covenant can run with the land in equity in certain circumstances.

TULK V MOXHAY 1848
Land in Leicester Square, London was sold to the covenantor who covenanted to keep the land in an "open state, uncovered with any buildings, in [a] neat and ornamental order", on behalf of himself, his heirs and assigns. The defendant subsequently bought the land with notice of the covenant and attempted to build on the land. The owners of the benefited land applied for an injunction against the defendant.

Held . . . .
❖ (Ch D) The owners of the benefitted lands could enforce the covenant against the defendant in equity because he had notice of the covenants when he bought the land. (1848) 41 E.R. 1143.

Commentary ....

The decision was the basis upon which the principles as to the transmission of the burden of the covenant evolved. The principles can be summarised as follows:

[1] the covenant must be negative or restrictive in nature;

[2] the covenantee must own land capable of benefiting from the covenant at the time the covenant is granted;

[3] the parties to the covenant must have intended that the burden of the covenant should run with the land; and

[4] the general equitable principles apply including the requirement for the successors in title to the covenantor to have had notice of the covenants.

In order for the burden of the covenant to run with the land, the covenant must be negative in nature. This is a question of substance not of form. Hence although the covenant in *Tulk v Moxhay* was to keep the land in an open state, the substance of the covenant is nonetheless negative or restrictive in the sense that it was effectively a covenant not to build on the land.

Key Principle ....

The parties to the covenant must have intended that the burden of the covenant should run with the land.

MORRELLS OF OXFORD LTD V OXFORD UNITED FOOTBALL CLUB LTD 2000

In 1962 the Oxford CC sold part of the land it was developing for a new housing estate to the purchaser. In cl.2 of the agreement, the purchaser covenanted on behalf of itself and its successors in title to build and operate a public house on the land. In cl.3, the Council covenanted, for the benefit of the land that was conveyed to the purchaser, not to permit the use of any land or building in its ownership in competition with the purchaser's business. The claimant was the successor in title to the purchaser and the defendants were the successors in title to the Council who wanted to build a new football stadium and associated leisure facilities. The claimant argued that this was a breach of cl.3.

Held ....

❖ (CA (Civ Div)) In construing cll. 2 and 3, it was clear that cl.2 was intended to bind the successors in title, whilst cl.3 was silent in this respect. It could be argued that this was deliberate and as such could be construed as a contrary intention in order to exclude the application of s.79 of the **Law of Property Act 1925**. Hence the burden of the covenant did not run with the land as this was excluded by contrary intention. [2001] Ch. 459.

Commentary
Section 79(1) of the **Law of Property Act 1925** deems that a covenant is made by the covenantor on behalf of himself, his successors in title and persons deriving title under him or them unless excluded by contrary intention. This is a form of conveyancing shorthand and the burden of the covenant runs with the land unless the operation of s.79 is excluded. This case is an example of how s.79 can be excluded.

Key Principle
The covenantee must own land which can benefit from the covenant at the time the covenant is granted.

> ### LONDON CC v ALLEN 1914
> Allen covenanted with the plaintiffs that he would not build on a plot of land, which lay across the end of a street. He covenanted for himself, his heirs and assigns, and other persons claiming under him, so far as practicable to bind the land into whosoever hands the same might come. The plaintiffs did not own any neighbouring land for the benefit of which this covenant was imposed. Allen subsequently sold the land to the defendant who had notice of the covenant but proceeded to build on the land without the plaintiffs consent.

Held
❖ (CA) The plaintiffs were not entitled to enforce the covenant against the defendant, as it did not own any relevant land capable of benefiting from the covenant. [1914] 3 K.B. 642.

Commentary
The reversion of a landlord qualifies as relevant land for this purpose. See *Hall v Ewin* (1887) L.R. 37 Ch. D. 74.

TRANSMISSION OF THE BENEFIT OF THE COVENANT IN EQUITY

Apart from satisfying the general requirements for the transmission of the benefit of the covenant, in order for the benefit of the covenant to run with the land in equity, it must be annexed to the land, assigned with the land or subject to a building scheme.

[1] ANNEXATION

[a] Express Annexation

Key Principle
The benefit of the covenant is expressly annexed to the land when the words of the covenant show that it is for the benefit of the covenantee's land.

> ROGERS V HOSEGOOD 1900
>
> A plot of land was conveyed by the owners to the then Duke of Bedford in 1869. The Duke covenanted that no more than one message or dwelling house should at any one time be erected or standing on the plot and that it would only be adapted for and used as a private residence only. It was stated that the covenant was entered into with the intent that, it might so far as possible, bind the premises thereby conveyed and every part thereof, into whosoever hands the same might come, and might enure to the benefit of the vendors, their heirs and assigns and others claiming under them to all or any of their lands adjoining or near the premises. The vendors, who were owners of other plots of land, subsequently conveyed another plot of land near to the Duke of Bedford's land to a purchaser who had no knowledge of the earlier covenant. The Duke of Bedford's successor in title to the plot of land proposed to build a block of residential flats on the land. The successors in title of the other plot of land sought to enforce the covenant.

Held
❖ (CA) The successors in title of the other plot of land could enforce the covenant against the successors in title of the Duke's land. The wording in the covenant showed an intention that the covenant was to run with the land and therefore was enforceable by the successors in title of the covenantee. The lack of knowledge on the part of the purdiaser of the other plot of land that it had the benefit of the covenant did not prevent him or his successors

in title from enforcing the covenant, provided that the benefit of the covenant had been annexed to the land. [1900] 2 Ch. 388.

> ## Renals v Cowlishaw 1878
> Land adjoining a residential estate was sold to the defendant's predecessors in title in 1845. The latter entered into covenants with the vendors and their assigns, which restricted their right to build on or use the land. The vendors subsequently sold the residential estate to the plaintiff's predecessors in title. This conveyance did not contain any reference to the restrictive covenants nor was there any representation or term in the contract that the purchasers of the residential estate would have the benefit of the covenants contained in the earlier conveyance. The plaintiff's conveyance contained a covenant limiting their use of the residential estate. The plaintiffs commenced an action to restrain the defendants from building on the adjoining land in contravention of the covenants.

Held

❖ (Ch D) Although the plaintiffs were the assigns of the covenantee, they were not entitled to sue upon the original covenants as the covenant failed to identify the land to be benefited by the covenant. (1878) L.R. 9 Ch. D. 125.

Commentary

The difference between the two cases is that in *Rogers v Hosegood*, the plaintiff could enforce the covenant as it had been expressly annexed to the land. Therefore, the fact that he was ignorant of its existence was irrelevant. In *Renals v Cowlishaw*, the covenant was not expressly annexed to the land as it had failed to identify the land which was to benefit from the covenant. As such although the plaintiffs were the assignees of the covenantee, the covenant was unenforceable. Ultimately it is clear that it is a matter of the construction of the relevant documents as to whether the covenant is annexed to the land and for the benefit of not only the covenantee but also his successors in title: *Rees v Peters* [2011] EWCA Civ 836. See also *Small v Oliver & Saunders (Developments) Ltd* [2006] EWHC 1293 (Ch), below.

Key Principle

Where the deed creating the covenant annexes the benefit of the covenant to the whole of the land, the annexation would be ineffective unless it is clear that the covenant confers an actual benefit on the whole of the land and not merely part thereof.

RE BALLARD'S CONVEYANCE 1937
The applicant was the purchaser of 18 acres of a 1,700 acre estate. He covenanted with the vendor, her heirs and assigns and successors in title on behalf of himself, his heirs and assigns, that they would be bound by the covenants contained in a schedule to the conveyance. The applicant applied for a declaration under s.84 of the **Law of Property Act 1925** that his property was no longer affected by the covenants contained in the earlier conveyance.

Held
❖ (Ch D) Where a restrictive covenant purports to be annexed to the land, but does not in fact concern and touch the whole of the land, (but merely part of it), the annexation is ineffective. The covenant does not run with the land and cannot be enforced by any owner of the land except the covenantee. [1937] Ch. 473.

Commentary
[1] Clauson J. stated that:

> "It appears to me quite obvious that while a breach of the stipulations might possibly affect a portion of that area in the vicinity of the applicant's land, far the largest part of this area of 1700 acres could not possibly be affected by any breach of the stipulations".

The conclusion was that as the covenants were not such as could benefit the whole of the land, the covenants could not be enforced by subsequent owners of the land. However, where it is made clear in the stipulation that the covenant benefits whole or any part or parts of the retained land, then the covenant is valid and effective: *Marquess of Zetland v Driver* [1939] Ch. 1 CA.

[2] The strict approach in *Re Ballard's Conveyance* has not always been followed. In *Wrotham Park Estate Co Ltd v Parkside Homes Ltd* [1974] 1 W.L.R. 798 Ch D, the court took the view that a covenant could benefit the whole of a 4,000-acre estate spread over three sites. The owners were satisfied that the covenant could be regarded as benefiting the whole of the land, which it was intended to protect.

[3] In *Small v Oliver & Saunders (Developments) Ltd* [2006] EWHC 1293 (Ch), below, the court had to resolve the issue of whether pre-s.78 of the **Law of Property Act 1925** an annexation to the whole of the land was also capable of being annexed to each and every part of the land, in the absence of any clear

statement in the conveyance. The court held that where a covenant was annexed to the whole of the land it was also annexed to each and every part. Hence, this is the reverse of the situation in *Re Ballard's Conveyance* in that whilst a covenant which is only annexed to part of the land is not annexed to the whole, where it is annexed to the whole it will also benefit each and every part thereof unless there is a contrary intention

[b] Statutory annexation

Key Principle

The benefit of the covenant can be annexed to the land by the operation of s.78 of the **Law of Property Act 1925**.

FEDERATED HOMES LTD V MILL LODGE PROPERTIES LTD 1979

M owned three plots of land which were described as the blue land, the red land and the green land. M sold the blue land to the defendant who agreed not to build more than 300 dwellings on it ("the covenant"). The other two plots of land were subsequently sold by M. The plaintiff later became the owner of both these two plots of land but had acquired it from different vendors. The benefit of the covenant was passed to the plaintiff, as owner of the green land, through an unbroken chain of assignments from the original covenantee. The defendant decided to build in contravention of the covenant not to build more than 300 dwellings on the land. The plaintiff sought to prevent this. The covenant was therefore enforceable against the defendant by the plaintiff as owner of the green land. The plaintiff further argued that the covenant was enforceable against the defendant, as owner of the red land. It argued that ss.62 or 78 of the **Law of Property Act 1925** allowed it to do so as the covenant "touched and concerned" the land.

Held

❖ (CA (Civ Div)) As the covenant touched and concerned the land belonging to the covenantee, the benefit of the covenant was therefore annexed to the land under s.78 of the **Law of Property Act 1925**. The covenant was enforceable against the defendant. [1980] 1 W.L.R. 594.

Commentary

Brightman L.J. stated that:

> "if the precondition precedent to s.78 is satisfied ... that is to say, there exists a covenant which touches and concerns the land of the covenantee ... that covenant runs with the land for the benefit

of his successors in title, persons deriving title under him or them and other owners and occupiers".

Therefore, it would appear that so long as the covenant is one which touches and concerns the land, the benefit of that covenant is one that is annexed to the land under s.78 of the **Law of Property Act 1925**. The successors in title to the covenantee or persons deriving title under him or them can enforce the covenant against the covenantor or his successors in title or persons deriving title under him or them. This has been subject to much academic criticism. See for example C.H.L. Preston and G.L. Newsom, *Restrictive Covenants Affecting Freehold Land*, 7th edn (London: Sweet & Maxwell, 1982). This decision has been accepted, without argument in *Robins v Berkeley Homes (Kent) Ltd* [1996] E.G. 75 (C.S.) Ch D but is now subject to *Crest Nicholson Residential (South) Ltd v McAllister*, below.

It had been accepted since that decision that s.78 of the **Law of Property Act 1925** had the effect of annexing the covenant to each and every part of the land since the court appear to assume that every successor in title or persons deriving title under them could claim under that statutory provision. This has been confirmed by *Small v Oliver & Saunders (Developments) Ltd* [2006] EWHC 1293 (Ch), below, where the court was of the view that a covenant which was annexed to the land (whether express or statutory) was annexed to each and every part of the land, in the absence of any contrary intention. In that case, as noted above, the court was also of the view that this was the same position pre s.78 of the **Law of Property Act 1925** and if that is the case then it is argued that s.78 is not as far reaching as originally envisaged.

Key Principle

Whilst s.78 of the **Law of Property Act 1925** provides for statutory annexation, the courts should take into account construction of the wording of the relevant conveyances and, where relevant, s.78 can be excluded by a contrary intention.

CREST NICHOLSON RESIDENTIAL (SOUTH) LTD V MCALLISTER 2004

The covenants in question in this case limited land to use in connection with a private dwelling house (impliedly, singular per plot) or professional purposes. There had been four groups of previous conveyances known as the Arthur, Humphreys, Roberts and Wing conveyances. These had divided the land into various plots one of which was owned by the respondent. The appellants sought a declaration that they were not prevented from erecting more than one dwelling house on a plot. The respondent came to own her land via one of the Wing conveyances. She sought to argue that she and her land were sufficiently referred to in the other conveyances as to be a beneficiary of the covenant and so prevent the building development in contemplation.

Held

❖ (CA (Civ Div)) It was held that whilst s.78 of the **Law of Property Act 1925** did not require that successors in title be expressly named it was a requirement that the land to be benefited was clearly identified. It was found that the Humphreys' conveyances and second Roberts' conveyance expressly referred to the vendors as beneficiaries. By inference land not owned by the vendors was not intended to be benefited. The respondent was not helped either by the Arthur and second Roberts' conveyances which did not expressly annex the benefit and the respondents plot was not clearly covered by the description of land benefited. The Court of Appeal affirmed that *Federated Homes Ltd v Mill Lodge Properties Ltd* was good if incomplete law. Furthermore, statutory annexation under s.78 is subject to construction of the wording used in the relevant conveyances. [2004] EWCA Civ 410.

ROAKE V CHADHA 1983

A house was sold in 1834 subject to a covenant that no more than one private dwelling house would be built on the land. The deed stipulated that the covenant would not enure for the benefit of any owner or subsequent purchaser of the covenantee's land unless the benefit of the covenant was expressly assigned. The plaintiffs were the successors in title to the covenantee's land and the defendant was the successor in title to the covenantor's land. The defendant proposed to build an additional house on the land. The plaintiffs sought a declaration that they were entitled to the benefit of the covenant and an injunction to restrain the defendant from erecting another house on the land.

Held

❖ (Ch D) The plaintiffs were not entitled to the benefit of the covenant. Although s.78 of the **Law of Property Act 1925** did not allow for its provisions to be excluded by contrary agreement, the covenant had to be construed as a whole to see if the benefit of the covenant was annexed to the land. Where the covenant was not qualified in any way, annexation could be readily inferred. However, as the covenant expressly stipulated that the benefit of the covenant could only enure for the benefit of any owner or subsequent purchaser by express assignment, the benefit of the covenant could not be said to have been annexed to the land. [1984] 1 W.L.R. 40.

Commentary

The issue of whether there is annexation under s.78 of the **Law of Property Act 1925** is therefore a matter of construction of the relevant document in each case rather than a question of automatic annexation and as such each case does not necessarily create a precedent (*Seymour Road (Southampton) Ltd v Williams* [2010] EWHC 111 (Ch)). The effect of the decisions is that s.78 of the **Law of Property Act 1925** can be excluded by a contrary intention. This is notwithstanding that s.78 is silent on this issue in comparison with s.79 of the same Act (which expressly allows for the latter to be excluded). This was considered in *Roake v Chadha* and confirmed in *Crest Nicholson Residential (South) Ltd v McAllister*. An application of this can be seen in *Sugarman v Porter* [2006] EWHC 331 (Ch) where it was held that the original covenants had been specifically intended to benefit the vendor in relation to her remaining unsold land. In this context and in the absence of express annexation it was held that statutory annexation had not taken place in that there was sufficient contrary intention. In a similar vein but leading to a different outcome is *Mahon v Sims* [2005] 39 E.G. 138 QBD where it was held that in the circumstances and purposive reading of the documents, the phrase "transferors" should be read to include transferors' successors in title.

Where there was a use of both the phrase "transferors" and "transferors and its successors in title" in the document, the court in *City Inn (Jersey) Ltd v Ten Trinity Square Ltd* [2007] EWHC 1829 (Ch) decided that on the construction of the document it was clear that the intention was to exclude s.78 of the **Law of Property Act 1925**. A similar conclusion was reached in *Norwich City College of Further and Higher Education v McQuillin* [2009] EWHC 1496 (Ch) where the court construed the words

> " ...for the benefit of the ... estate ... or the part or parts thereof for the time being remaining unsold and so as to bind (so far as may be) the property hereby conveyed into whosoever hands the same may come"

as meaning that it excluded benefitting the lands that were subsequently sold and hence excluded statutory annexation under s.78. See also *University of East London Higher Education Corp v Barking and Dagenham LBC* [2004] EWHC 2908 (Ch).

In *Margerison v Bates* [2008] EWHC 1211 (Ch) a covenant prohibited additions to or the enlargement of a bungalow without the written consent and approval of "the Vendor". The court held that as the phrase "the vendor" had been defined in the conveyance this meant that the benefit of the covenant did not include any successors in title and on her death the covenant would be discharged. A similar conclusion was reached in *Churchill v Temple* [2010] EWHC 3369 (Ch) where the restriction was deemed to have been discharged on the death of the "the vendors" as the restriction was interpreted as having effect only for a short duration of time and did not intend successors in title to have the benefit from it.

In the context of enfranchisement under the Leasehold Reform Act 1967 it was held in *Higgs v Nieroba*, Lawtel, December 12, 2005 that covenants previously in a lease should pass to the freehold where the landlord's retained adjoining land was materially enhanced and the restrictions were reasonable. Otherwise the enfranchisee would not just have gained a freehold rather than leasehold but would have gained a windfall release from building restrictions.

[c] Implied annexation

Key Principle
In the absence of express annexation and notwithstanding that the land to be benefited by the covenant is not identified in the covenant, the identity of the land could be implied from the circumstances of the case.

MARTEN V FLIGHT REFUELLING LTD 1961

In 1942, the Air Ministry requisitioned 200 acres of a farm of 562 acres, which was part of a large agricultural estate. The farm was conveyed in 1943 to the sitting tenant who, inter alia, covenanted with the vendors and their successors in title that no part of the land or any building on it would be used for any purposes other than agricultural purposes without the written consent of the vendors or their agents. The covenant was registered as a Class D(ii) land charge in 1943. In 1947 the Air Ministry let a commercial company into occupation giving rights over the aerodrome. The nature of the company's business included maintenance of the airfield and its facilities, design and development of air refuelling equipment and other miscellaneous industrial and commercial activities. In 1958, the Air Ministry compulsorily purchased a large part of the requisitioned land subject to the covenant. It also subsequently purchased the remaining part of the requisitioned land free of the restriction.

An action was commenced against the Air Ministry by the plaintiffs, alleging breach of covenant by the Air Ministry.

Held

❖ (Ch D) Having regard to the circumstances surrounding the 1943 conveyance, and taking a broad and reasonable view of the proof of the identity
of the estate, it could be shown with reasonable certainty that the covenant
was taken for the benefit of land belonging to the vendor. Therefore, it did not
matter that the covenant did not expressly annex or identify the land to be
benefited. As the plaintiffs together represented the whole legal and equitable interest in the covenant, they were therefore entitled to a declaration
that they were entitled to the benefit of the covenant. [1962] Ch. 115.

NEWTON ABBOTT COOPERATIVE SOCIETY v WILLIAMSON AND TREADGOLD LTD 1952

The covenantee was the owner of a property known as Devonia in
Bovey Tracey where she carried on the business of an ironmonger. The
original covenantor was the purchaser of a property belonging to the
covenantee opposite Devonia. The conveyance contained a covenant
by the purchaser not to carry on the business of an ironmonger on the
property. No reference was made as to the land that was to benefit from
this covenant. The business of the covenantee was subsequently
assigned by her son, together with the benefit of the covenant to a
cooperative society. The cooperative society subsequently amalga-
mated with the plaintiff society. The plaintiffs commenced an action
against the assigns of the covenantor to enforce the covenant.

Held

❖ (Ch D) There was nothing in the conveyance that identified the land for the
benefit of which the covenant was taken. However, the court was entitled to
look at the attendant circumstances to see if the land to be benefited was
shown otherwise with reasonable certainty. The plaintiffs were entitled to an
injunction enabling them to enforce the restrictive covenant. [1952] Ch. 286.

Commentary

Although *Newton Abbott Cooperative Society v Williamson and Treadgold Ltd*
suggested that the land to be benefited could be inferred from the circumstances, it was merely an obiter dictum. The case was decided on the basis of
the assignment of the benefit of the covenant (see later). It would therefore
appear that *Marten v Flight Refuelling Ltd*, is the only case where the court
was prepared to hold that there could be an implied annexation of the benefit
of the covenant. See also *J Sainsbury Plc v Enfield LBC* [1989] 1 W.L.R. 590.

[2] ASSIGNMENT

Key Principle

The successor in title to the original covenantee's land can enforce a restrictive covenant if he or she can demonstrate that the benefit of the covenant has been assigned to him or her.

> NEWTON ABBOTT COOPERATIVE SOCIETY V WILLIAMSON AND TREADGOLD LTD 1952
> (see above).

Held

❖ (Ch D) As the covenantee's son had the benefit of the covenant in equity he was entitled to assign it to the cooperative society. The assigns of the covenantee were therefore entitled to enforce the covenant against the defendants. [1952] Ch. 286.

Commentary

The assignees of the benefit of the covenant can enforce a covenant against the covenantor or his assignees. However, in order to do so, it is necessary for the former to be able to establish an unbroken chain of assignments from the original covenantee to the current owner of the land to be benefited from the covenant. If the chain of assignment is broken, then the covenant is not enforceable unless it can be shown that the benefit of the covenant has been either annexed to the land or it forms part of a scheme of development.

[3] BUILDING SCHEMES

Key Principle

Where the requirements of a building scheme are satisfied, the owners of the respective lots of land in such a scheme have the benefit of mutually enforceable covenants.

> ELLISTON V REACHER 1908
> In 1860, a Building Society acquired the title to an estate in Felixstowe. Part of the estate had been laid out in plots and was shown in the sale plans of the society. The plan contained conditions, which were to affect the different plots of land. The conditions stipulated that each purchaser was to execute a deed of covenant for regulating building on the respective plots and securing performance of the covenants contained in it. This included a covenant that no hotel should be built on

any lot and no building should be used as a hotel, without the vendors' consent. Three of the plots of land were sold to the plaintiffs' pre-decessors in title and another two plots were sold to the defendants' predecessors in title. The plaintiffs commenced an action against the defendants to restrain them from using a building as a hotel in breach of the covenant.

Held

❖ (Ch D) The covenant was enforceable against the defendants and therefore could be restrained by injunction. [1908] 2 Ch. 374.

Commentary

[1] The decision of Parker J. was affirmed on appeal by the Court of Appeal (reported at [1908] 2 Ch. 665). The importance of Parker J.'s decision is with respect to the conditions which are to be satisfied in order for a building scheme to be established, resulting in covenants being mutually enforceable by the owners of the respective plots of land in the scheme.

[2] He stated (at 384) that:

> "[I]t must be proved: (i) that both the plaintiffs and defendants derive title under a common vendor; (ii) that previously to selling the lands to which the plaintiffs and defendants are respectively entitled the vendor laid out his estate, or a defined portion thereof (including the lands purchased by the plaintiffs and defendants respectively), for sale in lots subject to restrictions intended to be imposed on all the lots, and which, though varying in details as to particular lots, are consistent and con-sistent only with some general scheme of development; (iii) that these restrictions were intended by the common vendor to be and were for the benefit of all the lots intended to be sold, whether or not they were also intended to be and were for the benefit of other land retained by the vendor; and (iv) that both the plaintiffs and the defendants, or their predecessors in title, purchased their lots from the common vendor upon the footing that the restrictions subject to which the purchases were made were to ensure for the benefit of the other lots included in the general scheme whether or not they were also to enure for the benefit of other lands retained by the vendors".

The purchasers must be aware that the covenants were to be mutually enforceable.

> **SMALL V OLIVER & SAUNDERS (DEVELOPMENTS) LTD 2006**
> The claimant commenced an action against the defendant alleging a breach of a restrictive covenant contained in a 1925 conveyance. The covenant provided that the land was not to be used for any purpose other than as private residences " ... to the intent that such covenant shall enure for the benefit of and be annexed to the remainder of the ... estate". The defendant was building a house on its land at the back of the original house and wanted to use part of the land for access to the new house which the claimant alleged was in breach of the covenant. The issue was whether the claimant had the benefit of the covenant and whether there was a breach.

Held ....
❖ (Ch D) The claimant had the benefit of the restrictive covenant on the basis of annexation rather than by way of a building scheme. The claimant was not able to prove that the purchasers of the various adjoining plots of land at the time were aware that there was to be mutually enforceable covenants—a suspicion that the covenants were to be mutually enforceable was not sufficient. On the facts there was a breach of the covenant but in the circumstances the court would grant an order of damages in lieu of a permanent injunction. [2006] EWHC 1293 (Ch).

Commentary ....
This case is a recent example on the enforceability of a restrictive covenant on the basis of either annexation or building scheme. The claim that the covenant was enforceable on the basis of a building scheme failed as the purchasers of the adjoining properties merely had a strong suspicion rather than being aware of the reciprocal nature of the covenants. The court found that there was a breach but decided not to grant a permanent injunction as it would have been oppressive to do so.

Key Principle ....
A scheme of development can be found to have been established, even though the scheme may lack a common vendor and the land was not laid out in plots.

BAXTER V FOUR OAKS PROPERTIES LTD 1965

C, the owner of a large estate conveyed part of it to H in 1891. By an indenture made at the same time between C, H and all other persons who might subsequently purchase any part of the estate, it was agreed that H and all other purchasers, their heirs, assigns and persons claiming under them should observe and perform the covenants and conditions set out in the schedule. It was further provided that the covenants and conditions were enforceable by any other person enti- tled for the time being of any other land forming part of the estate. There was no evidence that C had laid out the estate in lots prior to any sale taking place and C sold the lots in accordance with the purchaser's requirements. The plaintiffs and defendant were the successors in title to the original purchasers from C. The plaintiffs sought to enforce a restrictive covenant against the defendant.

Held

❖ (Ch D) Where it is clear that the intention of the parties was that the various purchasers from a common vendor of parts of an estate should have rights as against each other, the court would give effect to that intention, notwithstanding that the vendor had not laid out the estate in lots prior to the commencement of sales. [1965] Ch. 816.

RE DOLPHIN'S CONVEYANCE 1970

In 1871, two sisters who were the owners of a 30-acre estate sold four plots of land to four different purchasers with a covenant that they would build only detached houses of plots of no less than a quarter acre. The purchasers further covenanted that they would obtain similar covenants from subsequent purchasers of any part of the estate. One of the sisters died in 1873. The estate subsequently passed to their nephew who sold off the remaining estate in six parcels, obtaining similar covenants from the purchasers with the exception of the last parcel of land. The plaintiffs acquired part of the estate with notice of the covenants and wished to build dwelling houses in contravention of covenant. The plaintiffs applied for a declaration, inter alia, that their land was no longer subject to or affected by the restrictive covenants, arguing that there was no building scheme.

Held

❖ (Ch D) The plaintiffs' land was subject to the restrictive covenants. A building scheme existed where on the true construction of the various con- veyances, it is clear that the covenants were imposed for the common benefit of all the purchasers and vendors of the estate. It was evident that the covenants were to be enforceable between the purchasers against each other and all of them had a common interest in such enforcement. [1970] Ch. 654.

Commentary

[1] In *Re Dolphin's Conveyance*, Stamp J. was prepared to hold that a building scheme existed on the basis that it was clearly intended by all the parties concerned that a local law be laid down for the estate for the benefit of all the separate purchasers. He did so in reliance of the principle laid down in the earlier case of *Baxter v Four Oaks Properties Ltd* that the existence or evidence of mutual obligation and reciprocity were the main characteristics of a building scheme.

[2] Whether or not a building scheme is intended is a question of fact. In *Emile Elias & Co Ltd v Pine Groves Ltd* [1993] 1 W.L.R. 305 PC (Trin), the Privy Council was of the view that on the facts of that case no building scheme was intended. This was because as all the lots were all of a similar nature and were all intended for a high class development, a disparity of the covenants imposed was a clear indication that there was no intention to create reciprocally enforceable rights.

[3] There must, however, be a clearly defined area in order for a building scheme to be established: *Whitgift Homes Ltd v Stocks* [2001] EWCA Civ 1732.

DISCHARGE AND MODIFICATION OF COVENANTS

Key Principle
Under s.84 of the **Law of Property Act 1925**, the Lands Tribunal has the power to modify or discharge any restrictive covenant in accordance with the criteria set out in that section.

> RE BEECH'S APPLICATION 1990
> The owner of a council house applied for the discharge of a restrictive covenant restricting the use of the house as a private dwelling, so as to enable him to convert it into office accommodation.

Held
❖ (Lands Tr) The restriction would not be discharged, as it would have an adverse impact on the area.

Commentary ....

[1] The case is merely an example as to how the Lands Tribunal exercises its power under s.84 of the **Law of Property Act 1925**. Other examples on the application of s.84 can be seen in cases such as *Re Love's and Love's Application* [1994] 67 P. & C.R. 101 Lands Tr, *National Schizophrenia Fellowship v Ribble Estates SA* (1993) 25 H.L.R. 476 Ch D and *Re Davies Application* [2001] 03 E.G. 134. A practical example of modification by the Lands Tribunal of restrictive covenants is *Turner's Application*, Lawtel, February 24, 2006 where in respect of the building of a bungalow in the rear garden of a plot it decided that the neighbours would not be deprived of any substantial benefit of value under s.84 that could not be adequately compensated. This was confirmed on appeal in *Shephard v Turner* [2006] EWCA Civ 8.

In *Attorney General of Hong Kong v Fairfax Ltd* [1997] 1 W.L.R. 149 PC (HK), the Privy Council recognised that there were circumstances outside s.84 where it would be possible to deem that a restrictive covenant had been abandoned by the dominant owner. In the case, by allowing skyscrapers to be built on the land, the dominant owner was deemed to have abandoned the covenant allowing only villas to be built on it.

[2] In respect of the approach to be taken by the Lands Tribunal, the Privy Council in *McMorris v Brown* [1999] 1 A.C. 142 PC (Jam) at 151 adopted a statement from *Re Snaith and Dolding's Application* (1996) 71 P. & C.R. 104. Bernard Marder QC stated that:

> " ... the position of the tribunal is clear. Any application under section 84(1) must be determined upon the facts and merits of the particular case, and the tribunal is unable to bind itself to a particular course of action in the future in a case which is not before it ... It is however legitimate in considering a particular application to have regard to the scheme of covenants as a whole and to assess the importance to the beneficiaries of maintaining the integrity of the scheme ...".

[3] The Law Commission published a Consultation Paper, *Easements, Covenants and Profits à Prendre* (Law Commission, March 2008), CP No.186. with a view to their reform and rationalisation. Such reforms are intended to take into account commonholds and the requirements of the **Land Registration Act 2002**. The Paper proposes the modernisation by statute in the way in which restrictive covenants can be discharged and modified.

Read the decision in *Austerberry v Oldham Corp* (1885) L.R. 29 Ch. D. 750 CA, do you think that there is any real basis for the proposition that the burden of a covenant does not pass at common law? Look at the Law Commission's Consultation Paper on *Easements, Covenants and Profits à Prendre*—what are the changes being proposed by the Law Commission in respect of positive and restrictive covenants?

Read the decision in *Crest Nicholson Residential (South) Ltd v McAllister* [2004] EWCA Civ 410 in detail and consider whether the covenant in question was intended to run with the land or whether the covenant was purely for personal benefit.

Index

LEGAL TAXONOMY
FROM SWEET & MAXWELL

This index has been prepared using Sweet and Maxwell's Legal Taxonomy. Main index entries conform to keywords provided by the Legal Taxonomy except where references to specific documents or non-standard terms (denoted by quotation marks) have been included. These keywords provide a means of identifying similar concepts in other Sweet & Maxwell publications and online services to which keywords from the Legal Taxonomy have been applied. Readers may find some minor differences between terms used in the text and those which appear in the index.
Suggestions to **taxonomy@sweetandmaxwell.co.uk**.